LEGENDARY LOCALS

OF

RUTHERFORD COUNTY

NORTH CAROLINA

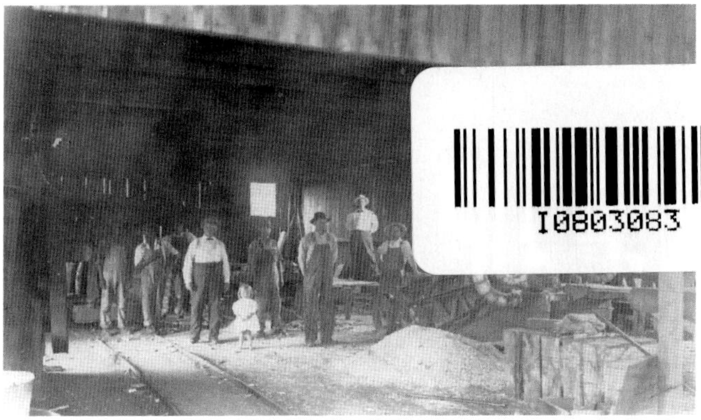

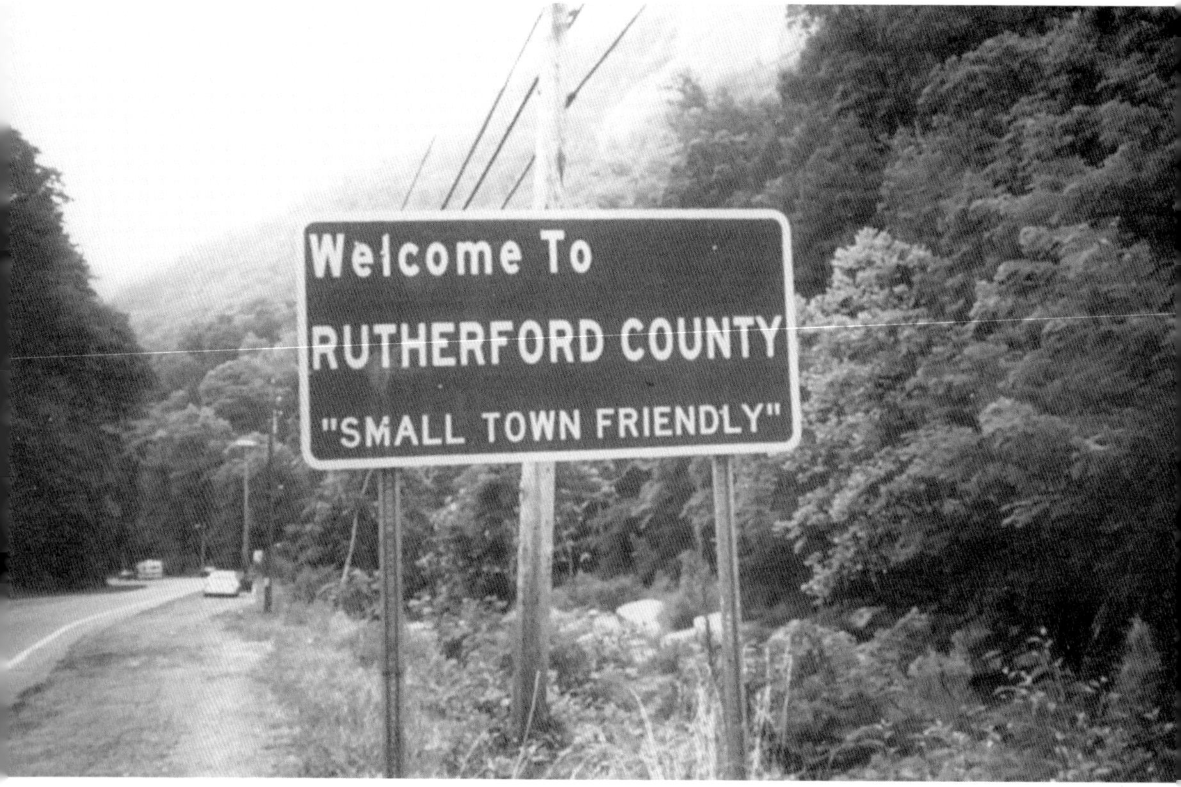

Small Town Friendly

The signs at the entrances into the county present Rutherford County's slogan: "Small Town Friendly." The concise motto suggests both the population size and the social atmosphere of the county; its 2011 population was approximately 67,538, and its land area is 564.14 square miles. Its population density of 119 persons per square mile is less than 198.2 for the state of North Carolina. (James M. Walker.)

Page 1: Withrow inside Hollis Gin

See page 59.

LEGENDARY LOCALS

OF

RUTHERFORD COUNTY

NORTH CAROLINA

DR. ANITA PRICE DAVIS

LEGENDARY LOCALS

ISBN 978-1-4671-0064-9

Legendary Locals is an imprint of Arcadia Publishing
Charleston, South Carolina

Printed in the United States of America

Library of Congress Control Number: 2012950611

For all general information, please contact Arcadia Publishing:
Telephone 843-853-2070
Fax 843-853-0044
E-mail sales@arcadiapublishing.com
For customer service and orders:
Toll-Free 1-888-313-2665

Visit us on the Internet at www.arcadiapublishing.com

Dedication

For the Rutherford County residents—you volunteer information, make suggestions, help in every way possible, encourage, and overlook my many flaws. Thank you!

On the Cover: From left to right:
(TOP ROW) Cpl. Arthur Fred Price, gave his life in World War II (Author's collection; see page 72); Victoria Simmons Hicks Goode, a former slave and the great-grandmother of Milton Robinson Jr. (Courtesy of Milton Robinson Jr.; see page 44); Coran Toney, local farmer and World War II veteran (Courtesy of J.V. and Rachel Toney Jones; see page 25); Nelle Butler Wright, employee of Union Trust Company and BB&T (Courtesy of Sandra Butler Weeks, see page 54); John Brooks, World War II veteran and mica miner in the county (Courtesy of John Brooks, see page 28).
(MIDDLE ROW) "Cowboy" Ralph Spicer, singer, recording artist, and movie actor (Courtesy of Ralph Spicer, see page 98); Chess "Goat Man" McCartney and author Anita Price Davis (Author's collection, see page 39); George S. Mills, Vietnam Cross of Gallantry Winner (Courtesy of Ruby Mills and George S. Mills, see page 119); Plato Rollins Price, merchant (Author's collection, see page 39); Hernando De Soto, Spanish explorer (Courtesy of Library of Congress, see page 10).
(BOTTOM ROW) Capt. Wilbur J. Burgin, 31-year military veteran and founder of Rutherford County Farm Museum (Courtesy of Capt. Wilbur J. Burgin, see page 41); Nell Daves Price Burns, widow of Arthur Fred Price, wife of Robert Ewart Burns, and deputy sheriff of Rutherford County (Author's collection, see page 72); Robert Ewart Burns, resident of Rutherford County, employee of Duke Power Company, and farmer (Author's collection, see page 27); Walda Carpenter, employee of Public Welfare Department and interviewer for the Civilian Conservation Corps (Courtesy of Walda Carpenter, see page 38).

CONTENTS

ACKNOWLEDGMENTS

I—the author—herewith acknowledge the generous contributions of images and information, the helpful attitude of each person consulted, and the willingness of others to volunteer to share photographs, suggestions, and information. The encouragement of those about me was a much-appreciated gift.

To me, there is no other place on earth that displays the kindness that Rutherford County represents. I hope to capture some of that giving spirit on these pages.

I was a full-time resident of Rutherford County from my birth in 1943 until 1969, when I took the position of professor at Converse College in Spartanburg, South Carolina, about 35 miles away. With my parents residing in Rutherford County, I made several trips to the county each week and maintained contact with them, with the county, and with the residents. After the deaths of my parents, the 35 acres with the Burns family home became mine to love. I still maintain contact with the people in the county; the number of people who "drop in" when they see we are "home" indicates that they still feel welcome and free to visit at will.

The people throughout the county have helped with *Legendary Locals of Rutherford County*. These current residents (like those before them) exemplify the slogan "Small Town Friendly."

INTRODUCTION

Rutherford County, originally Anson County and later Tryon County, lies in the Piedmont Region of North Carolina and at the borders of North and South Carolina. In the early history of the county, the Cherokee and Catawba tribes had used the area primarily for hunting. Located in the piedmont area of the state, Rutherford County includes some primarily flat and/or gently rolling land and also encompasses some of the majestic mountains and the rugged terrain so appealing to locals and travelers alike.

Chapter 1 highlights some of those early people who were intrigued by the area, who explored in what is now the county, and/or who invested their lives in its settlement. Many were from European countries. These explorers braved the elements and the hazards of their journeys to find what might be awaiting them in the Rutherford County area. These important explorers and early founders include Hernando De Soto and William Tryon. In 1906, the later explorer Thomas Alva Edison gave many people of the county their first view of the automobile and a glimpse of what was to come when he spent some time exploring in the county during May and June of that year. Edison was seeking cobalt and manganese in the area, particularly around Henrietta; he needed cobalt and manganese for his inventions. Tourists still explore the Rutherford County area in large numbers during the summer and during the autumn when the leaves reach their peak.

Europeans who were not afraid of frontier living had begun settling in the area in the 1700s. Their relations with the Native Americans, however, were not always peaceful.

African American settlers in the county began arriving in the 1800s. Their arrival—though somewhat later than that of some of the other groups—was vital to the county and to the state.

Residents of Rutherford County have exhibited many ways of earning a livelihood. Their proper management of the resources of the area has been important in the past and will affect the future. Mining, lumbering, farming, tourism, textile working, producing energy, communicating, caring for others, entertaining, educating, protecting others, helping with spiritual needs, and retailing were particularly important to the county and to its people. Chapter 2 considers the agriculturalists and conservationists and acknowledges their importance to Rutherford County.

By 1856, railroads began to find their niche in the county. Such men as Ray Mauney, Ed Price, and John Tedder later found their place on the rails. One town in the county, Ellenboro, supposedly took its name from an engineer's daughter.

In the late 1800s and the early 1900s, manufacturing and farm-related occupations began to prosper throughout Rutherford County. Raleigh Rutherford Haynes and Simpson Bobo Tanner became household names. Textile mills sprang up about the county in such places as Cliffside, Henrietta, Caroleen, Avondale, Alexander Mills, Spindale, Rutherfordton, Forest City, and Ellenboro. Villages near the mills and the power plants gave workers a choice of housing. When some of these plants closed, ceased supplying residences, and/or outsourced production abroad, particularly in the late 20th century, many families of Rutherford County had to change their occupations, their residences, and their lifestyles. Some people, however, purchased their houses and currently still occupy them. Chapter 3 examines the managers of the resources of the area.

Vital to the well-being and health of the county are the communicators. Those who conveyed information to the residents through broadcasts, newspaper articles, speeches, and books remain vital to Rutherford County residents. Chapter 4 examines some of these important communicators in the county and their roles.

Traditionally, the hardworking residents of Rutherford County have made time for entertainment and recreational activities. This "down time" has helped locals to maintain their physical and mental health. Rutherford County has been the "stomping ground" of many internationally known people. Such entertainers as "Snuffy" Jenkins, Earl Scruggs, "Cowboy" Ralph Spicer, Vince Carmen, and Bobbi Staff (Barbara Jean Grindstaff Whitehurst) have performed here and shared their talents abroad. Chapter 5 considers entertainers and entertainment in the county.

Ministers, teachers, principals, doctors, and dentists have played important roles and continued to improve the lives of the people through the years. Chapter 6 looks at these caregivers and their service to the locals.

Chapter 7 focuses on those who have served Rutherford County, the state, and the nation through law enforcement, the military, and the government. These unselfish people represent the storied past of the county and the promise of a new day.

Legendary Locals of Rutherford County will present a brief history of the county, detail its 14 townships, include information on the economics and the culture of the area, and share some exquisite scenes of the people and the area. This book gives a tour of the county and its people through photographs, captions, postcard images, memorials, markers, and monuments. In this volume, one will also discover just how diverse the area is with urban and rural scenes, mountains and foothills, landmarks and natural wonders, churches and schools, work and leisure-time activities, and things old and new.

Most importantly, *Legendary Locals of Rutherford County* includes Rutherford County people: the young and the old, the white-collars and the blue-collars, those who used to live or are currently living in the county, the rich and the poor, and the workers and the unemployed. The volume, however, is devoid of unwelcoming crowds, bustling cities, and hostile neighborhoods; they do not exist here.

The most important component of the tour and of Rutherford County is its people. Their lives, their services, and their sacrifices are all part of *Legendary Locals of Rutherford County.* The traveler through this book or through an actual trip through the county will find that Rutherford County does indeed live up to the nickname: Small Town Friendly.

CHAPTER ONE

Explorers and Founders of Rutherford County

The first European explorers of what is now Rutherford County, North Carolina, were most likely Spaniards; their explorations date from the 1500s. These early Spanish explorers found no European or Native Americans settled in the piedmont and mountain areas of what would become Anson, Tryon, and Rutherford Counties. When English traders passed through the region on their way to the Cherokees (1673), there were still no permanent European or Native American settlements within the present bounds of Rutherford County.

For thousands of years, the Cherokee and Catawba tribes had used the rich areas in Anson, Tryon, and Rutherford Counties as hunting grounds. The region continued to serve both tribes in the 1600s and early 1700s. The Broad River was usually the dividing line between the two groups.

Writer Clarence W. Griffin indicates that the first European settlements in what is now Rutherford County may date from the 1730s. He notes that settlements in the Brittain community (Westminster) and even Presbyterian services occurred here before 1740. Not everyone, however, agrees with Griffin's dates.

In 1748, Anson County included the land from Lumberton to the Mississippi River. Even part of the present state of Tennessee was within the Anson County boundaries at that time. The first land grants in the area date from 1754, about 80 years after the first English traders came through and during the French and Indian War (1754–1763). The hostilities among the Indians, the French, and the English, however, discouraged many explorers and settlers.

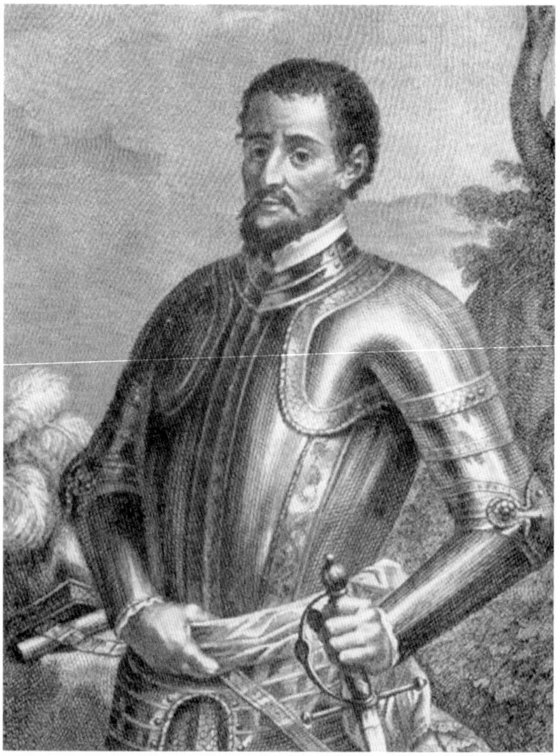

Hernando De Soto, First Spanish Explorer

De Soto and his men were likely the first Europeans to explore Rutherford County. J. Maca's engraving of Hernando De Soto (c. 1500–1542) dates from about 1791. Other Spaniards followed De Soto, including Juan Pardo and his Spanish explorers, who passed through a part of Anson, Tryon, and Rutherford Counties in 1566–1567. These explorers may have spent a brief time in the area and possibly constructed a fort near present-day Morganton in Burke County and/or near Marion in McDowell County, North Carolina. The fort(s), however, did not become permanent. (Library of Congress.)

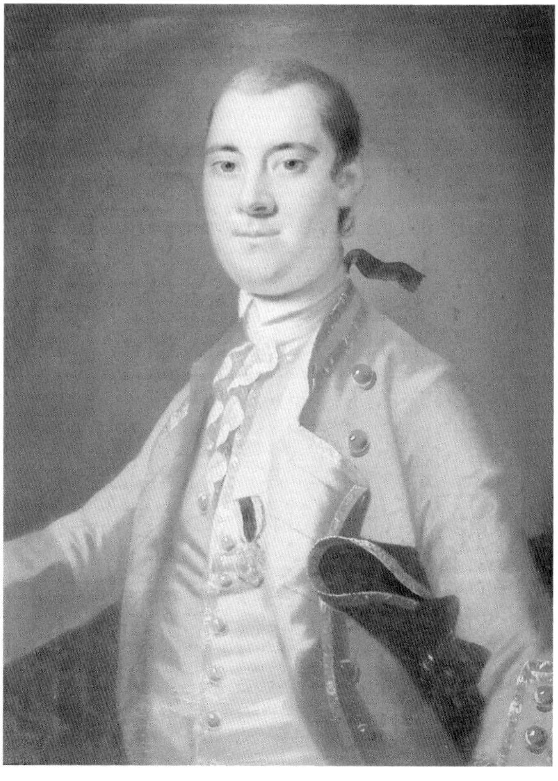

William Tryon, Fourth Royal North Carolina Governor

The North Carolina State Archives identifies this painting as one "believed to be a portrait of William Tryon." Royal Governor Tryon (1764–1771) spent much time in the area that would become Tryon County, named for him; part of Tryon County is now Rutherford County.

Tryon was one of the earliest, most easily identifiable, and most powerful of the legendary locals who came from Europe, visited the western parts of Anson, Tryon, and Rutherford Counties, expressed a personal interest in the area, and served the area significantly and controversially. Tryon was the fourth royal governor of North Carolina. Tryon had been born in Surrey County in England the same year (1729) that North Carolina changed from a Proprietary Colony to a Royal Colony ruled by governors appointed by the king of England. Tryon (1729–1788) was a descendant of "the Earl of Essex, Queen Elizabeth's sometime favorite, and from the Royal House of Plantagenet." (North Carolina State Archives.)

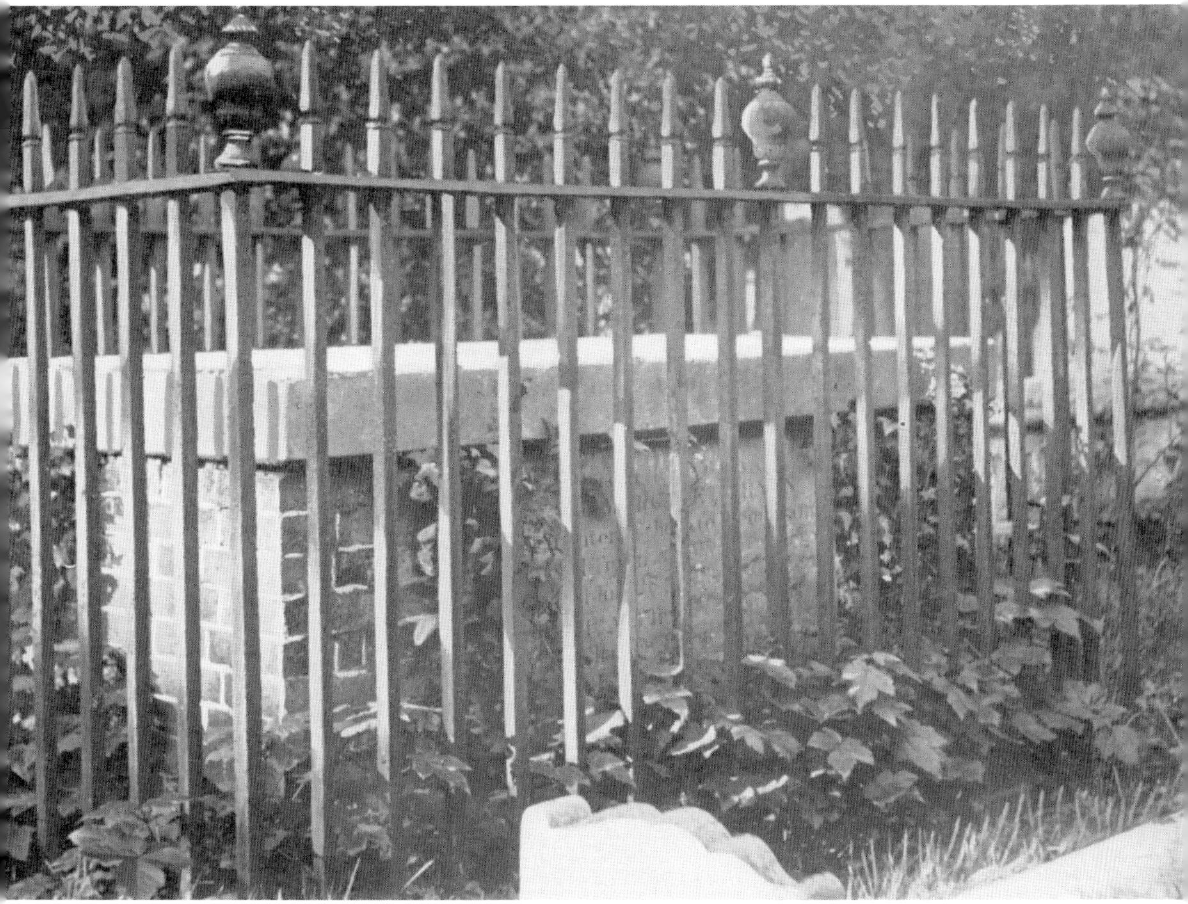

William Tryon's Later Years

Tryon had served as captain in the 1st Regiment of Foot Guards. On April 26, 1764, King George III commissioned William Tryon as the lieutenant governor of North Carolina.

On October 10, 1764, Tryon arrived in Brunswick. Accompanying him were his wife, Margaret Wake Tryon, their four-year-old daughter Margaret Tryon, the servant boy John Hawks, and Fountain Elwin, who was a cousin of Margaret Wake Tryon and the secretary to the lieutenant governor.

Tryon served during a difficult time in North Carolina's history. American resentment against the British was growing during the 1700s. The Cherokees, the Catawbas, and the settlers argued about the land. Disputes with adjacent colonies about the boundaries were bothersome. Governor Tryon himself led a surveying party with militia to view the western area and to determine boundaries. By 1767, Governor Tryon had already begun to make plans to form a new county to carry his name.

Tryon's popularity changed during his term from an accepted governor of the area to a less popular official who tried to prevent assemblies by the people. *NCpedia* even describes his practices as "savagely brutal."

Tryon left North Carolina to hold the position as colonial governor of New York (1771–1780). After returning to England, he continued his career in the military until his death.

Gov. William Tryon died on January 27, 1788. His interment was at the old Parish Church of St. Mary's in Twickenham, Middlesex. (Marshall DeLancey Haywood.)

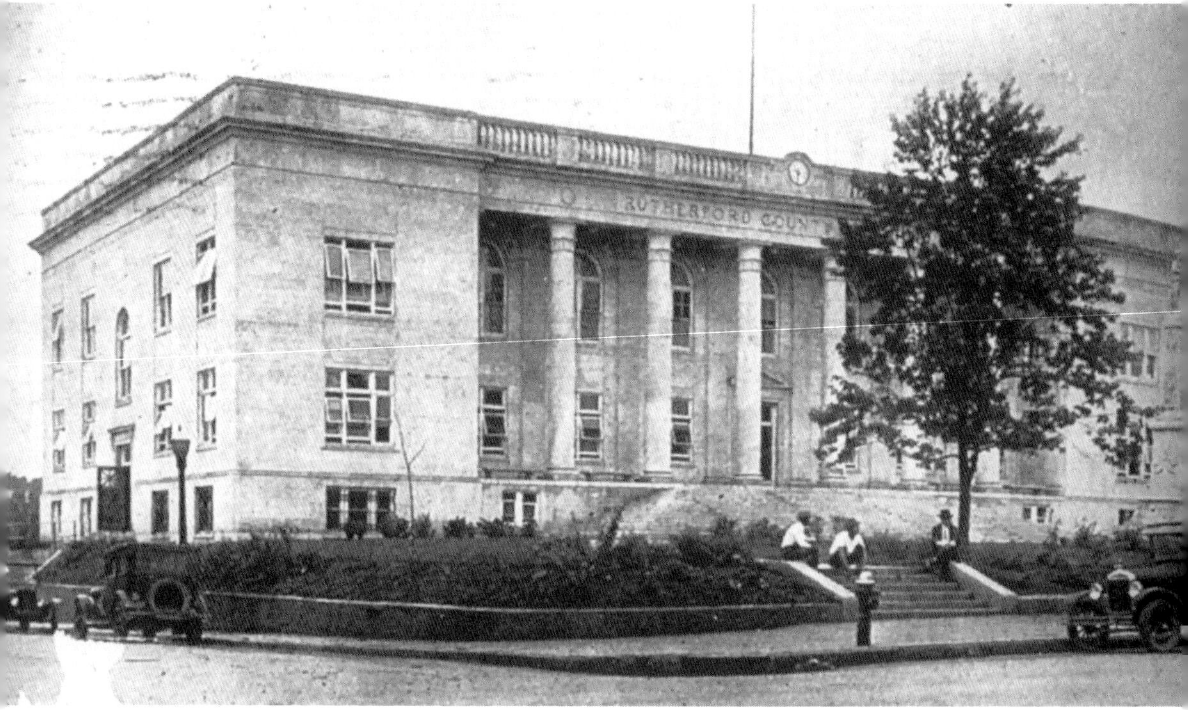

Griffith Rutherford

In 1777, Tryon County (North Carolina) took a new name: Rutherford County. The new name came from Griffith Rutherford (1721–1805). The January 13, 1926, laying of the cornerstone of the current Rutherford County Courthouse was in the county seat of Rutherfordton, which also takes its name from Griffith Rutherford; this granite courthouse in the town and county named for Griffith Rutherford has been in the National Register of Historic Places since 1977.

No photograph or portrait of the red-haired Griffith Rutherford exists. There are, however, many reminders of his life, including the Rutherford County Courthouse.

Griffith Rutherford was born in Ireland in 1721. In 1729, his family came to America. After the death of his parents while he was still a child, relatives in New Jersey or Pennsylvania assumed the responsibility for his care. Griffith Rutherford began surveying in the early 1750s. He moved to Rowan County and served as a captain in the militia during the French and Indian War. Despite having fought with William Tryon at the Battle of Alamance, Rutherford became an early supporter of the American Revolution. Griffith Rutherford received the appointment of brigadier general in April 1776.

Rutherford's influence and his military excursions extended to the adjacent state of Tennessee, where he spent his last years. Rutherford perceived a threat from the Cherokees in the western part of Tryon County, which extended into what is now the state of Tennessee. He led about 2,500 men into this westernmost area. Rutherford and his men ruined Cherokee camps, destroyed some 36 homes, and decimated the Cherokees' winter food supplies.

Between 1777 and 1780, Griffith Rutherford was active in state politics in both North Carolina and Tennessee; he served as a representative from Rowan County, North Carolina. Rutherford and his troops continued to attack the small Tory groups around Rowan County.

In 1781, British forces took General Rutherford captive in Camden, South Carolina, after he received a shot in the leg and a saber wound to the head. It was 10 months before Rutherford's release. He and his troops were able to take control of Wilmington for the Patriots. (Postcard Company, Auburn, Indiana.)

General Rutherford's Tennessee Marker

Rutherford accumulated extensive property and wealth through speculation. He moved to Tennessee and received appointment as the first president of the legislative council (1794).

Eighty-four-year-old Griffith Rutherford, the father of 10, died in his sleep in Sumner County, Tennessee, in 1805. No portrait of the 180-pound, red-haired, five-foot-eight man exists, but a memorial to him stands in Rutherford County, Tennessee; counties in both North Carolina and Tennessee bear his name. The State of Tennessee prepared a memorial to Gen. Griffith Rutherford in Rutherford County, Tennessee. (Brent Moore.)

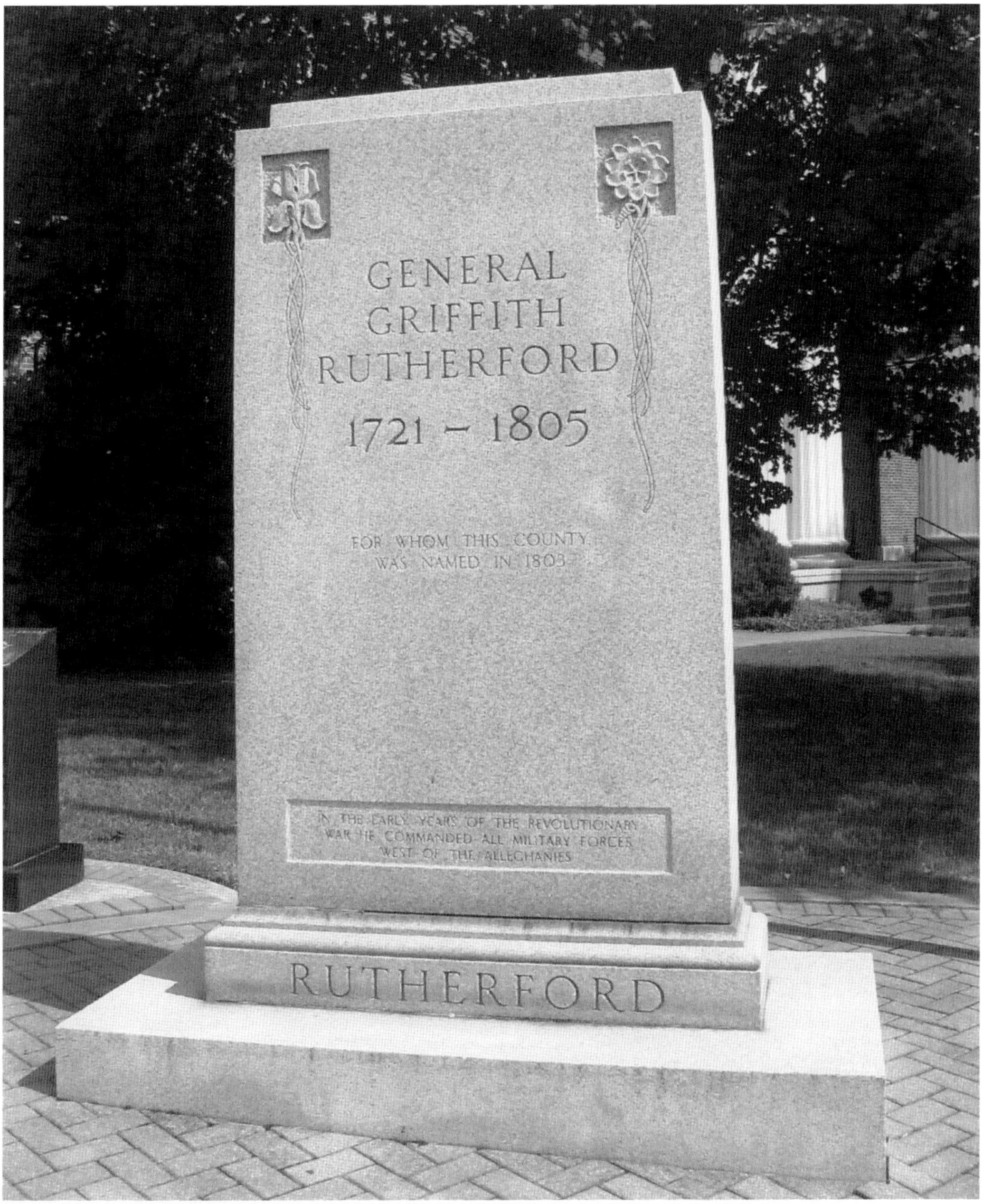

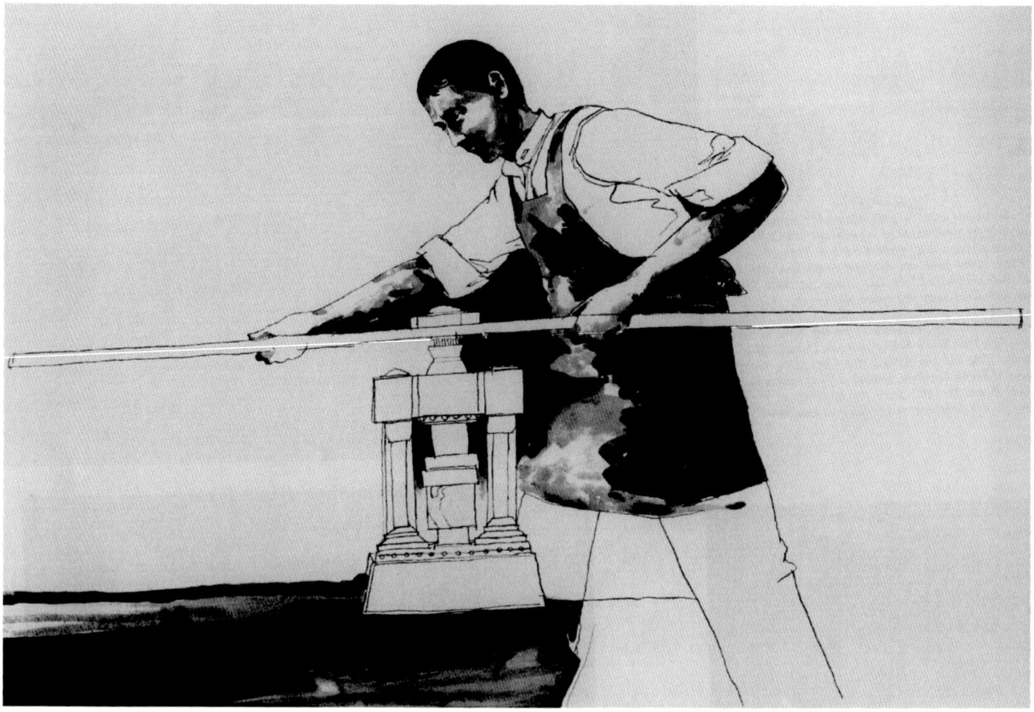

The Bechtlers, Their Mints, and Coins

Rutherford County, particularly Rutherfordton, was the nation's leading gold-producing area from 1790 until the California Gold Rush in the 1840s. Prior to 1849, prospectors rushed to North Carolina to strike it rich. Anson, Tryon, and Rutherford Counties, North Carolina, were at the heart of the fever.

Born in 1782 in the city of Pforzheim in the German state of Baden, Alt Christoph Bechtler was an apprentice to a gunsmith and gold and silver metallurgist. Christoph (later Christopher), his sons August and Karl, and his nephew Christoph Jr. came to the United States and landed in New York on October 12, 1829. They opened a Philadelphia-based jewelry store and clock repair business and immediately applied for American citizenship.

In early 1830, the Bechtlers moved to a land tract 3.5 miles north of Rutherfordton. A July 1830 advertisement in the *North Carolina Spectator and Western Advertiser* announced their jewelry store and clock repair business in Rutherfordton. On July 2, 1831, Bechtler advertised in the *Spectator* that he could assay gold and produce gold coins in his home.

This is an artist's rendering of Christopher Bechtler Sr. (1782–1842), who minted gold coins in Rutherford County. No photograph of Bechtler exists.

The Bechtlers made their own presses, dies, and other equipment. They produced the first gold dollars in the United States; after August 1, 1834, they placed dates on their coins.

Bechtler minted three denominations: $1, $2.50, and $5. James Gray noted the coins were "in three finenesses: 20 carats, 21 carats, and 22 carats. . . . [They] were of honest weight and any variation in fineness was due solely to the limited technology at the time."

Between 1831 and 1840, Bechtler coined $2,241,840, according to a report filed with the US Treasury Department. Production began declining after the launching of the Charlotte and Dahlonega Mints in 1838, however. (Bruce Roberts and Duke Energy.)

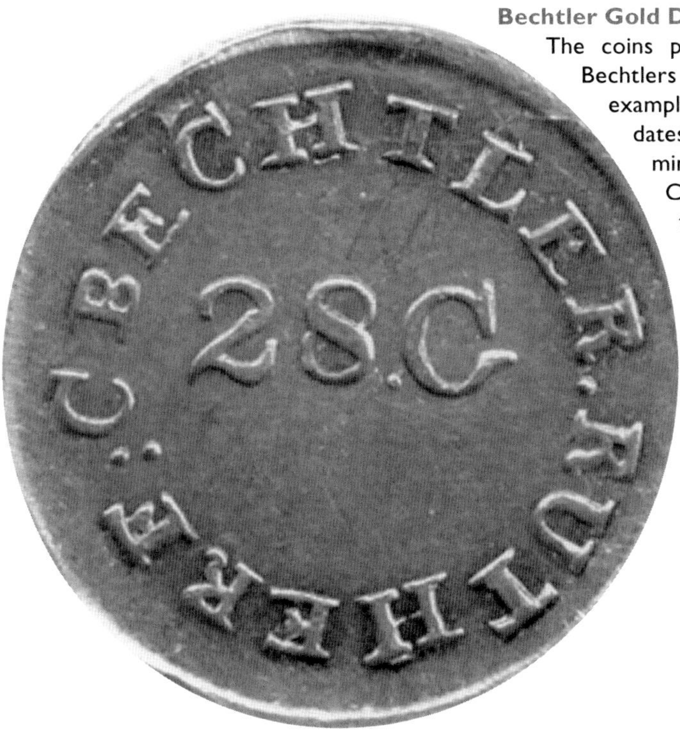

Bechtler Gold Dollar

The coins pictured here are ones that the Bechtlers minted. The first coin is an example of the Bechtler Gold Dollar and dates from 1830–1837. The place of the minting was Rutherfordton, North Carolina. August Bechtler received the Bechtler Mint from his father in 1840. August labeled his $1 gold pieces "A. Bechtler" to distinguish them from his father's coins. These $1 pieces have become the most common of the Bechtler coins. (Courtesy of North Carolina Collection Numismatic Collection, University of North Carolina at Chapel Hill.)

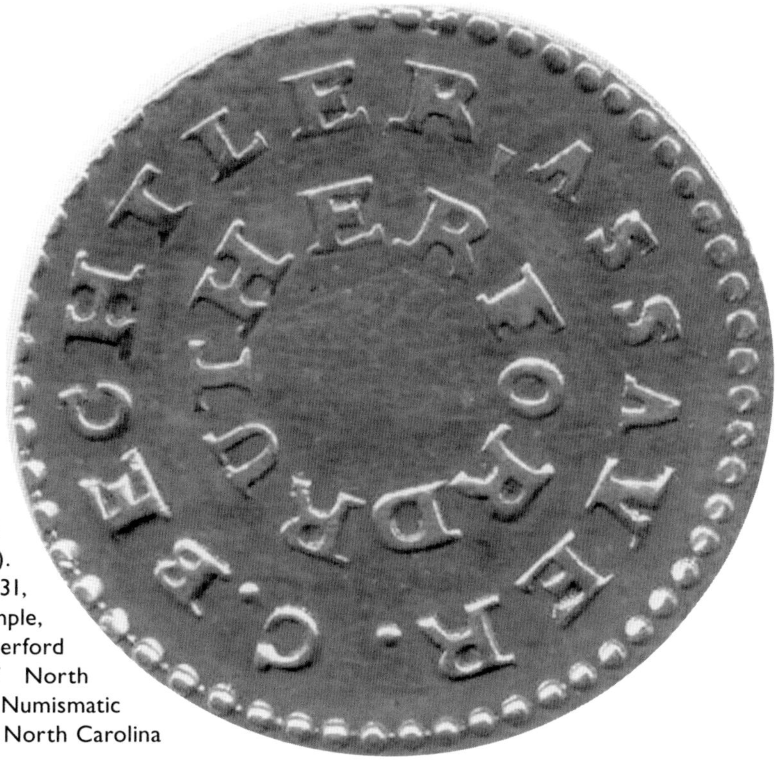

Bechtler Gold Quarter-Eagle

This coin is an example of the Bechtler Gold Quarter-Eagle ($2.50). This coin dates from 1831, and, like the first example, its minting was in Rutherford County. (Courtesy of North Carolina Collection Numismatic Collection, University of North Carolina at Chapel Hill.)

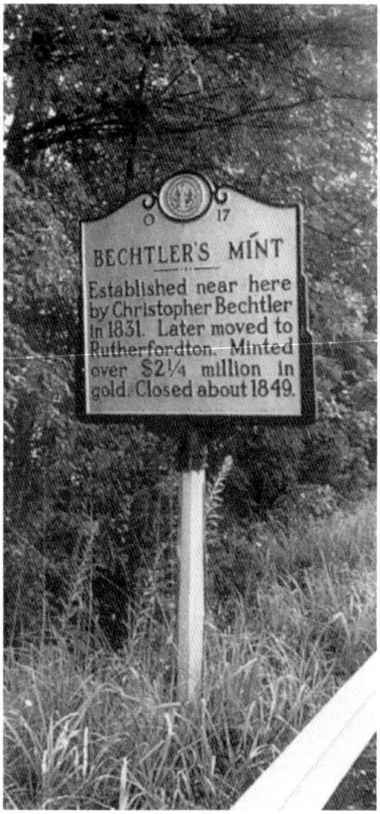

Site of Christopher Bechtler's Mint and the Bechtler Home

On April 14, 1997, the North Carolina Division of Archives and History provided a roadside marker to indicate the original site where Christopher Bechtler established his 1831 mint. The marker commemorated where the Bechtlers coined over $2.25 million in gold. The Bechtler Mint later moved from this site.

Below is the home of August Bechtler. Bechtler moved the coining to a house at 130 West Sixth Street in Rutherfordton after the death of Christopher Bechtler in 1842. Now called the Bechtler House, the site is still open to the public. Christoph Jr. took over the mint after August's 1846 death, but he produced only the A. Bechtler $1 pieces.

Christoph Jr. struck the $1 coins from rusted dies; many were of questionable weight and fineness. The mint finally closed about 1850.

The Bechtlers were "the most successful, prolific and long lasting of all the pioneer and territorial minters." James Gray observed that their "coins were well accepted across the Southeast."

On October 2, 2012, UNC-TV aired the film *Gold Fever and the Bechtler Mint.* Shot on location in Rutherford County, the film is available online. The Bechtler House and views of the coins are important to the video. (Left, James M. Walker; below, Jackie Wallace, Rutherford County Tourism Development Authority.)

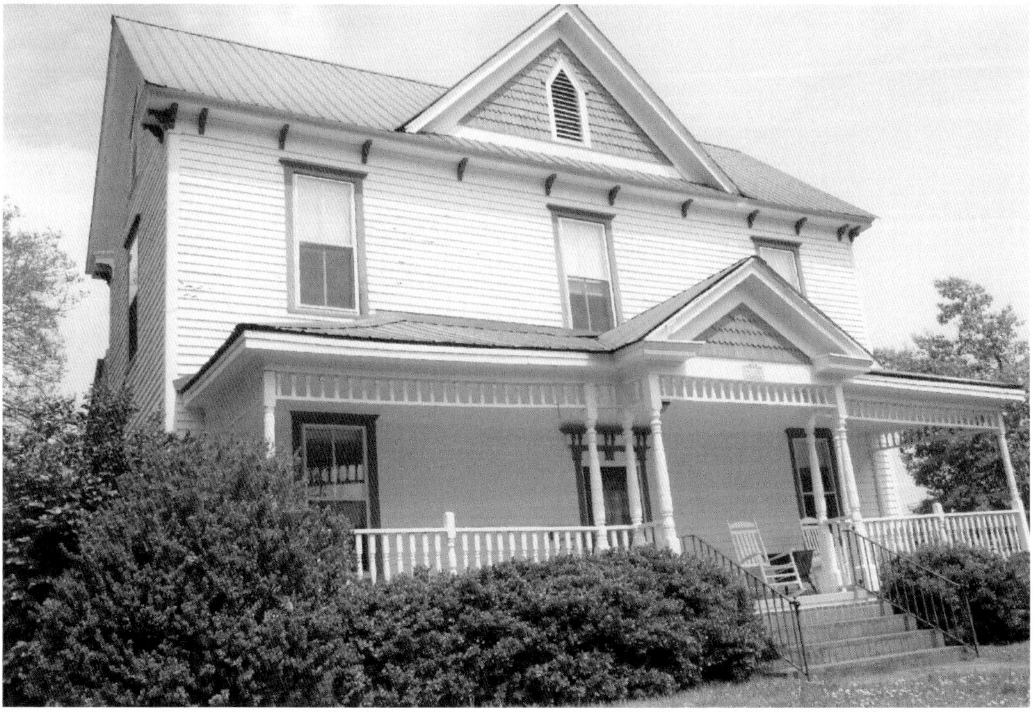

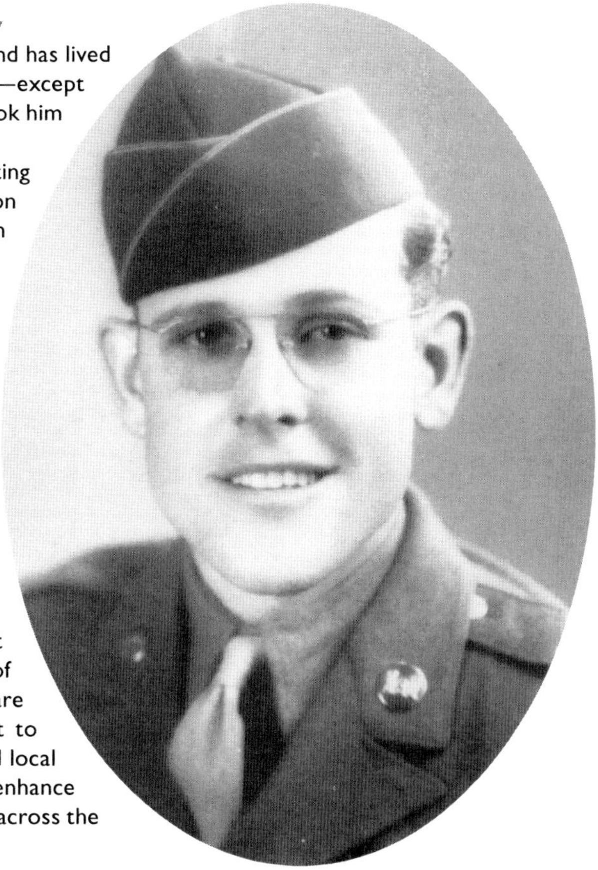

Veteran and Preservationist Ivey Ray Mauney

T-5 Ivey Ray Mauney is a veteran of World War II and has lived his entire life of 80-plus years in Rutherford County—except for when he was in the military. Mauney's service took him both stateside and abroad.

Mauney served in the 718th Railway Operating Battalion during World War II and went ashore on Utah Beach on D+70 (August 15, 1944); he was soon operating trains on the liberated French Railway System. His unit transported fuel, rations, and heavy equipment. Mauney's main duty was that of a locomotive engineer. After his return from active duty, Mauney became interested in preserving and documenting the past of his county.

In 1965, an opportunity arose that Mauney seized to help him document and preserve the history of Rutherford County. Mauney was able to purchase McKinney Mill, shown below, and preserve it. The mill dates from 1860. In 1910, the owner moved the mill 300 yards to its present location on McKinney Mill Road on Sandy Run Creek. The mill had ground both corn and wheat for the locals for many, many years. Still places of scenic beauty, McKinney Mill and Sandy Run Creek are popular destinations for photographers who want to capture the serenity on camera and for tourists and local historians. Preservationist Mauney continues to enhance the landmark he purchased in 1965; his home is just across the road from the historic site. (Ivey Ray Mauney.)

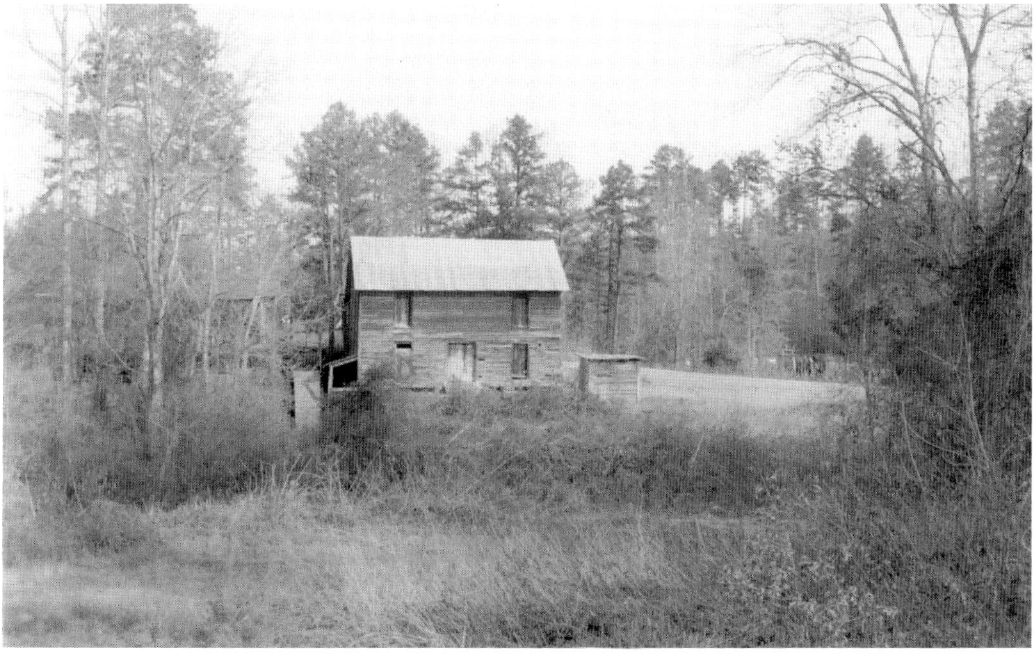

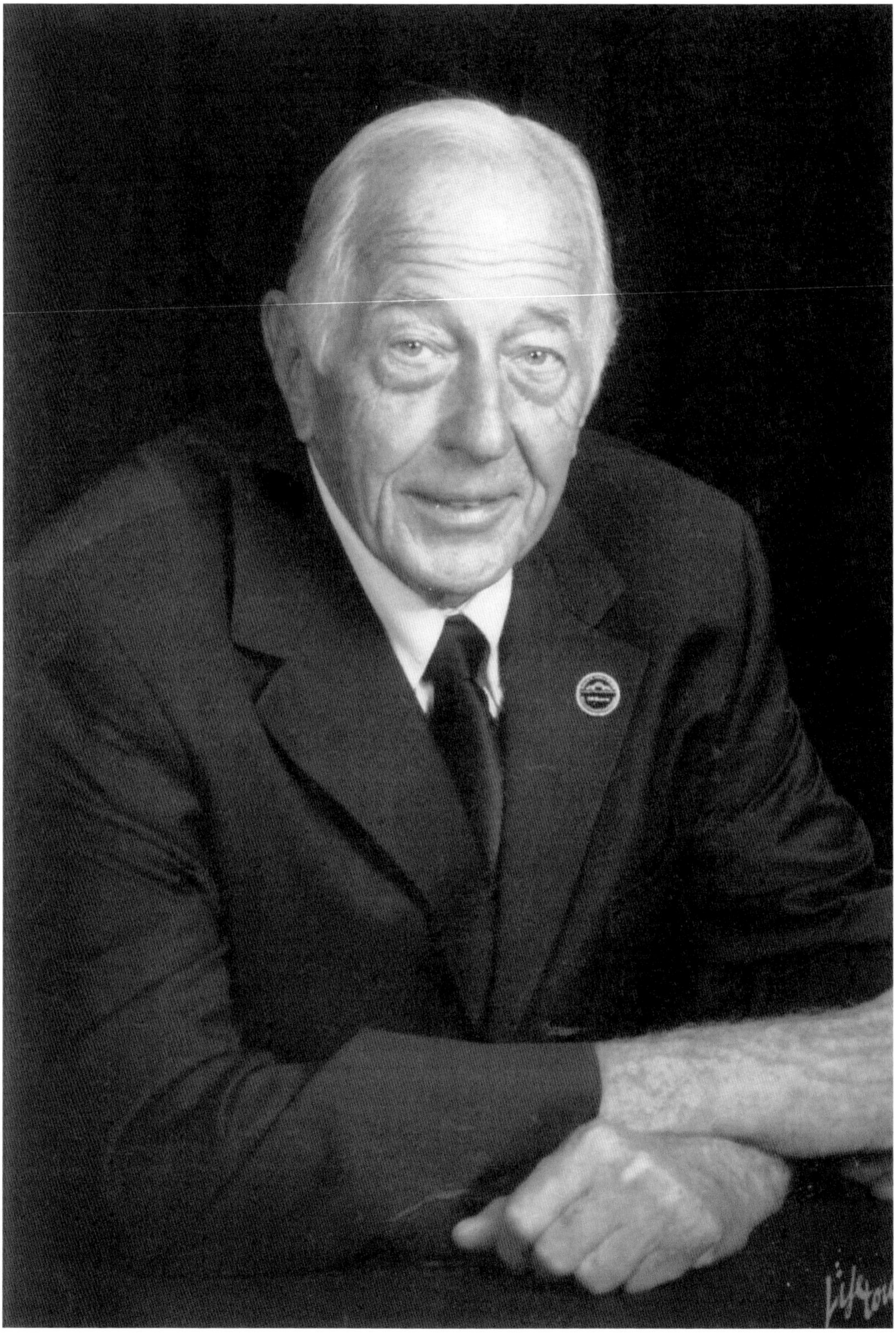

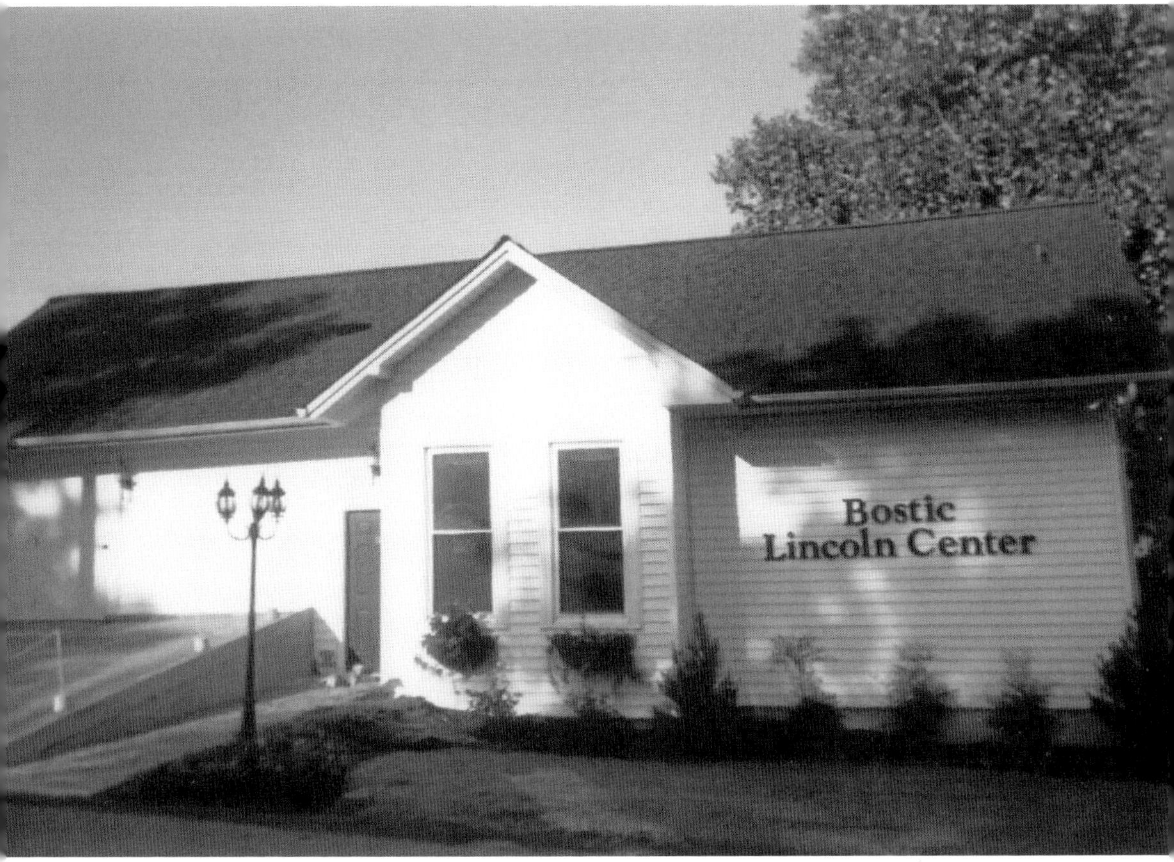

P. Keith Price, a Bostic Lincoln Center Founder (BOTH)
Korean War veteran P. Keith Price led the 2008 founding of the Bostic Lincoln Center in Rutherford County. He, along with others, wanted the local truths about the true parentage of Abraham Lincoln to be shared and preserved; he also wanted the lifetime works of research-historians, such as William Henry Herndon, James H. Cathey, and James Caswell Coggins, to be appreciated properly and assimilated to describe Lincoln's full character, borne of family and community genetics.

As one of North Carolina's most significant counties, old Rutherford County, the "Mother of 16 Counties," is genesis for many pivotal events and personages of the entirety of humanities, creations, and course changes. None are more honorable than the long-held and fundamentally established truths of the birth meanings of the 16th president, Abraham Lincoln. P. Keith Price and others want to disseminate the proof that Lincoln was born to the young Nancy Hanks in Rutherford County around 1805; Lincoln seems to be a Rutherford County native.

Despite the now-understood causes for Lincoln's birth circumstances having been so long hidden and disparaged, the work of all those who preserved, researched, and recorded has, nonetheless, been prepared and printed. The work of the Bostic Lincoln Center is now widely publicized and it increasingly accepted across the nation. (P. Keith Price.)

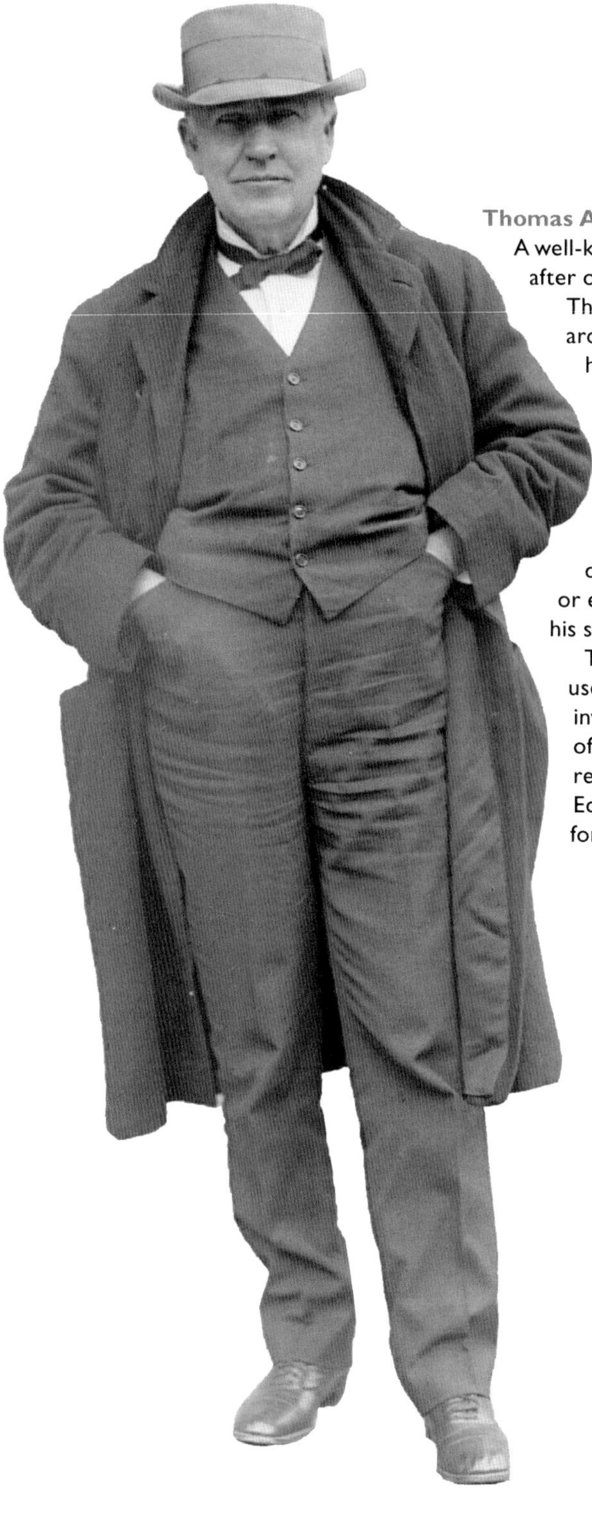

Thomas Alva Edison, Explorer in Rutherford County

A well-known inventor explored in Rutherford County long after one would expect explorations to be necessary. Thomas Alva Edison (1847–1931) examined the area around Henrietta and Caroleen in 1906. He was hoping to discover cobalt and manganese for a new invention. Thomas Alva Edison needed the two minerals to help him with perfecting his new invention, a steam-powered automobile. Edison indicated that if he could find a vein of cobalt in the county, the purchase of gasoline for automobiles would be a thing of the past. Edison did not find what he needed in Rutherford County or elsewhere. The gasoline-powered engines trumped his steam version.

Thomas Alva Edison's exploration did serve some useful purposes, and many of the locals met the inventor. Edison alerted them to the significance of his work, and his visit gave county residents a renewed sense of importance. Traveling in 1906, Edison's vehicle was the first glimpse of a motorcar for many locals. (Library of Congress.)

CHAPTER TWO

Agriculturalists, Conservationists, and Entrepreneurs

Rutherford County has always been rich in good soils, abundant water, plentiful minerals, and many forests. These natural resources contribute to the economic health and to the people of the county, state, and nation.

The ultimate source of all water is, of course, precipitation. North Carolina usually fares well with 49 inches of yearly precipitation. Typically, available water is combined with the rich Carolina soil to ensure distinguished agricultural products. Fruit vines and trees cultivated by farmers grow well here. Farmers who dedicate some of their land to orchards and vineyards find that pecans, grapes, apples, and peaches thrive in the area.

In the 1930s, sweet potatoes became an important cash crop for Rutherford County farmers. Agriculture professor and future Ellenboro World War II air raid warden A.B. Bushong helped make sure that potato houses were available for farmers to cure and store their harvests of the cash crop that he had encouraged.

Millers, like the Andrews family, often placed their gristmills near flowing water and used waterpower to turn the wheels. North Carolina was not highly mechanized. It was one of the slowest states in the nation to change from mules to tractors. In 1930, the state had only 3.9 percent of its farmers using tractors; the rest of the nation had an average of 13.5 percent of the farms relying on tractors. It was 1945 before the state had achieved the 13.5 percent the rest of the nation had seen in 1930. A reason was the small size of the farms. Another reason was the readily available cheap farm labor, consisting of tenant farmers, sharecroppers, and family members.

Lumber and mill products were important to the growers, the harvesters, the lumber companies, and the consumers. The lumberyards were important to the county. In addition to its people, Anson, Tryon, and Rutherford Counties had the gifts of minerals, water, soil, and trees. Used wisely, these natural resources helped the county to progress.

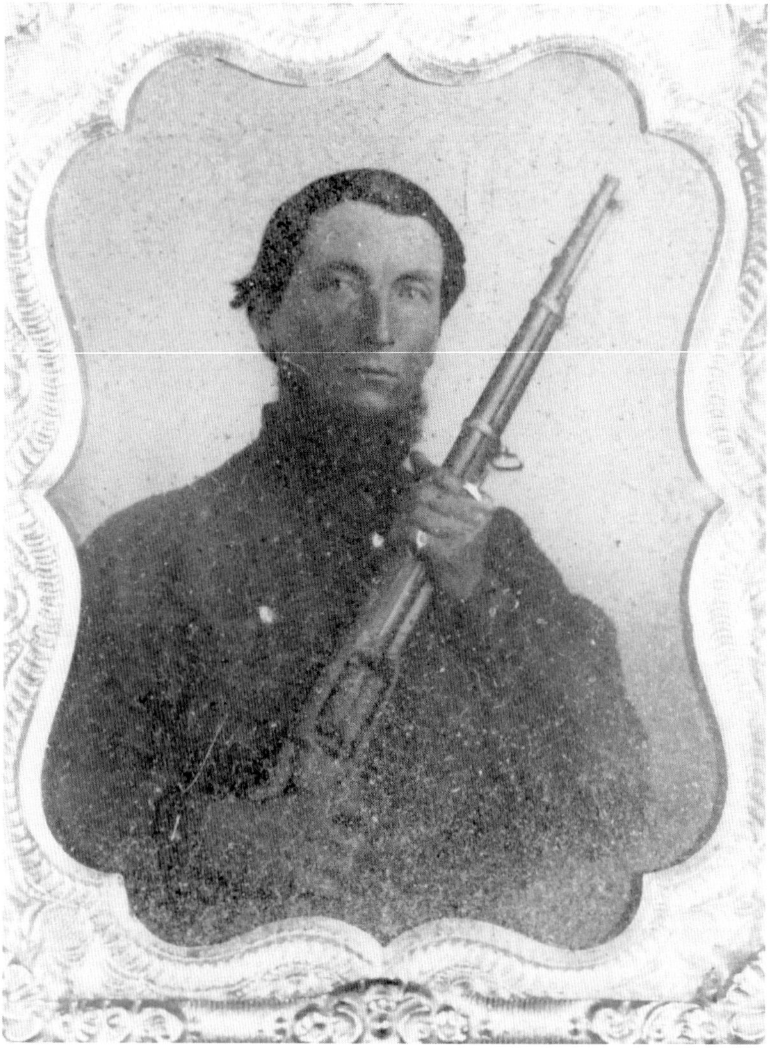

Amos Owens, Civil War Veteran

A truly legendary local in Rutherford County was Amos Owens (February 2, 1821–September 18, 1906). Amos Owens left his mountain home and his "stills" to serve in the Civil War. He volunteered under the command of Capt. H.D. Lee in the 16th North Carolina and served about 12 months. After a medical discharge, he reenlisted 12 months later on October 16, 1863, in Company I of the 56th North Carolina Infantry. He was said to ask God's blessing on the soul of each "blue-coat" after each firing. Having been captured at Five Forks, Virginia, he was released on June 29, 1865, at Point Lookout, Maryland. His military service; his annual celebration in June of "Big Day," which the area now observes on the Fourth of July; and his use of the fruit of the land have all helped to keep his memory alive.

Born on Sandy Run Creek in 1821, Amos made a reputation for himself in the Cherry Mountain section of the South Mountains in Rutherford County and as far away as the Mississippi River. Originally called Flint Kill, Cherry Mountain received its new name from the wild cherries that were numerous there and for the "cherry bounce" brewed by the blockader Amos Owens.

For his cherry bounce product, Amos blended 44 Blue Steel Whiskey, honey, and the juice from the cherries grown on the mountain. Cherry bounce became popular for its taste and for medicinal purposes—even though it was illegal. (Joe Stockton and Susan Todd.)

Amos Owens's Home, "The Castle"

Amos called his home, located on the side of Cherry Mountain, "The Castle." He bragged that it was three stories long and one story high. This photograph of Amos Owens's home on Cherry Mountain dates from 1875. The oxen-drawn wagon was typical of that age.

Amos and his wife, Mary Ann Sweezy Owens, accumulated 1,000 acres on Cherry Mountain where Amos continued to distill cherry bounce under the cover of the laurel, the rhododendron, and the other vegetation. Rumor suggests that Owens hid the profits from his cherry bounce and the annual "Big Day" celebration on the mountain; these caches have never been found even though some people still look for the riches.

Owens continued to run his distilleries despite arrests and a term in a prison in Albany, New York. A judge who was hesitant to incarcerate the elderly Owens offered to pardon him if he would promise to give up his illegal trade; Owens said that he could not promise, and so the judge gave him a prison sentence. (Joe Stockton.)

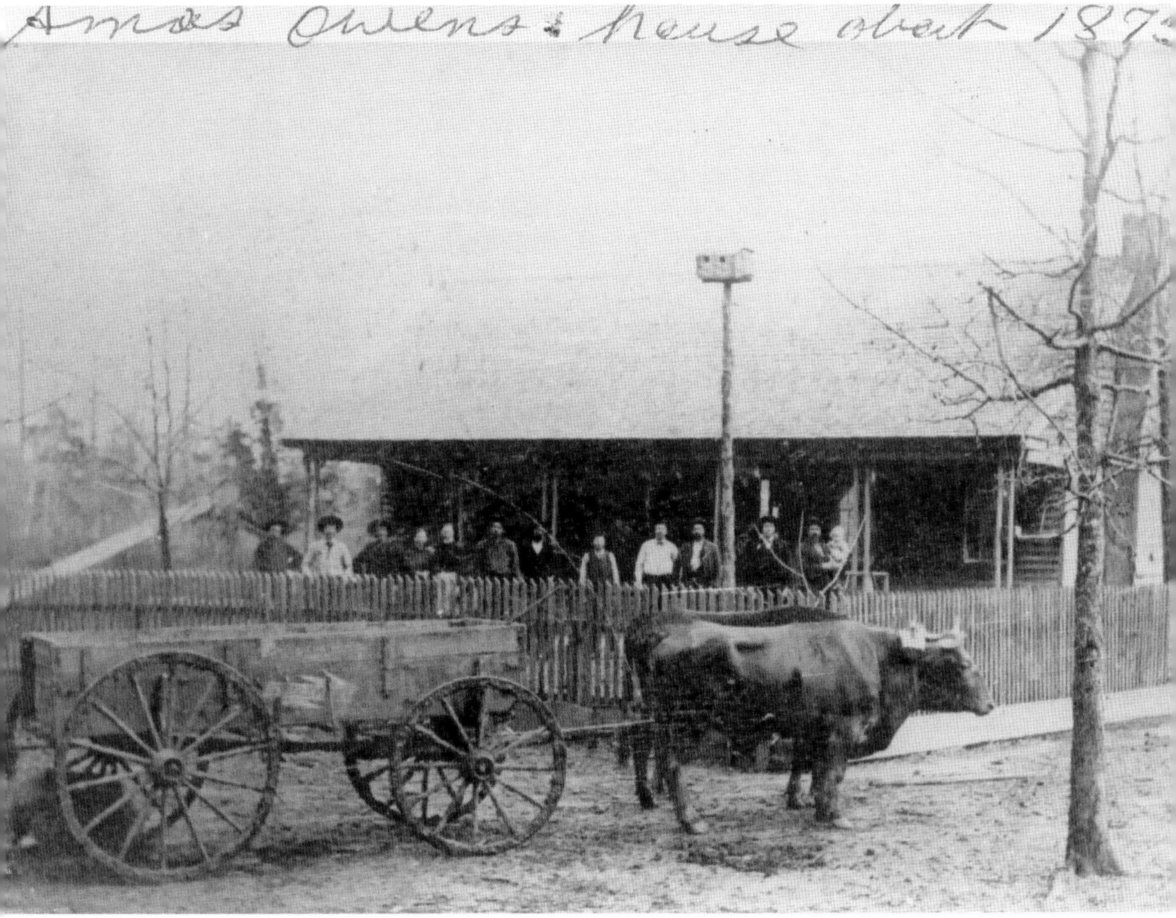

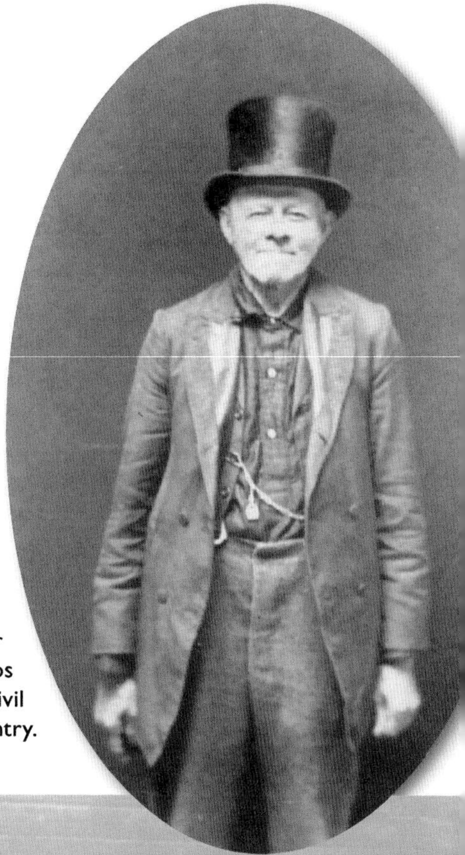

Amos Owens in Beaver Hat

In 1892, after one of his trials for illegal distilling, the judge, the lawyers on both sides, and his friends gave Amos Owens money for a beaver hat and a Prince Albert coat. This attire became his trademark.

The Big Day celebrations of the cherry harvest that Owens, his family, and friends had enjoyed so much still continue today in Ellenboro each Fourth of July. No Cherry Bounce is available, however!

In both the individual and the group photographs, Amos Owens wears his beaver hat; in the group photograph, he has his hand upon the shoulder of his wife, Mary Ann Sweezy Owens, sitting on the left. The occasion was probably a Big Day celebration; if so, it would have been complete with Cherry Bounce. Owens died on September 18, 1906. His burial was in Wall's Church Cemetery. Amos Owens's marker in Wall's Church Cemetery shows his Civil War Unit was Company I of the 56th North Carolina Infantry. (Both, Joe Stockton.)

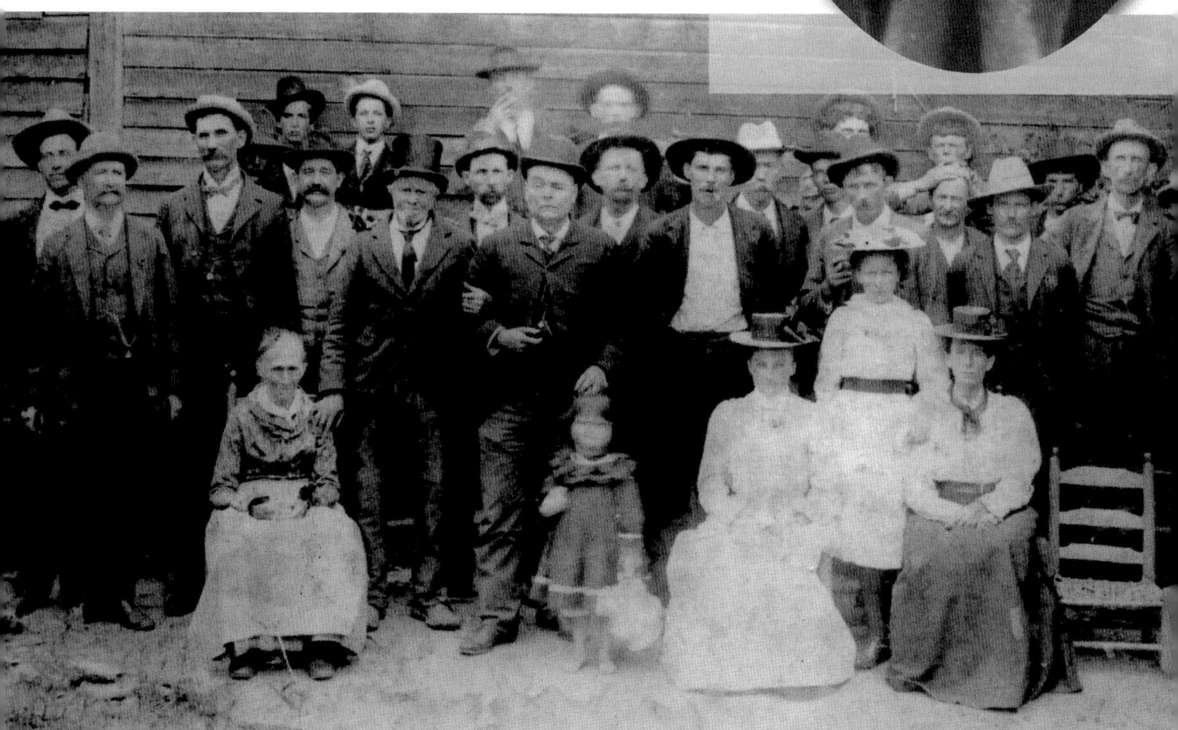

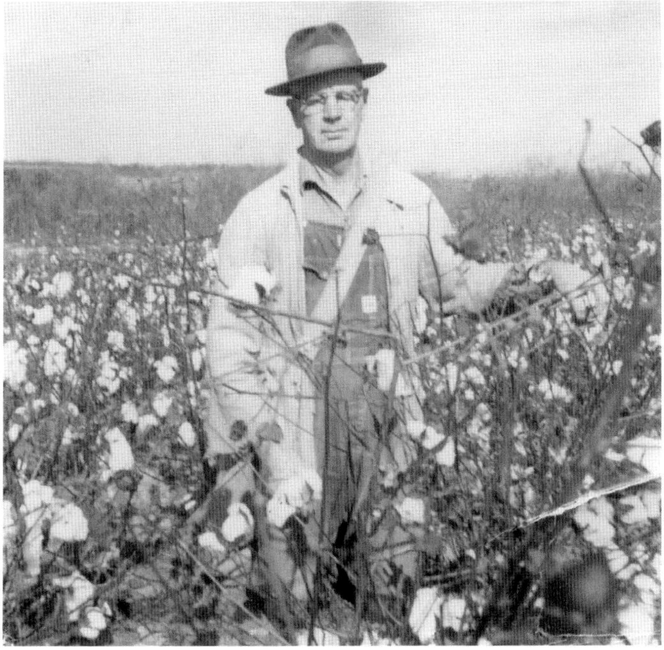

Coran Toney in Cotton
The Toney family's produce and other farm products were arguably some of the finest in the area. Here, local farmer Coran Toney, a World War II veteran, poses with his bumper crop of cotton. Cotton was an important cash crop in much of the county. The Toney family always tried to have a bale of cotton at the gin by the time of the local fair. (Mike Rhyne, Rachel Toney Jones, and J.V. Jones.)

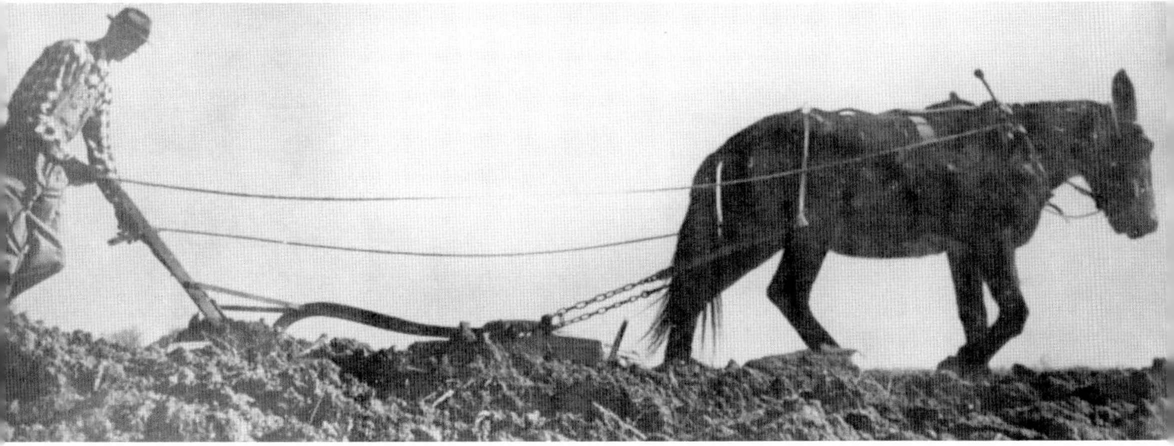

Fay Toney Plowing
Fay (February 3, 1909–July 23, 1994) was another representative of the Toney family and the many small farmers in Rutherford County. This photograph is of Fay using a mule-drawn plow, which, even into the 1960s, was typically preferred by most of the smaller Rutherford County farms. Like most of the Rutherford County men who had been of age during World War II, Fay served willingly. He achieved the rank of Tech-4 in a medical branch before the end of the war and before his honorable discharge.

A remarkable thing about Fay was the generosity that he showed to others. When he was in service, a ship carrying Fay and others sank. Fay remained aboard until the very end to help others in their evacuation. His kindness to others continued throughout his life.

Fay married Geneva Hughes (1913–1997). Visitors to their home were always welcomed. Their guests left with produce, grapes, apples, peaches, or whatever was in season; children were especially recipients of their generosity. Sharing was typical of many Rutherford County farmers, but Fay and Geneva were extremely bighearted. Those who knew him still remember his kindness, and his example continues. He was buried in Cleveland Memorial Park. (Betty Toney Davis.)

The Burns Family

This photograph shows the Burns family in 1910. Some remained farmers like many others in the county, but others opted for different lines of work. Interestingly, the photographer superimposed two deceased members of the family: the father (seated on the far left) and the son (standing behind his father). The deceased William Meredith Burns (January 20, 1846–August 19, 1907) and his son William Bryant Burns (May 15, 1899–November 3, 1909) appear even after their deaths and before computer imaging.

Other family members are, from left to right, mother, Fannie Lou Hamrick Burns (March 4, 1866–June 11, 1939); daughter Mary Cleo Burns (August 2, 1882–November 29, 1966), a polio survivor and a much-remembered teacher and artist who painted Baptisteries throughout the county for 40 years; farmer Clarence Leander Burns (December 25, 1883–October 22, 1959); Cora Burns Beam (September 7, 1985–July 1, 1970), a devoted wife, mother, and churchgoer; electrician and farmer Robert Ewart Burns (May 6, 1904–November 5, 1984) (See page 27.); the chaplain's wife, Bernice Burns Long (October 24, 1901–March 5, 1981); (second row) Zina Burns Dycus (March 26, 1890–March 3, 1949), Adelaide Burns Greene (January 12, 1897–July 2, 1978), Lolar Burns Hamrick (September 22, 1894–January 9,1969), Blanche Burns Lattimore (January 31, 1988–December 15, 1981); and telegrapher and former-farmer Ulys G. Burns (February 12, 1892–February 21,1968). (Author's collection.)

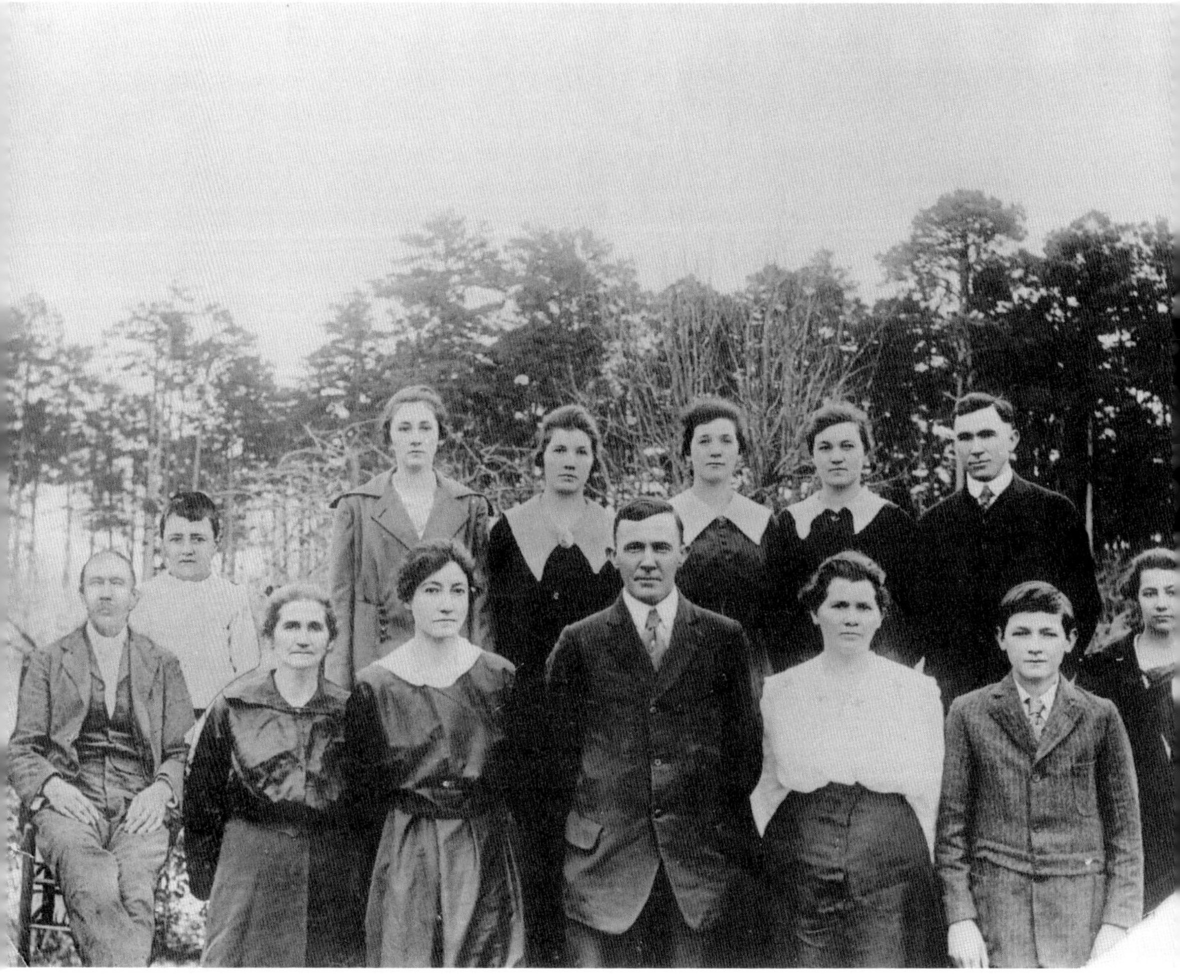

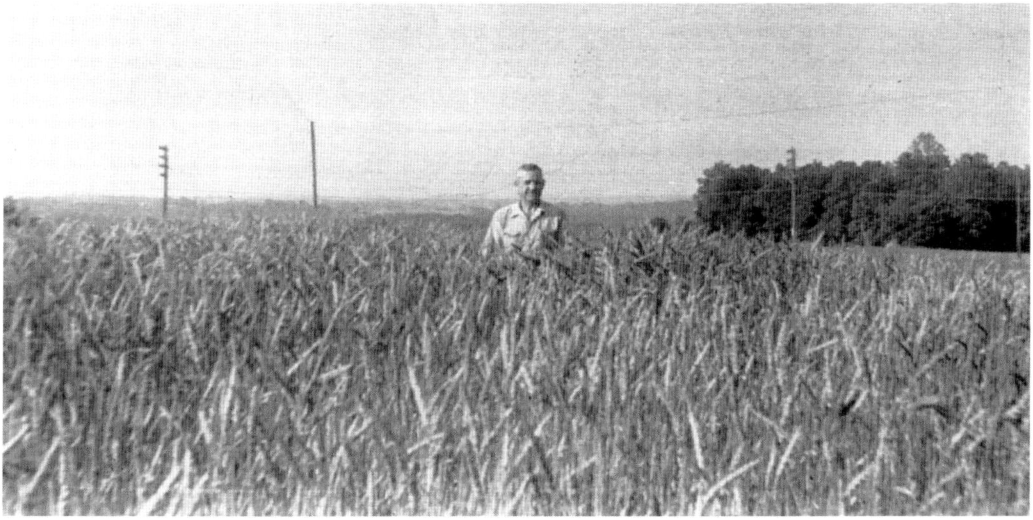

Robert Ewart Burns in Wheat Field

Electrician and farmer Robert Ewart Burns (1904–1984) stands in his Ellenboro wheat field outside his home at 2013 Highway 74 Business. His crop that year was mostly straw. Ewart was six feet, two inches tall, a measurement that helps indicate the height of the grain and its stalk.

Robert Ewart Burns worked outside jobs in addition to farming. First, he worked as an electrician and radio repairman at C.J. Hicks Store in Forest City and then he took a position in 1942 at the newly constructed Duke Power Steam Station. Ewart Burns also found time to help others with repairs. (Author's collection.)

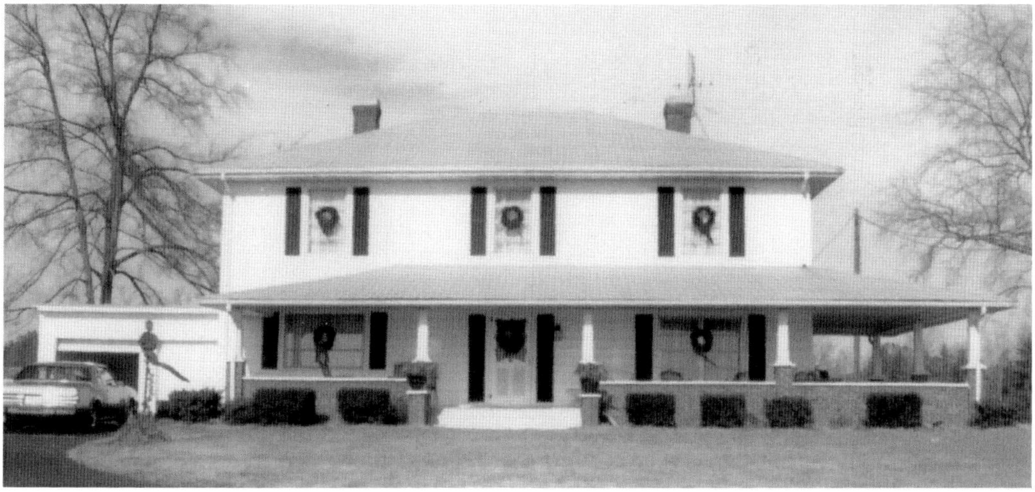

Ewart Burns's Home

Ewart resided most of his life in the Burns family home at 2013 Highway 74 Business. Without compensation, Ewart spent several days each year from 1929 to 1984 wiring the grounds of the Ellenboro School for the Colfax Free Fair; electricity was necessary for the rides and displays. He always promptly removed the cables after the event. In appreciation of Ewart's kindness and his often-free repair work for others, in the fall of 1985 Burns's hometown of Ellenboro decided to host a surprise event, which was to be called Ewart Burns Day in recognition of his good deeds. Ewart suffered a stroke on September 25 of that year before the event could unfold; the stroke would prove fatal. (Author's collection.)

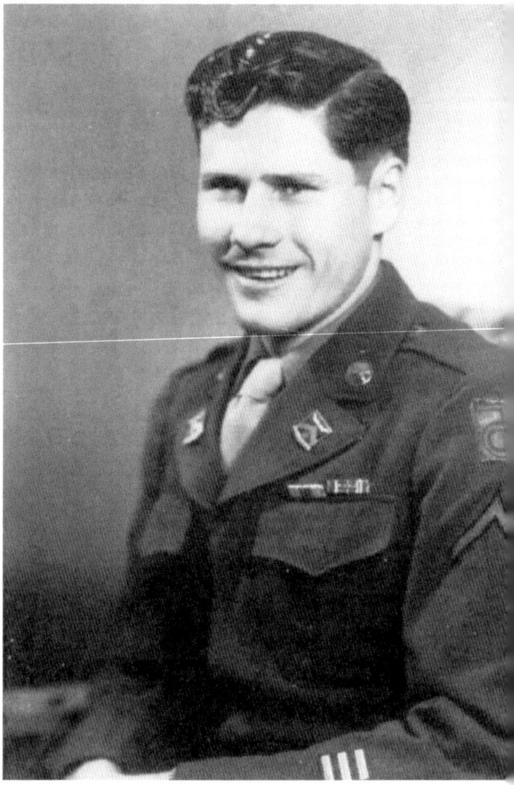

John Brooks: Veteran, Miner, and Merchant

Pfc. John Brooks served with the 740th Field Artillery during World War II. His unit was in the advance across the Rhine.

Before his entry into the military, John of Ellenboro worked on his father's farm. The Brooks family's Rutherford County farm had an unusual feature: B.B. Brooks, John's father, was able to mine mica on their property. John remembers that there was a lot of work involved in extracting and trimming the mica crystals, but a cigar box full of the mica sold for \$20–\$40, which was a windfall in the 1930s and early 1940s. The mica was used for "glass" in stoves and furnaces, for capacitors and insulators in electronics, and for insulation in fighter planes. Seventy percent of the nation's mica came from North Carolina, but such mining in the county was unusual. After World War II, Brooks operated a general store. (John Brooks.)

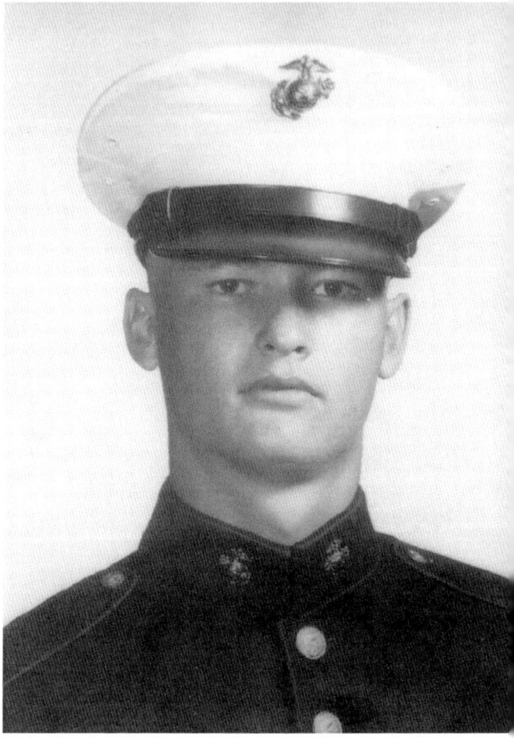

Cpl. Gaston David Godfrey

Having grown up on a farm in the county, Corporal Godfrey (February 23, 1942–March 18, 1966) was unable to return to it at the end of the Vietnam War. While serving in the Marine Corps, he was 1 of 10 Rutherford County men who died in the war.

A Purple Heart recipient, Godfrey died in hostile ground action in Quang Nam, South Vietnam. The Wall That Heals honors Godfrey on Panel 6E, Row 20. (Shirley Godfrey Guest.)

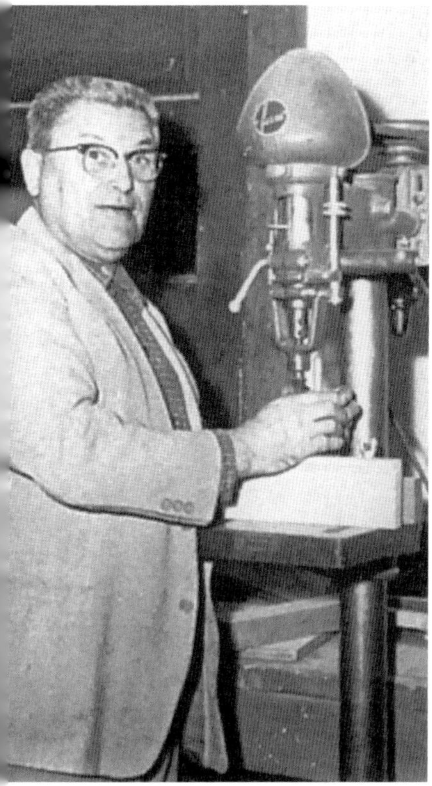

A.B. Bushong

Albert Bauman Bushong (March 3, 1894–January 9, 1978) was an agriculture teacher at Ellenboro School. He started a chick hatchery in the county with a capacity of 7,000 eggs. A.B. also instituted a cannery; taught agriculture classes for adults; served as chief observer of aircraft warning during World War II; provided training for returning veterans; organized tours to Washington, DC, for members of the community and high school classes; organized the installation of 600 mailboxes; and advised area residents on agriculture. In addition to organizing the Colfax Free Fair and performing the above community services, A.B. Bushong advised farmers in the area to begin developing a new cash crop, sweet potatoes. (Frank Wall.)

Bushong's New Cash Crop for County

A.B. Bushong met with the Rutherford County farmers in the 1930s and 1940s and gave suggestions for planting, tending, and harvesting the sweet potato crop on a large scale. Bushong offered a strategy for providing the large "potato houses" necessary for curing and storing the crops at the time. Bushong's recommendations increased the income of the individual farmers and of the county as a whole. Many of these 80-year-old potato houses instituted by A.B. Bushong in the 1930s and 1940s still stand today. (James M. Walker.)

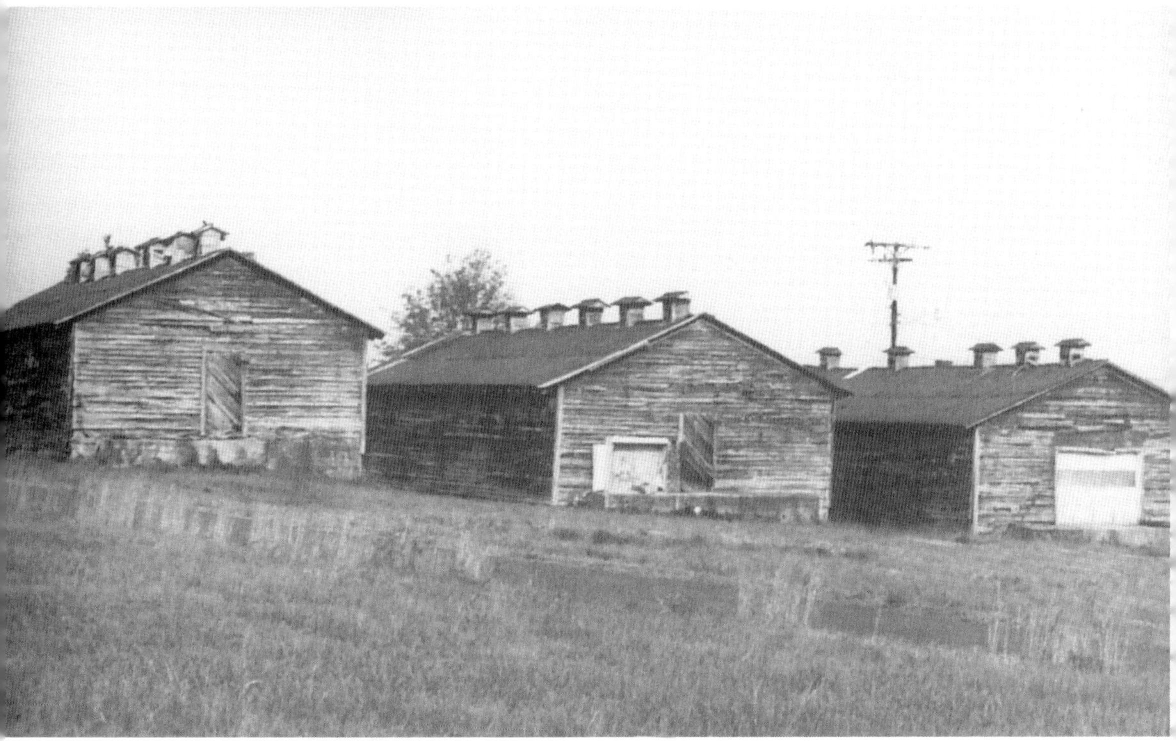

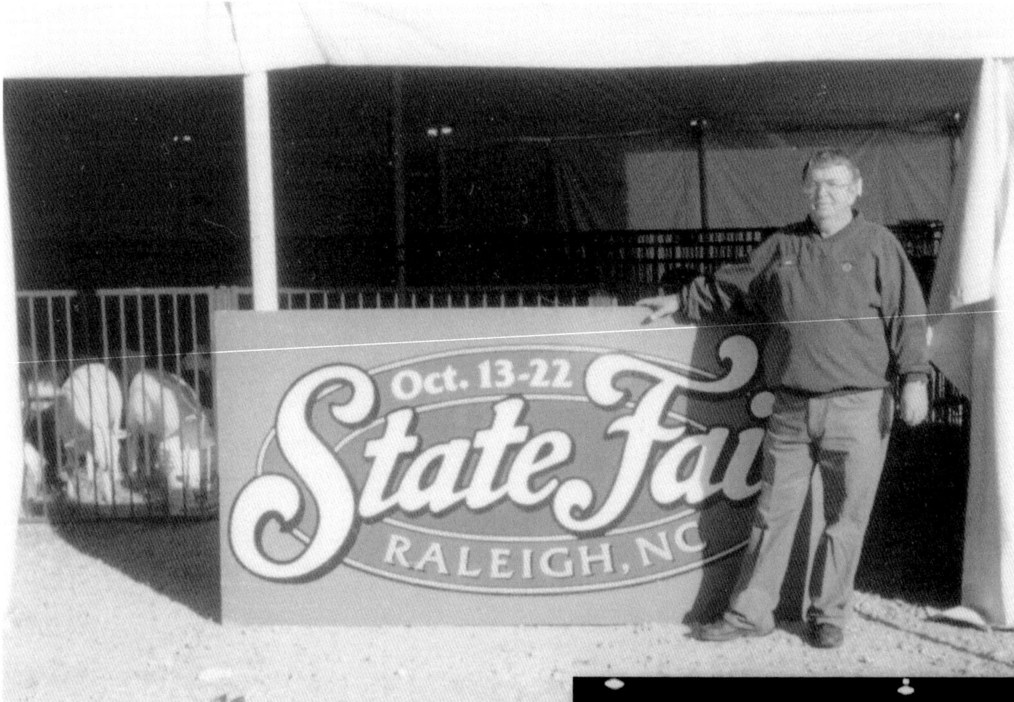

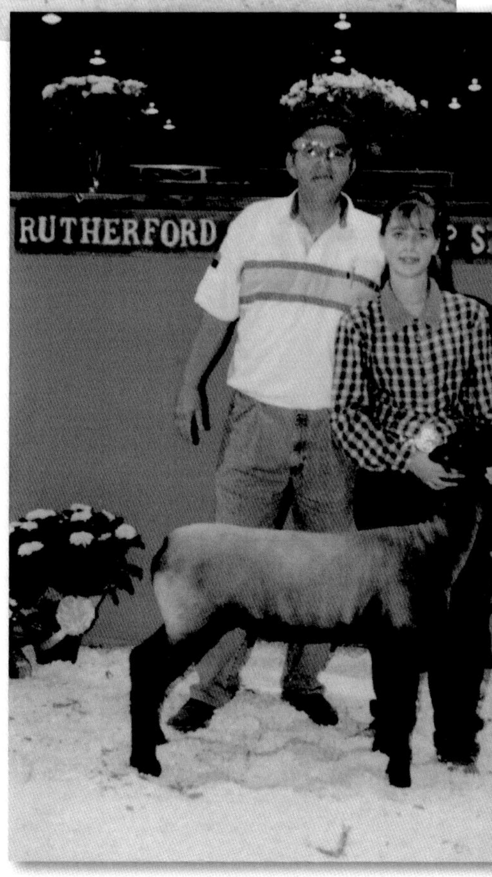

Bruce Hoyle and His Farm
Here, North Carolina native Bruce Hoyle stands near the 2000 North Carolina State Fair sign. Hoyle had entries in the state fair as well as in the local fairs. For 37 years, he was the corporate executive officer of Hoyle Insurance Company, just below the courthouse in Rutherfordton, North Carolina. While Hoyle was still in insurance, he began a new venture. He began raising goats, sheep, llamas, and even parakeets. He called his farm the Hoyle North Carolina Farm.

Hoyle's love of his animals spread to his three children, his nine grandchildren, and his three great-grandchildren. He and his family have been actively raising and exhibiting animals in competition for years. (Bruce Hoyle.)

Bruce Hoyle and Joy Blanton, Grand Champion Lamb
Here, Joy Blanton and Bruce Hoyle show their Grand Champion Lamb at the Rutherford County Fair. This is only one of the many prizes Hoyle animals have taken through the years. Hoyle is extremely pleased with the success and the effort that his family has put into the Hoyle North Carolina Farm. Bruce Hoyle proudly claims, "All the winners from this family would fill a book!" (Bruce Hoyle.)

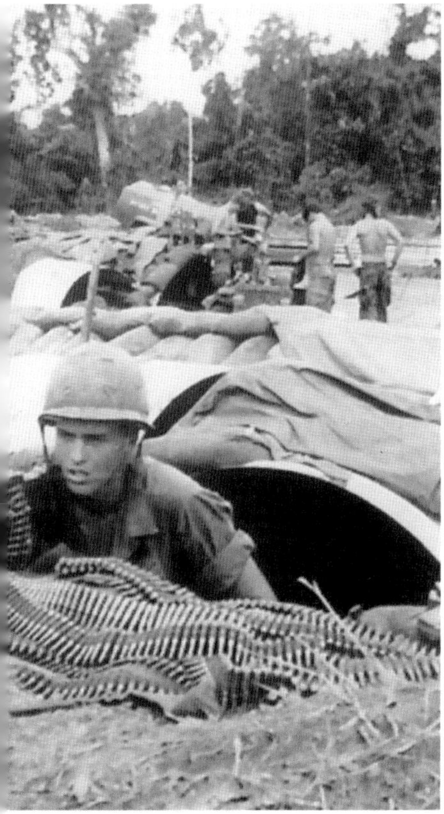

Veteran Jerry D. Nelon

Sgt. Jerry D. Nelon served his country with distinction during the Vietnam War. Nelon earned the National Defense Service Medal; the Vietnam Service Medal with two Bronze Service Stars; the Combat Infantryman Badge; the Republic of Vietnam Campaign Medal; the Air Medal; the Army Commendation Medal with one Oak Leaf Cluster and "V" Device; and the Sharpshooter Award (Rifle). Jerry D. Nelon's military training enabled him to use the M-60. In this photograph, Nelon is in position at a Forward Fire Support Base in Vietnam. (Jerry D. and Robin Nelon.)

Bison Farmer Jerry Nelon and Knoll Farms

Nelon and his wife, Robin, call their family-owned and family-operated bison ranch Knoll Farms. In August 2011, the Nelons had 70 head of animals.

The Nelons do not allow hunting of the bison on their Knoll Farm, but they do conduct prearranged tours of the farm. They also rent the facilities for scheduled events. (Jerry D. and Robin Nelon.)

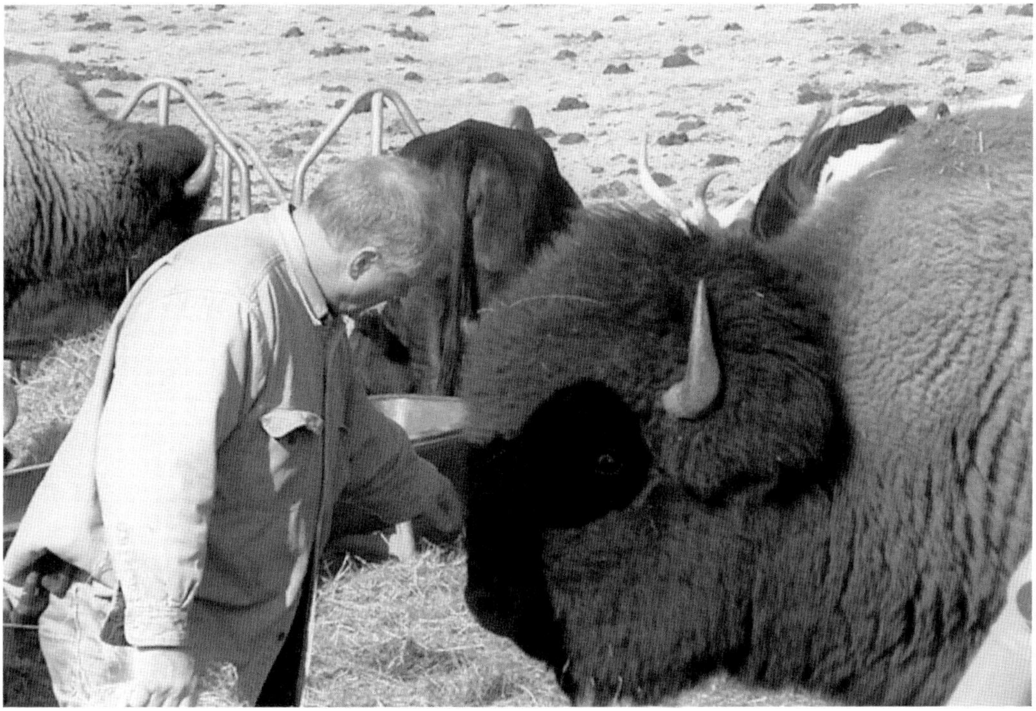

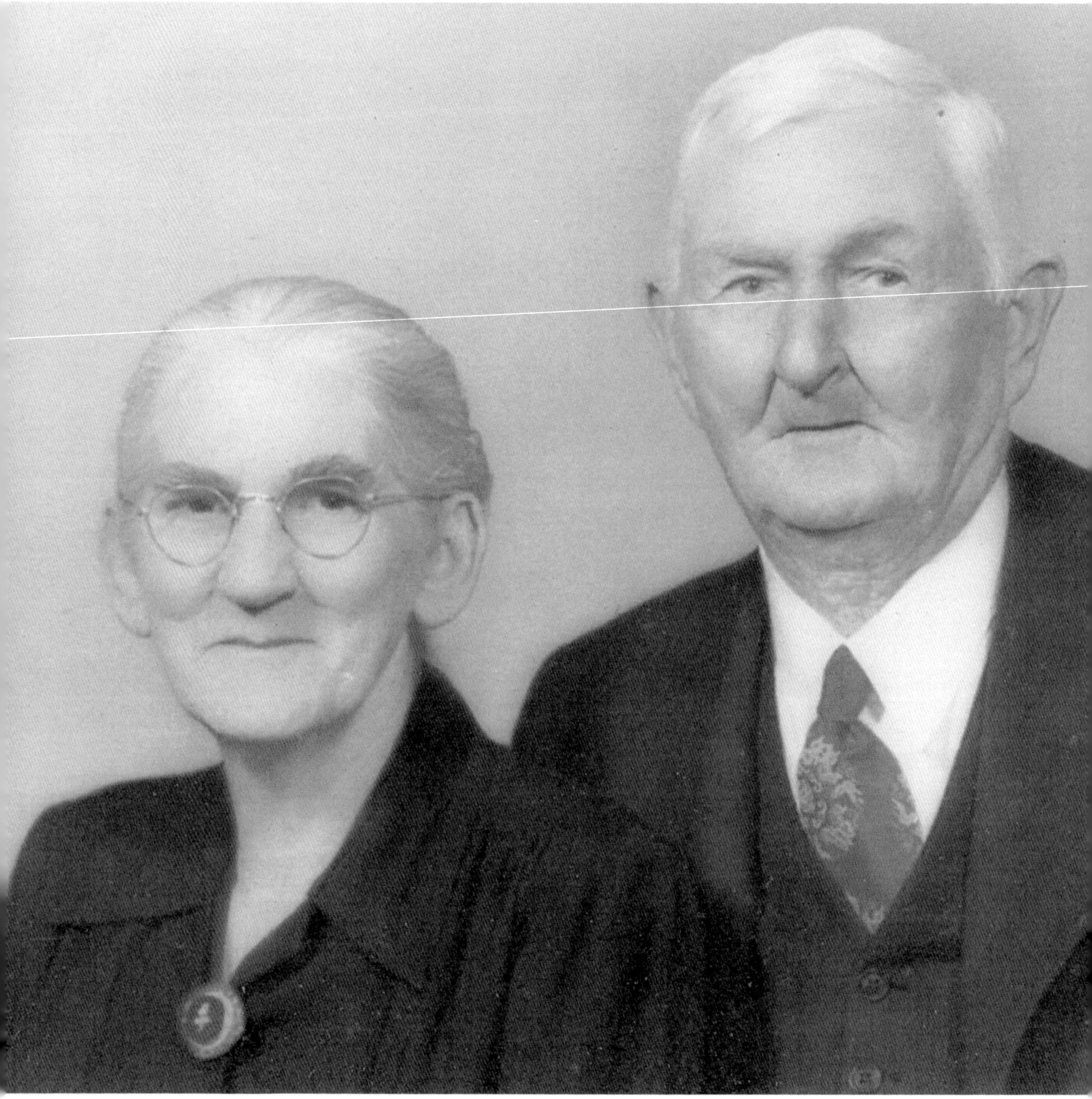

James Louis Hamrick and Sarah B. Hamrick
Pictured here are James Louis Hamrick (1869–1970) and his wife, Sarah B. Hamrick (1874–1956). They were original owners of Hamrick Lumberyard in Ellenboro. Jimmy Louis lived to be 101 years old. He was considered the resident historian on the Civil War veterans from the area because he remembered listening to their stories when he was only a child. Jimmy Louis and Sarah were the parents of seven children; one of them, Eldon Hamrick (1894–1979), helped in the operation of the lumberyard, which endured for more than half a century. Eldon and his family, which included his sons Dick and Bob, assumed responsibility for the establishment after his father's death. (Colfax Museum and Mike Rhyne.)

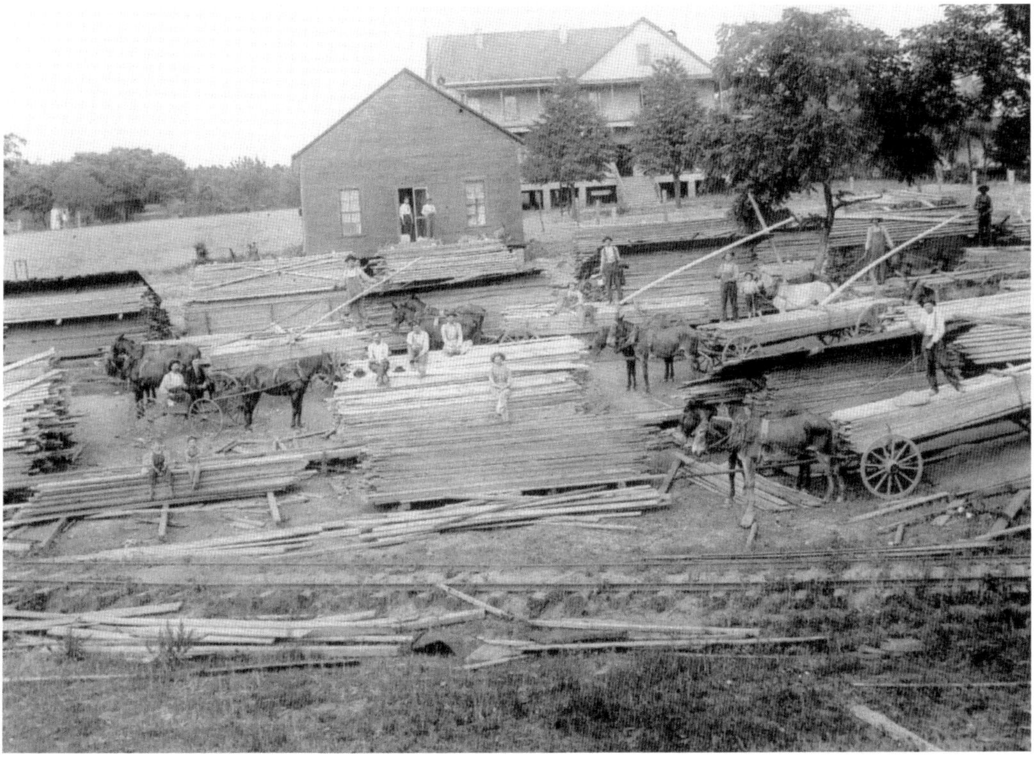

Hamrick's Lumberyard

For more than half a century, Jimmy Louis Hamrick's home and Hamrick Lumberyard were landmarks on the much-traveled main road between Forest City and Shelby, North Carolina. This is a 1910 photograph of the lumberyard—even before the completion of Highway 74 Business in Ellenboro. In the background of this photograph of the Hamrick Lumberyard in Ellenboro, one can see the Hamrick residence near the yard. The inclusion of the mules and horses and the antiquity of the equipment help indicate the age of the image. (Beulah Pruette and family.)

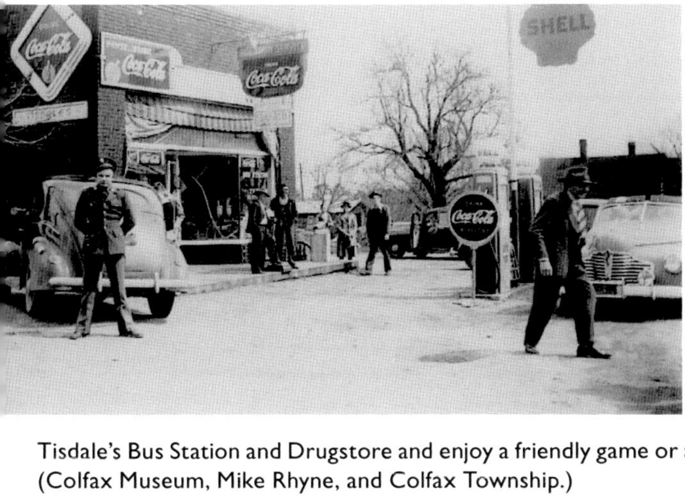

Jimmy Louis Hamrick

Jimmy Louis (1869–1970) remained active and alert for most of his 101 years. Here, Hamrick (in the suit) is walking in front of Tisdale's Bus Station and Drugstore in Ellenboro. T. Lawson appears in the law enforcement uniform.

Hamrick and his lumber business were familiar sights in Ellenboro. After his semiretirement from the lumber company, Hamrick and some of his friends would set up their checkerboard or domino game in the shade at the side of Tisdale's Bus Station and Drugstore and enjoy a friendly game or attempt to solve the world's problems. (Colfax Museum, Mike Rhyne, and Colfax Township.)

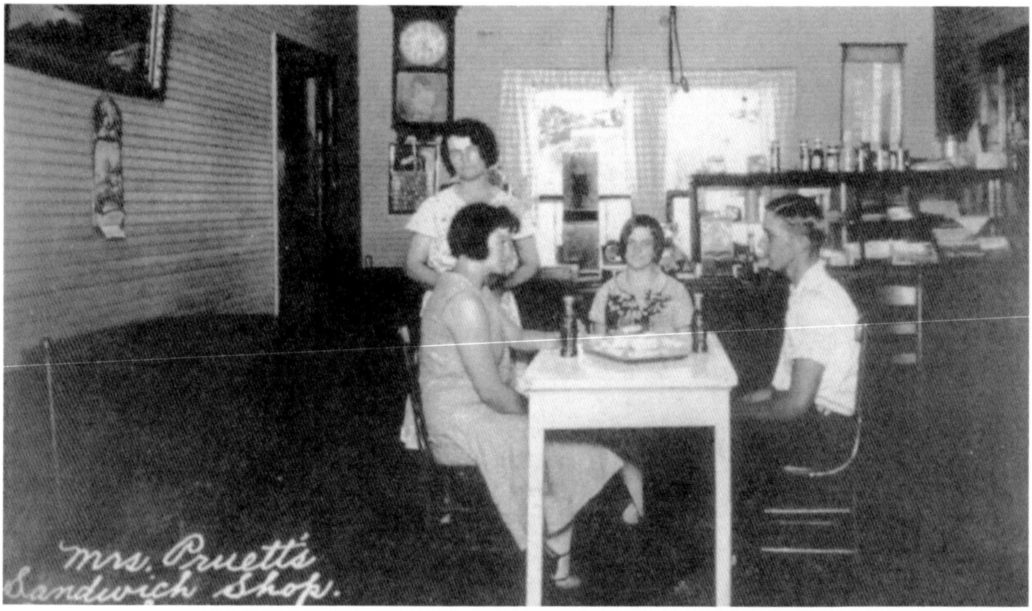

Beulah Bessie Glover Pruette's Sandwich Shop
Beulah Bessie Glover Pruette lived near the Hamrick Lumberyard. Like most people in the area, she could not help but notice the business and the traffic around the Hamrick Lumberyard. Beulah and her husband, Edgar Thomas Pruette, had an idea: she would establish a sandwich shop to serve the locals, the loggers, and the travelers on the road between Forest City and Shelby. Beulah, who is standing in the photograph and who had previously owned a tea shop, set an example of hard work, responsibility, and enterprise for the community and for her family, especially her daughter Nelle Pruette Butler Wright (page 54). Pruette's Sandwich Shop became a gathering place for the community from about 1927 to 1940. Seated from left to right are Beatrice Edwards Hamrick (December 20, 1906–February 3, 1998), Iva May Jones, and Forest Harrill. (Beulah Pruette and family.)

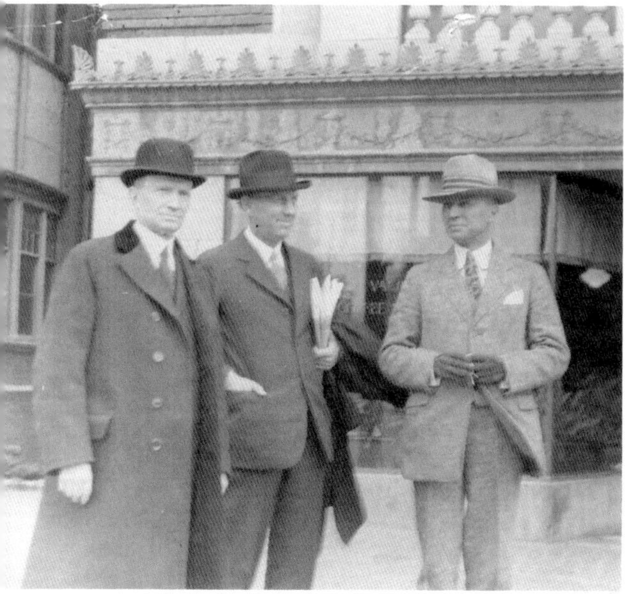

Lucius Morse and His Twin Brothers
Also at work in the county in the 1920s were entrepreneurs, especially Lucius Boardman Morse (1871–1946) and his twin brothers, Hiram and Asahel. Born in Warrensburg, Illinois, Lucius Morse graduated from Valparaiso University and Chicago Medical College (1897). He practiced medicine in St. Louis for only one year before developing tuberculosis. After two years of recuperation, he renewed practice in Asheville, which had the reputation of hosting a healthy climate for TB victims. Morse fell in love with nearby Chimney Rock and brought his brothers to see the area. Pictured from left to right are Lucius, Hiram, and Asahel Morse. The brothers bought Chimney Rock and 64 acres for $5,000 from Jerome Freeman; they planned to develop the area into a resort and park for the tourist trade. (Chimney Rock Park Media Room, Mary Standish.)

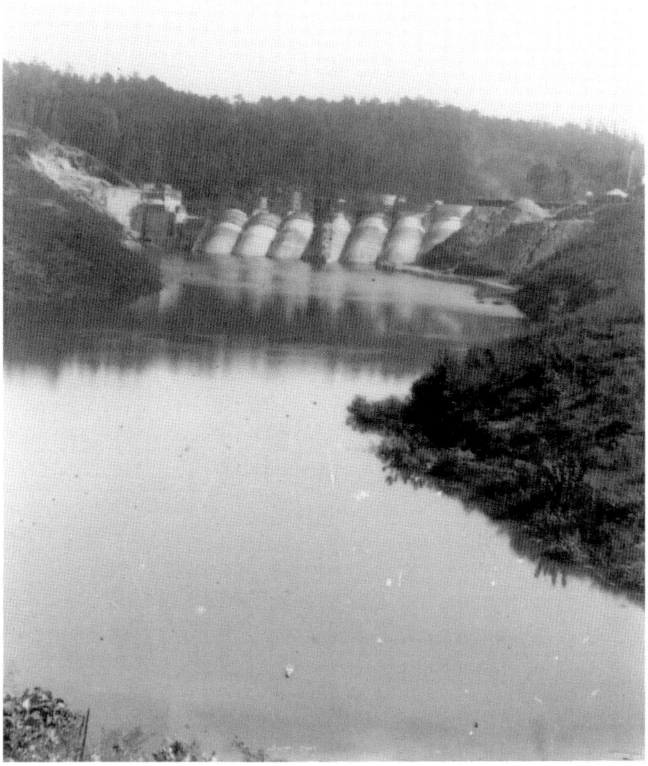

Morse Begins Lake Lure and Inn

Planning for the Lake Lure Inn began in 1925; the Lake Lure Inn would draw many people, including notables, such as Pres. Franklin Delano Roosevelt, Emily Post, and F. Scott Fitzgerald. During World War II, the inn provided a safe place for servicemen needing rest and rehabilitation.

In 1925, bonds helped finance a contract for building a dam across the Rocky Broad River. The dam would help generate power and would form a 1,500-acre mountain lake, which would have a 27-mile shoreline. The dam closed on September 20, 1926. This photograph shows the dam beginning to impound the water of the Rocky Broad River into a lake. (W.H. McArthur; photograph by "Will" McArthur.)

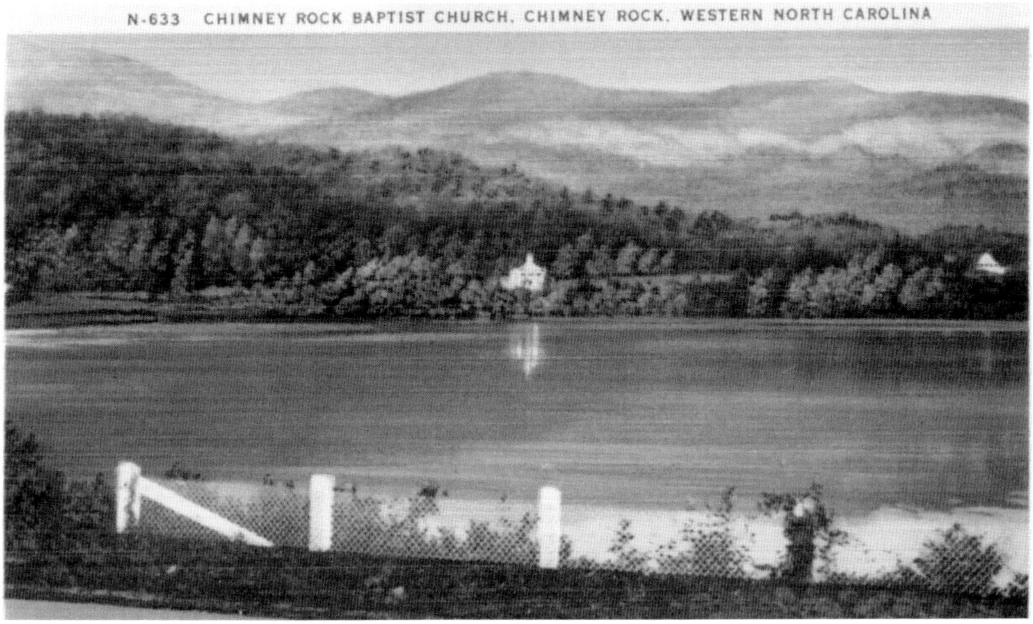

Chimney Rock Baptist Church Cemetery

Lucius B. Morse and park superintendent and builder Guilford Nanney are interred in the cemetery of Chimney Rock Baptist Church, pictured here. Lake Lure is evident in the foreground of this card. (Asheville Postcard Company, Asheville, North Carolina.)

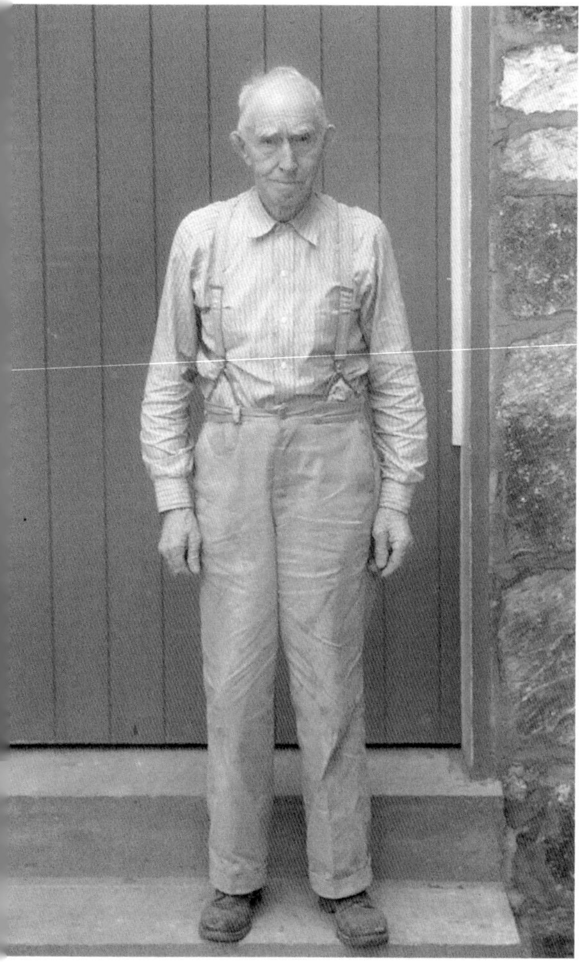

Guilford Nanney

By the time the Morses purchased Chimney Rock from Jerome Freeman, the 2,280-foot, wooden stairway to Chimney Rock that Freeman had had installed was 17 years old. Exposed to the elements for almost two decades, the stairs were no longer safe. The Morses contacted local builder Guilford Nanney to consider rebuilding the 472 steps so that visitors could reach the top of Chimney Rock.

Born in Henderson County, Guilford Nanney (January 10, 1871–November 10, 1952) designed tall houses "in his head" and built them for others. Several of the houses he designed and built are in the National Historic Register. Nanney agreed to complete the work in two weeks. (Chimney Rock Park Media Room, Mary Standish.)

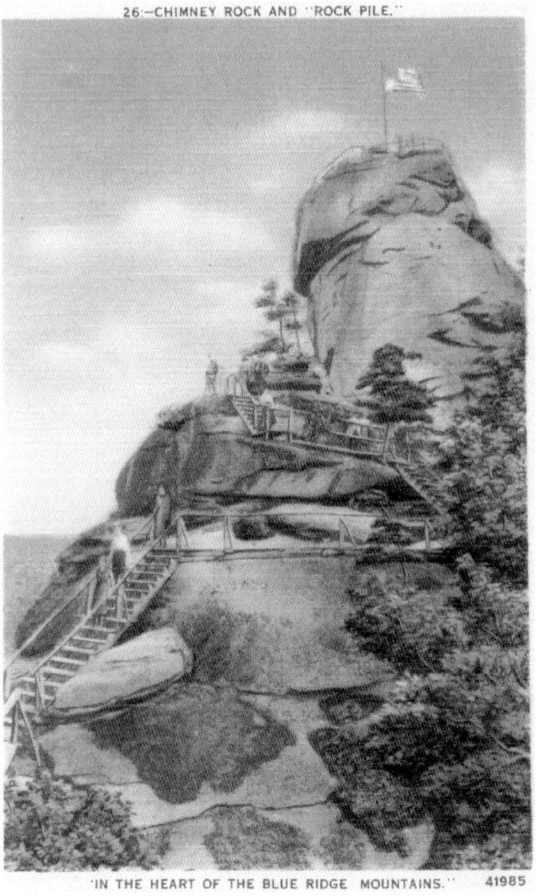

Nanney's Work

This early postcard shows some of the 472 steps, landings, and lookouts that visitors had to climb to reach the top of Chimney Rock before the installation of the elevator in 1949. Nanney had used locust wood, which became "like iron" with age.

Nanney also designed a network of paths and lookouts in Chimney Rock Park. He spent his later years serving as Chimney Rock Park superintendent. Nanney lived to see the installation of the Chimney Rock elevator in 1949. (Asheville Postcard Company, Asheville, North Carolina.)

Civilian Conservation Corps Workers in North Carolina

To encourage the conservation and preservation of the natural resources and to increase the employment of the citizens, Pres. Franklin Delano Roosevelt ordered on April 5, 1933, the institution of the Civilian Conservation Corps (CCC). Rutherford County benefitted directly from this action. The development of Western North Carolina and Rutherford County resulted from President Roosevelt's brainchild. The construction of the Blue Ridge Parkway and the enhancement of the Great Smoky Mountains National Park drew many travelers into Rutherford County. (North Carolina Division of Archives and History.)

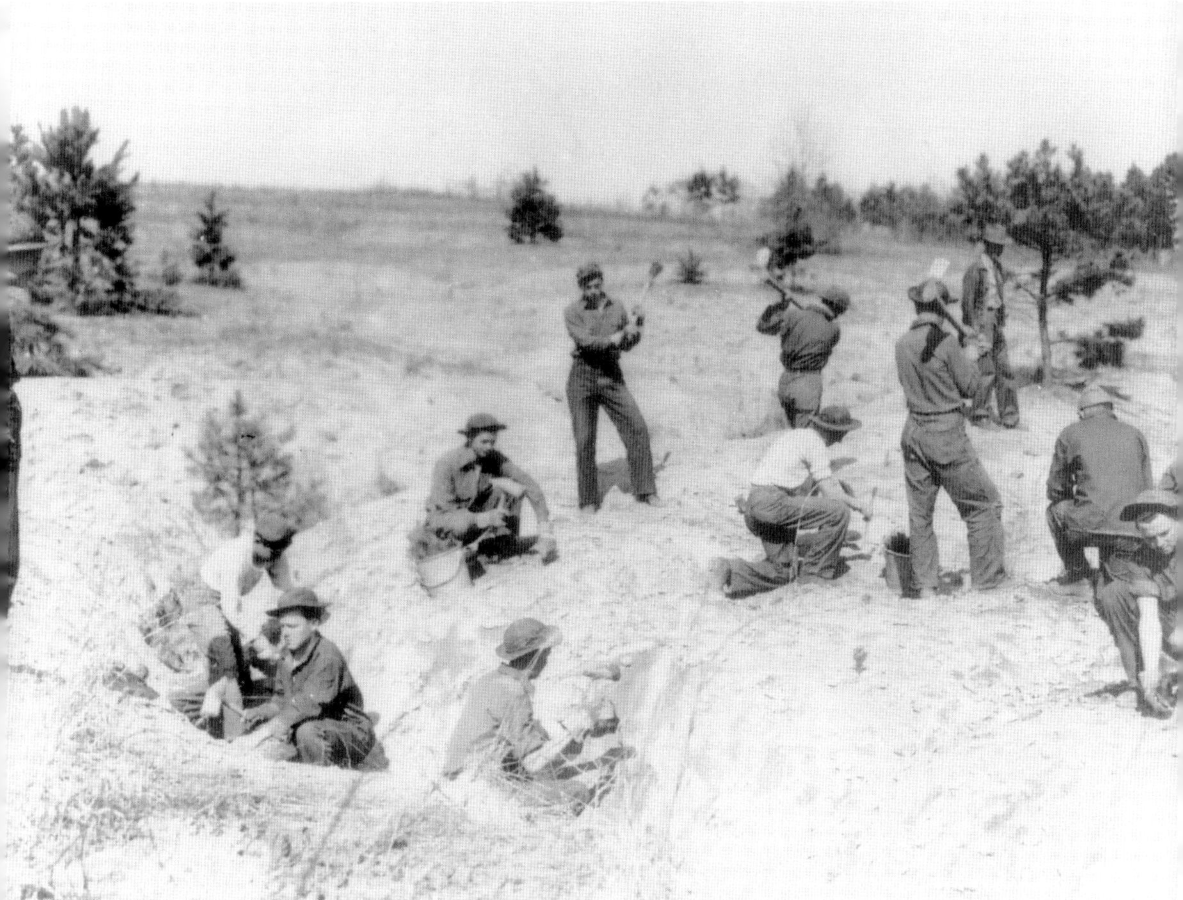

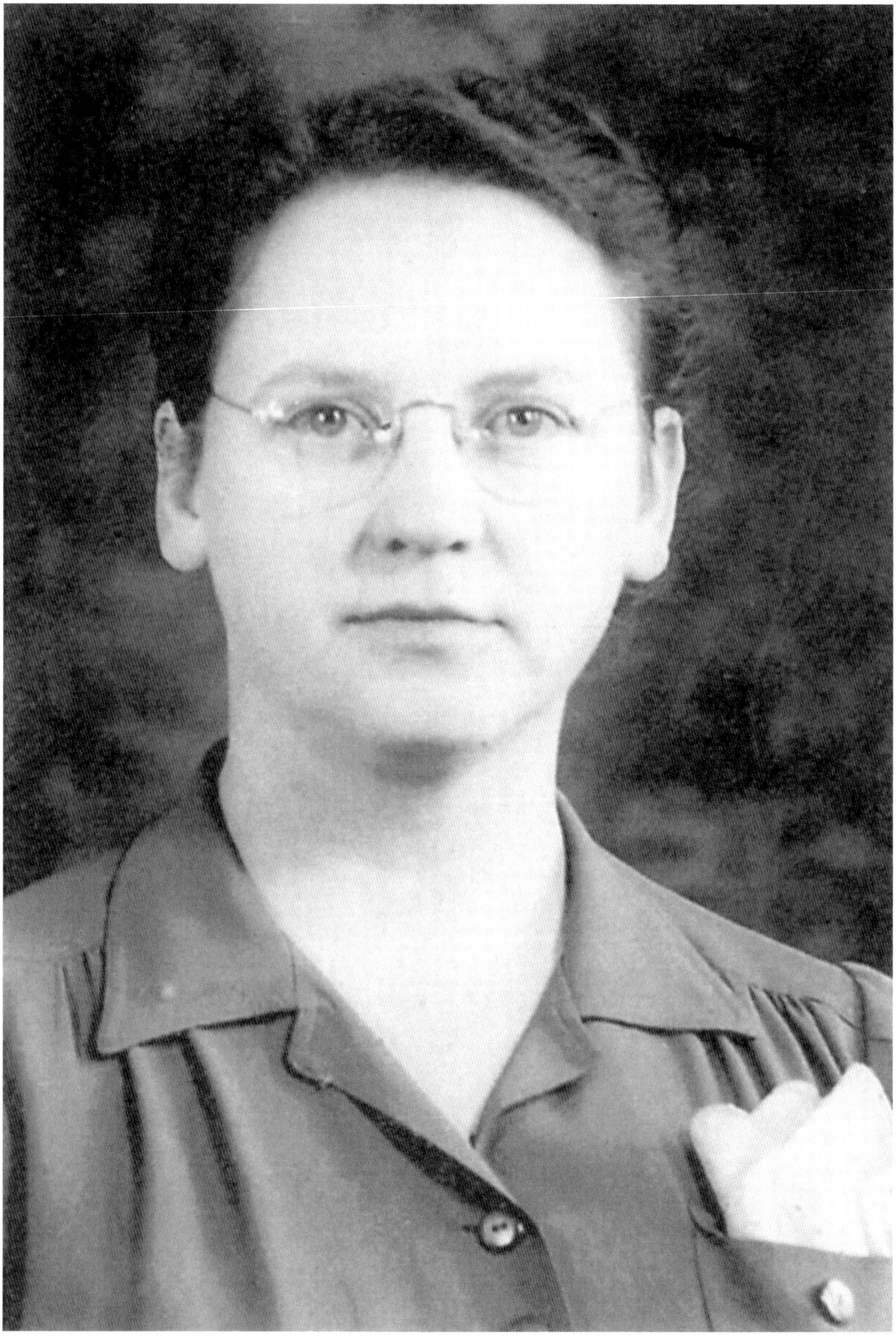

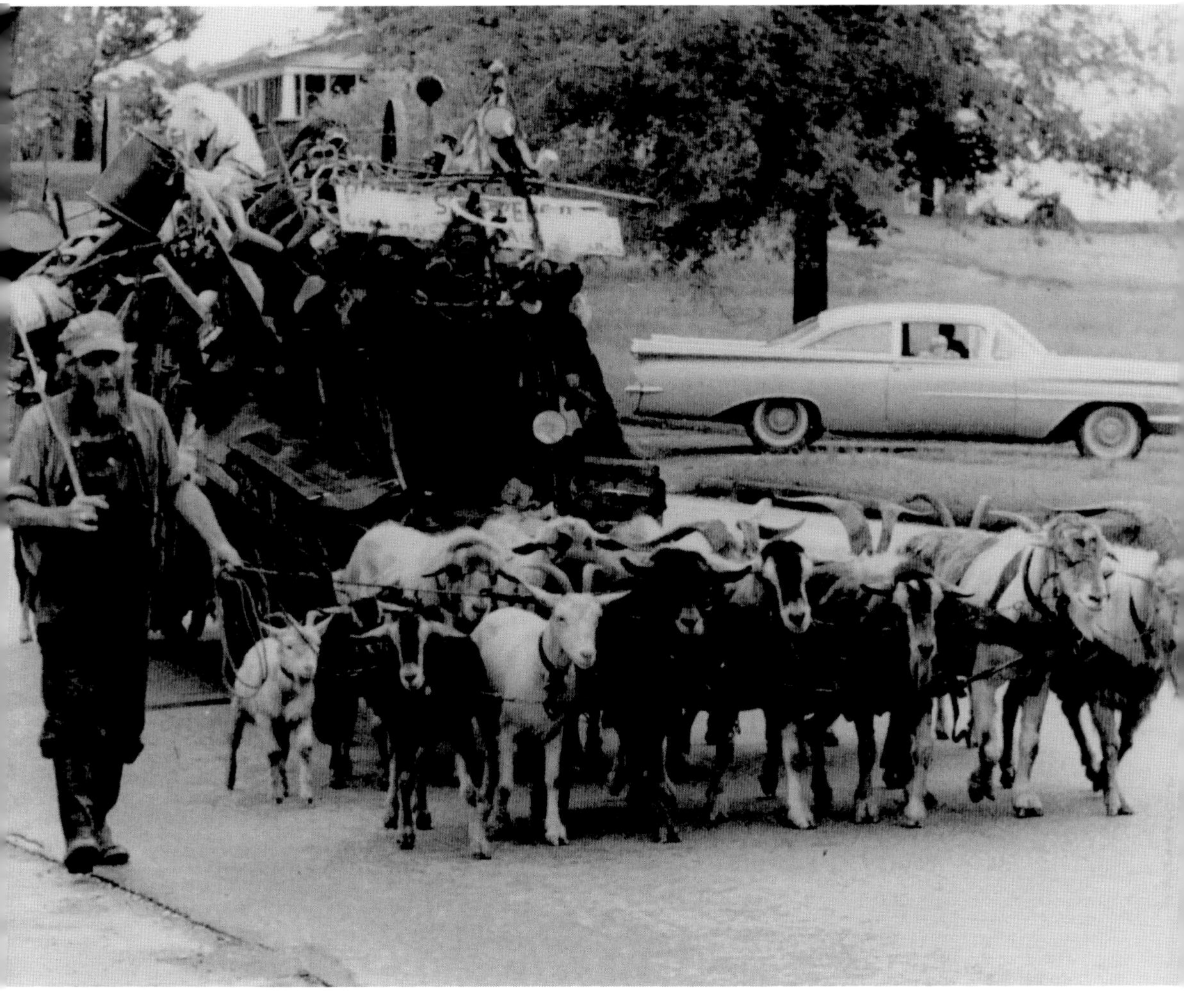

Charles "Chess" McCartney

Charles "Chess" McCartney (July 6, 1901–November 15, 1998) was a traveling animal husbandman. He was not a permanent resident of Rutherford County, but his yearly visits in his goat-drawn wagon for several decades made him a familiar sight throughout the county. Born in 1901 in Sigourney, Iowa, the "Goat Man" began traveling in the late 1930s. He bragged of visiting each of the contiguous states at least once. He lived off donations, contributions after his sermons, and the postcards that he sold. This photograph of Chess McCartney shows him with his goat caravan on Main Street in Spindale, North Carolina. (Author's collection.)

Walda Morris Carpenter, Welfare Worker (OPPOSITE PAGE)

The employment of some of the CCC workers was a direct result of an interview with Walda Morris Carpenter in the Welfare Department of Rutherford County. In her job, she had to certify those who were eligible for employment in the CCC. Carpenter (1906–2003) left teaching to work with the Welfare Department of Rutherford County. She had as one of her duties the interviewing of young men to work with the Civilian Conservation Corps; she believed controlling the erosion in the county benefitted the area farmers and the state in general. Rutherford County welcomed the tourist trade enhanced by the Blue Ridge Parkway and the Great Smoky Mountains National Park. (Walda Morris Carpenter.)

Author and Chess McCartney, 1990s

In 1990, "Chess" McCartney was living in a retirement home in Easton, Georgia. Chess talked eagerly of the peace of sleeping under the stars or in the wagon in bad weather; he spoke of sleeping with the goats for warmth. He talked of some strange lights in the sky he had seen. He recalled Price's Store and his visits there. (Author's collection.)

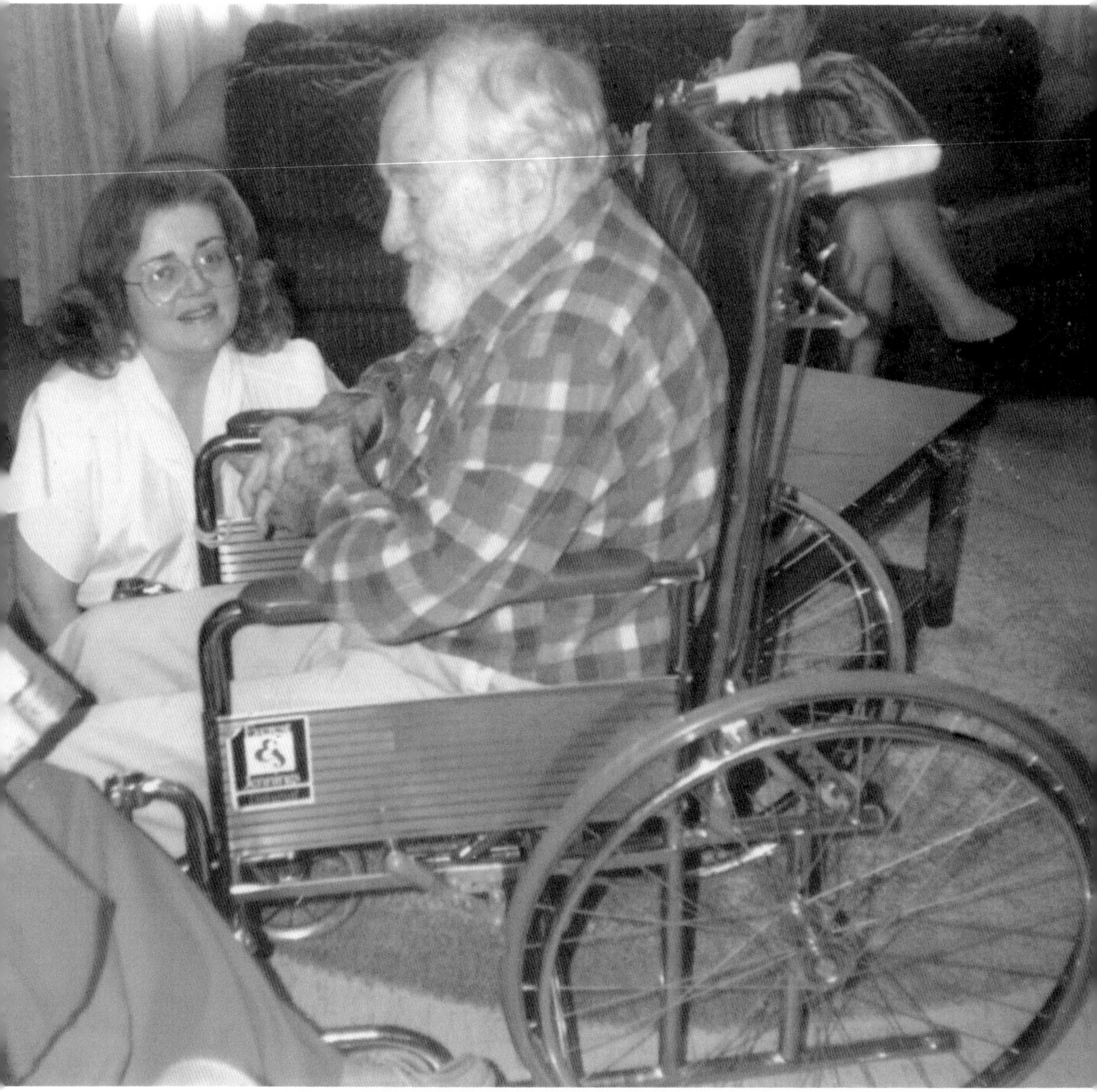

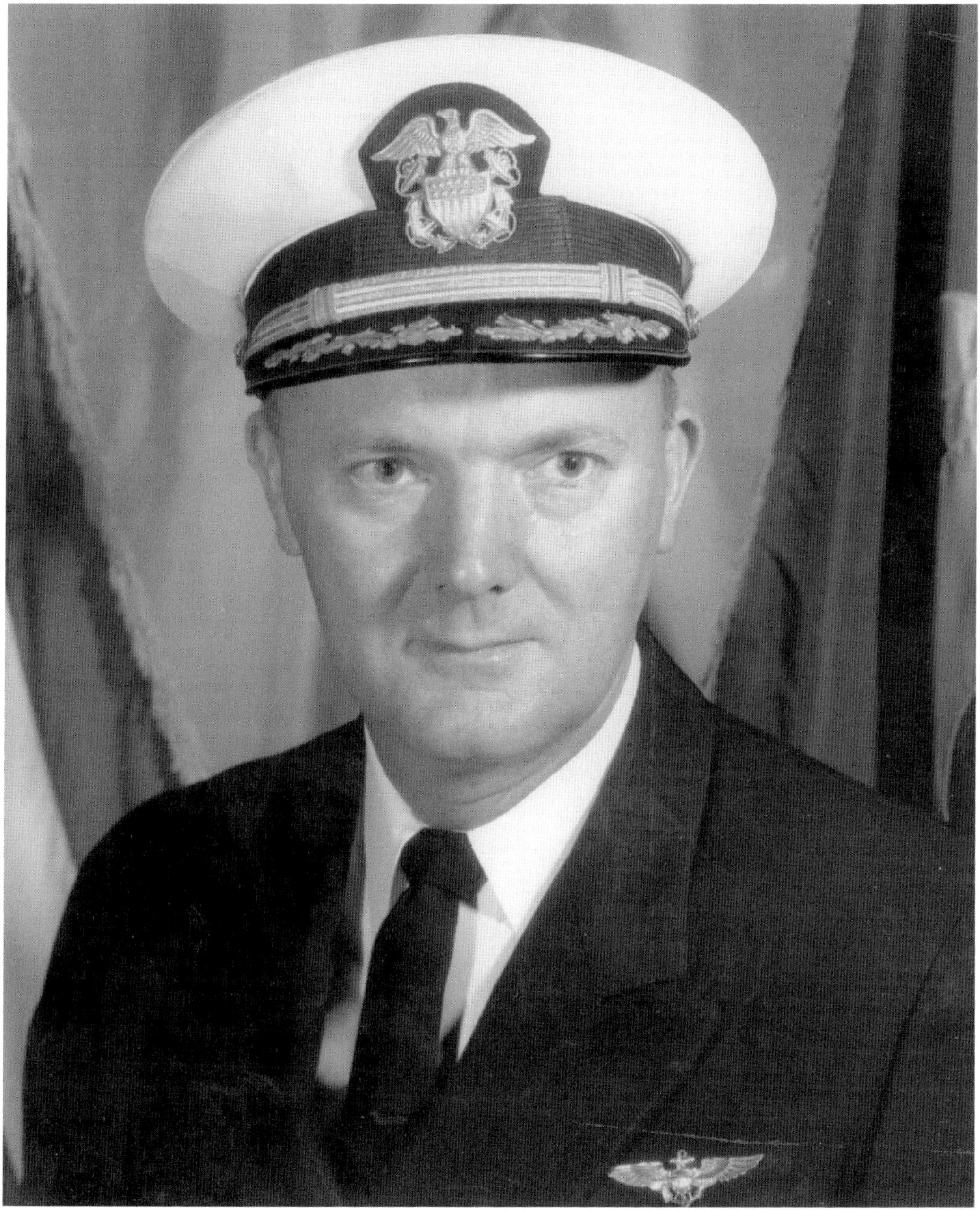

Capt. Wilbur J. Burgin

Burgin entered military service on May 6, 1943, and retired on August 1, 1974. During his military career, Captain Burgin had over 5,000 flight hours and over 500 carrier landings. His military service encompassed three wars: World War II, the Korean War, and the War in Vietnam. After retiring from the military, he worked his own and his brother Max's farm. However, he had something else in mind. (Wilbur J. Burgin.)

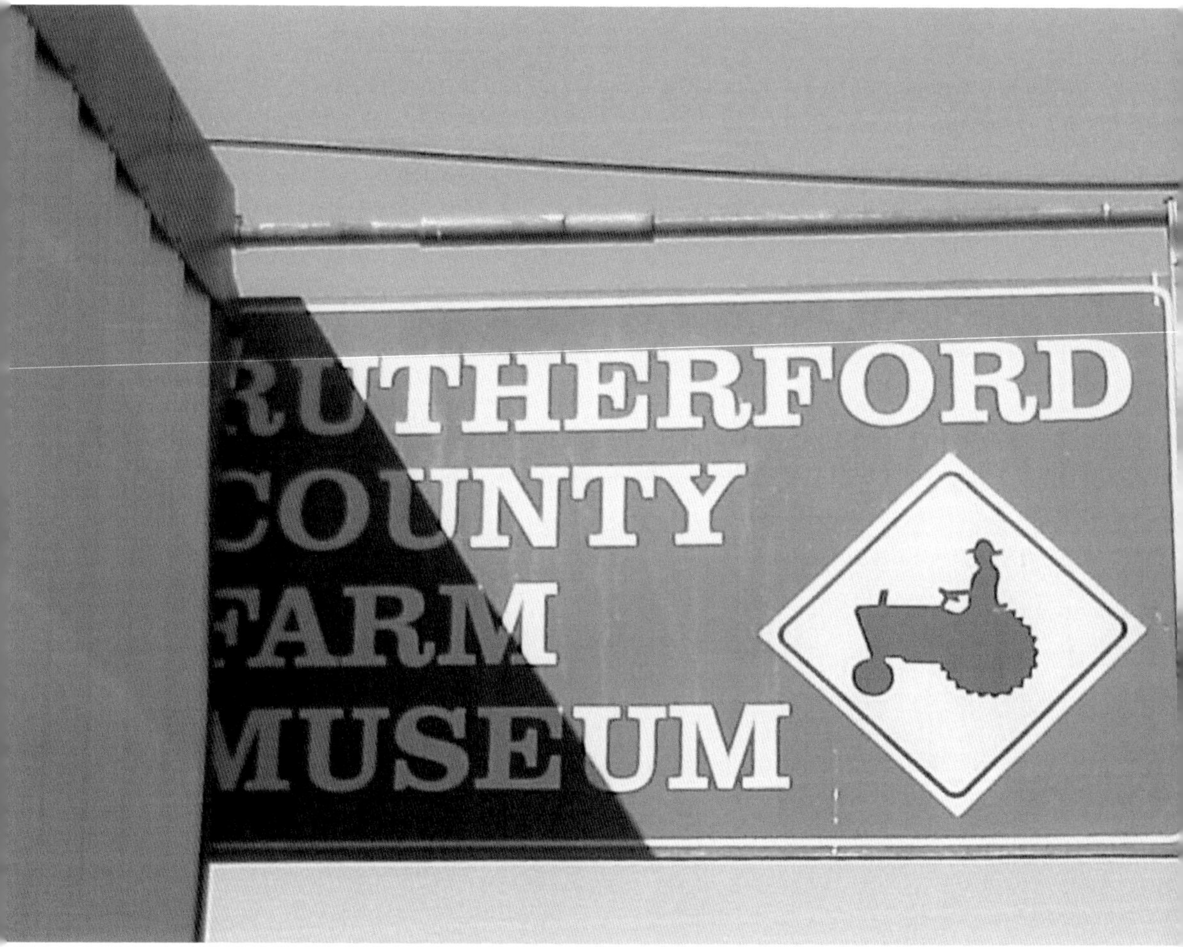

Rutherford County Farm Museum and Captain Burgin

In 1993, retired US Navy captain Wilbur J. Burgin helped establish the Rutherford County Farm Museum. He prepared proposals, spoke at meetings, went to homes to secure artifacts, and set up displays to solicit interest in his project. His work paid off well. The Rutherford County Farm Museum is still (in 2012) at 240 Depot Street in the J.W. Davis Building, with Burgin still serving as a director. Displays include farm implements, hand-sewn items, and even washing machines. The museum welcomes donations and loans. (Wilbur J. Burgin.)

CHAPTER THREE

Managers of Resources

Many of the businesses in Rutherford County used as their bases the area's natural resources: its land, water, timber, agricultural products, minerals, and, most importantly, its people. Hardworking, ethical employers and employees continue to give back to the county and to care for its resources. The previous chapter discussed the agriculturalists, conservationists, entrepreneurs, and their works. This chapter is a tribute to those who have successfully managed the many rich natural resources of the county and the products of those resources. This chapter looks also at the people at the local funeral homes, mortuaries, and crematories that offer dignified last memorials for residents.

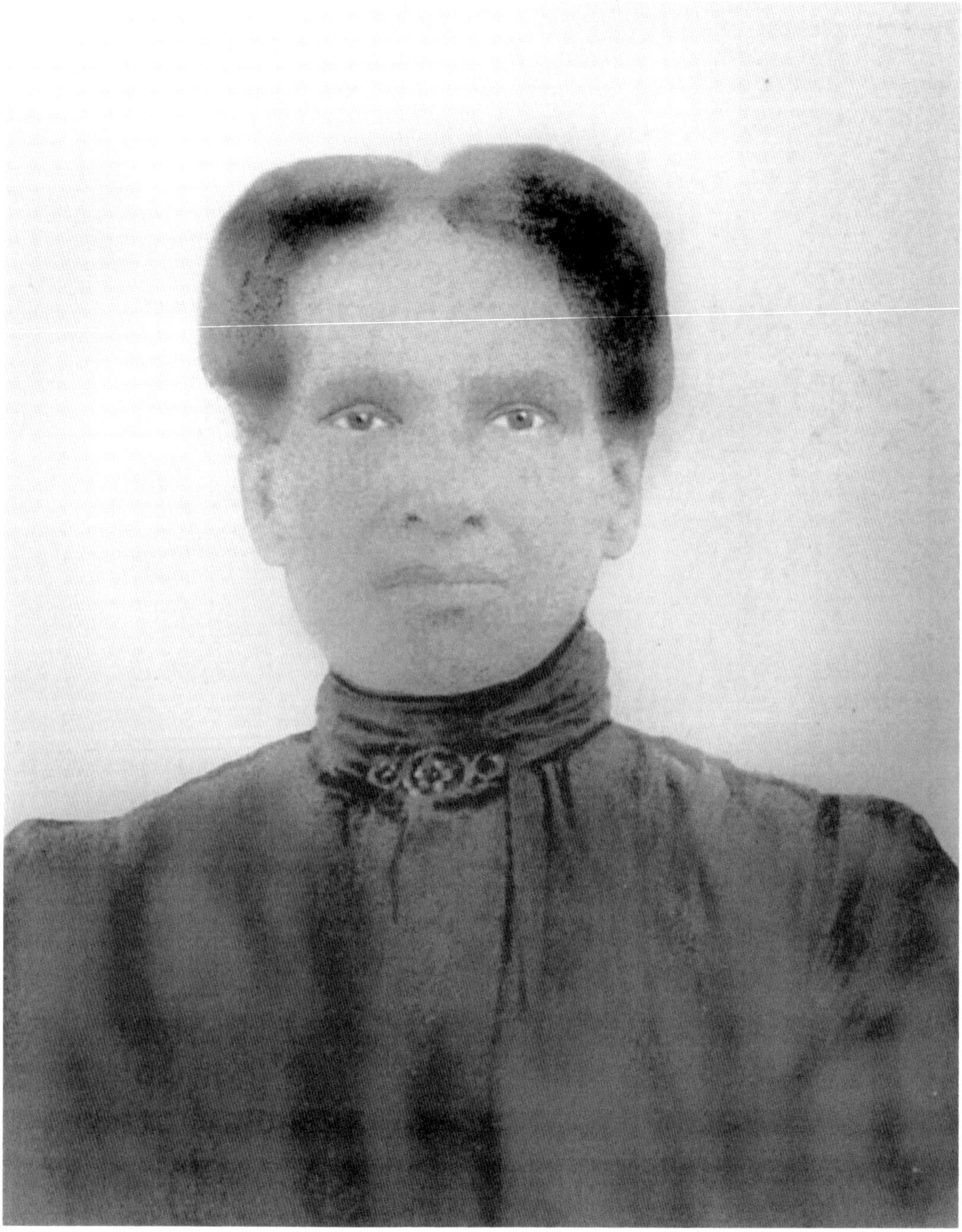

Victoria Simmons Hicks Goode, Former Slave

Victoria Simmons Hicks Goode of Rutherford County was a former slave born in 1851. She had several name changes because her last name changed when her master changed. Goode (her married name) lived to see freedom before her death in 1932. She was the great-grandmother of Milton Robinson Jr., an Army veteran and a retiree of Bell South in Atlanta. Robinson's father, Milton Robinson Sr., was the publisher of the newspaper the *Harris Herald*. (Milton Robinson Jr.)

Tildon Rucker "T.R." Padgett and Cleo Padgett

Padgett (1876–1953) and his wife, Cleo (1881–1971), served their county well. T.R. and his brother-in-law Grover King began the Padgett and King Furniture Store in 1903 on the south side of the square in Forest City. They soon established a good reputation as businessmen. About a year later, King sold his interest in the store to Padgett, who continued the furniture business and purchased the Florence Mill Company Store. In the stock, Padgett obtained from the Florence Mill Store a number of caskets.

While selling the caskets he had received, Padgett realized that the county needed the services of a funeral director and mortician. He purchased a horse-drawn hearse in 1916 and established a funeral home in a Forest City house on Main Street in the 1920s.

In 1932, Padgett constructed a brick facility on the same site as his original house on East Main Street. Padgett and King Mortuary remains both the oldest mortuary in the county and the oldest Forest City business operating under its original name. It is the first purpose-built funeral home in Rutherford County. Tildon and Cleo also served the community through their volunteer work. Cleo was instrumental in developing the Main Street Beautification Project in Forest City; the landscaped medians and the beautiful fountain still are highlights of the area. The couple rest in the Cool Springs Cemetery in Forest City. (Melinda Griffin Peterson.)

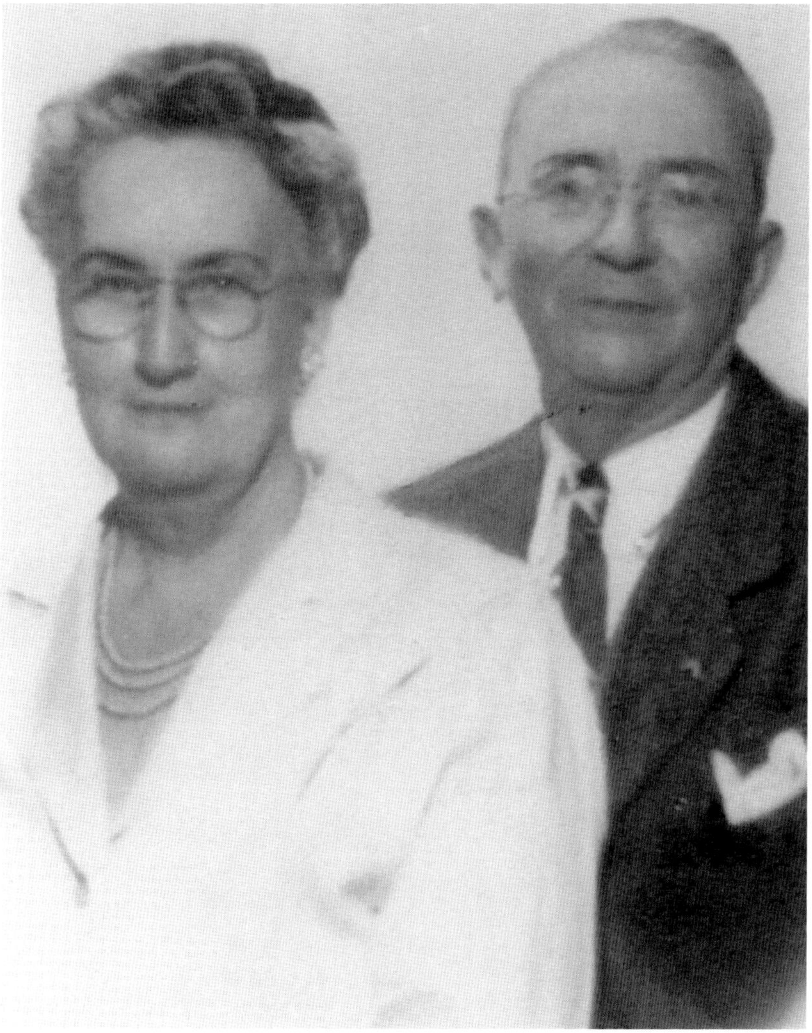

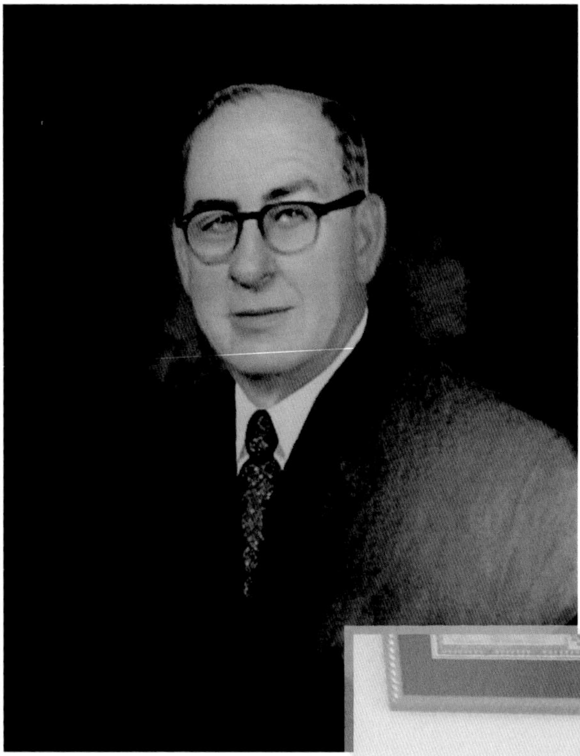

James T. Padgett and Shane Earley
Through the years, Padgett and King Mortuary has had a succession of family members carrying on the business. James T. Padgett (left), son of Cleo and T.R., operated the company after his father's death. James's son-in-law Ron Guy and his cousin D.G. Padgett continued the business. When Elizabeth Padgett (the wife of James T. Padgett) died in 1989, Guy and a longtime employee formed a partnership. After Ron Guy died in 2005, Shane Earley (right) purchased the Padgett and King Mortuary. He and his staff continue the tradition of caring service begun more than a century ago. (Shane Earley.)

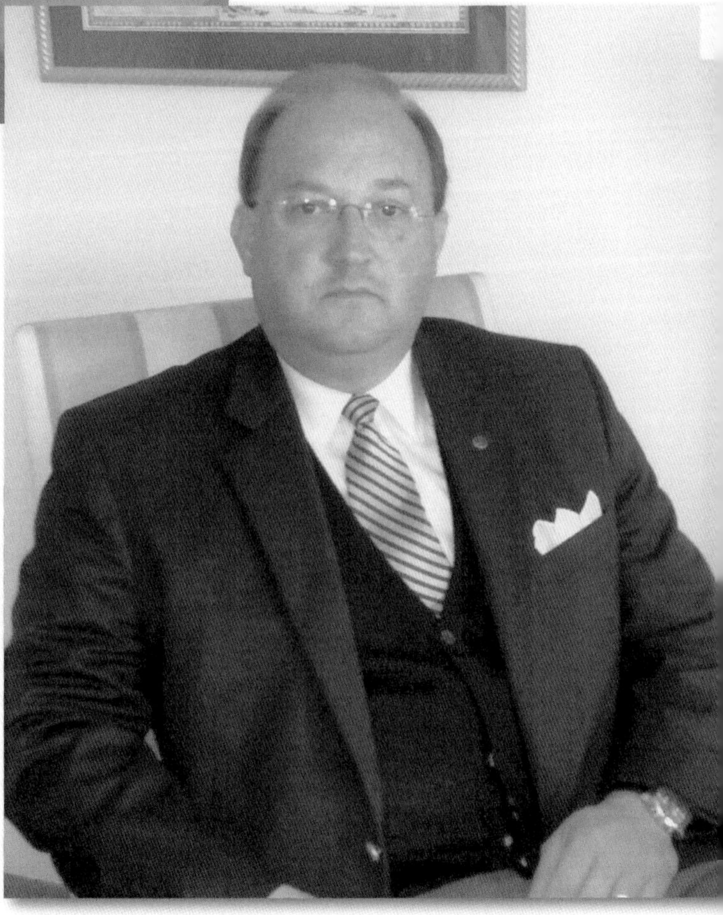

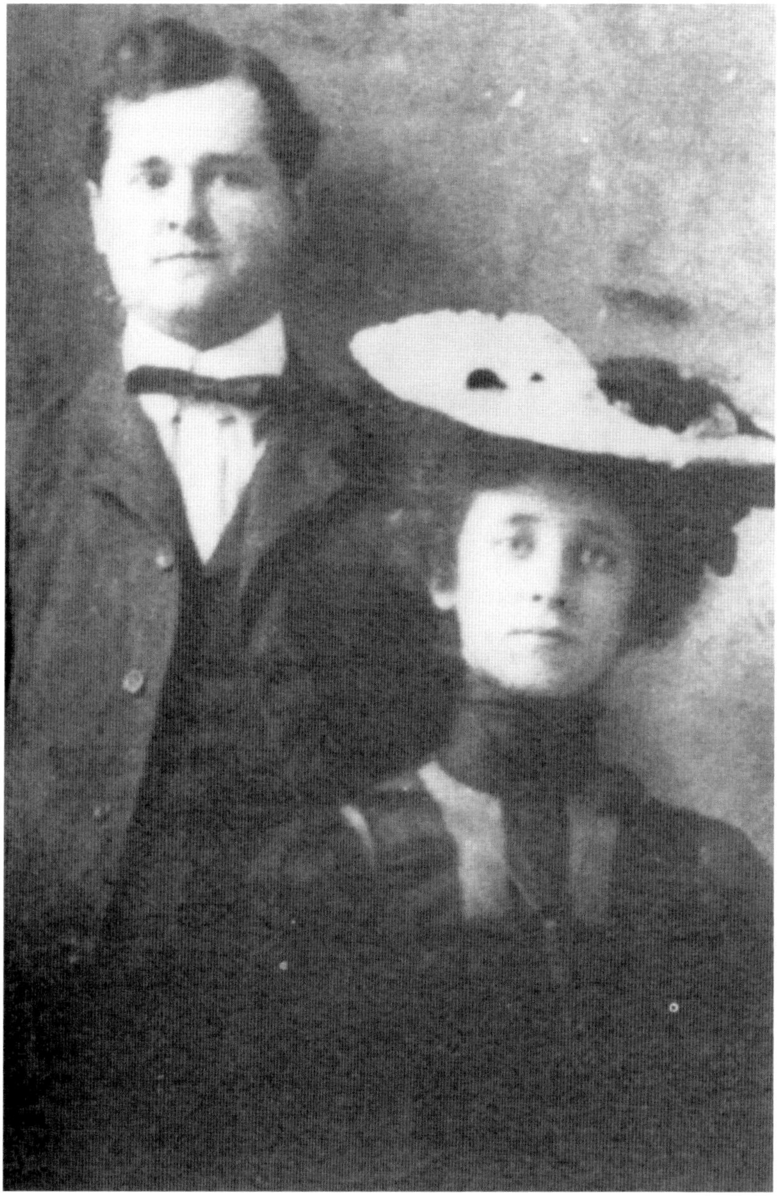

Edgar Nollie Washburn I and Grace Elizabeth Harton Washburn
The Washburn family name is an easily recognizable one in Rutherford County. Benjamin Washburn (1806–1863) was the first Washburn to open a store (1831) in North Carolina. Reuben Washburn (1829–1904), Edgar Nollie Washburn (1874–1935), E.N. Washburn (1902–1971), and Edward "Ed" N. Washburn (1930–) continued the mercantile tradition. Often, the Washburns helped with the final services of the people.

Edgar Nollie Washburn I operated the post office for the Washburn community from 1900 until 1906, when the office closed. As have other Washburns, Edgar Nollie attempted to meet the consumer needs of the community, particularly the area between Bostic and Sunshine, North Carolina. Here, Postmaster Edgar Nollie Washburn I is pictured with his wife, Grace Elizabeth Harton Washburn. (Catherine Sinclair Washburn.)

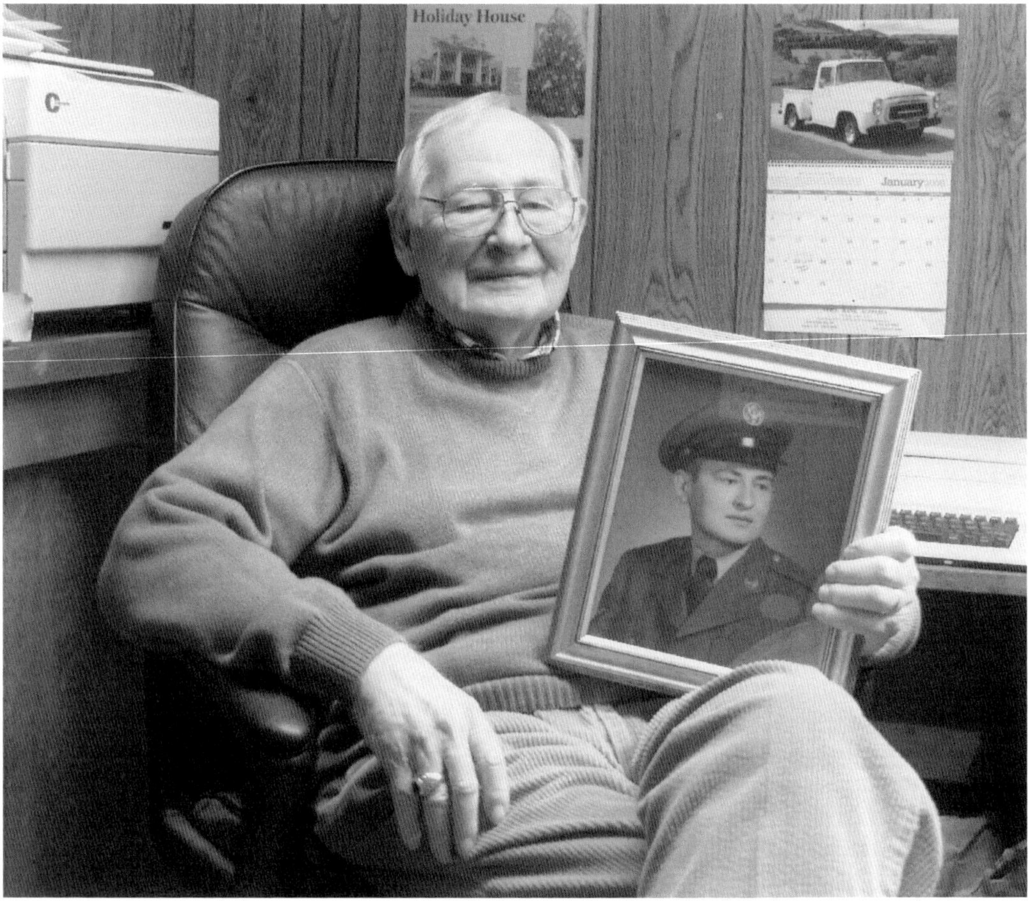

Edward "Ed" N. Washburn in Washburn's General Store Office

The current managers of the Washburn's General Store are Korean War veteran Edward "Ed" N. Washburn and his beautiful, intelligent wife, Catherine Sinclair Washburn. Ed Washburn is the son of E.N. Washburn; he began helping his father with the business in 1945.

Ed's motto is, "If I do a good service, the money will take care of itself." Pictured here in Washburn's General Store, which dates from the early 1830s, is Ed Washburn. Ed is holding his military portrait from the Korean War; he had enlisted in the military in 1951. After serving at Lackland Air Force Base and in Cheyenne, Wyoming, Washburn received his discharge and returned to Rutherford County. He continued working in his father's store. Determined to do more for the community, E.N. Washburn entered into the funeral business.

By 1957, his Wofford graduate son Ed had also earned his license as a funeral director. The Washburn Funeral Service was important to E.N., Ed, and Catherine. The building beside the store was the site of the embalming room, arrangement room, and an office.

By the late 1960s, the health of E.N. Washburn had declined to the point that Ed and Catherine were completing most of the work for the business. Ed and Catherine held E.N. Washburn's final services in the historic Washburn house after he passed in 1971. Ed and Catherine assumed full responsibility for the business and continue to live in the Washburn house in 2012. The couple sold the funeral portion of the business but has kept the general store in the family.

The national *DAR* magazine, *Our State* magazine, and UNC-TV have all featured the store. The publicity has brought people to the store from all sections of the country. (Edward N. Washburn and James M. Walker.)

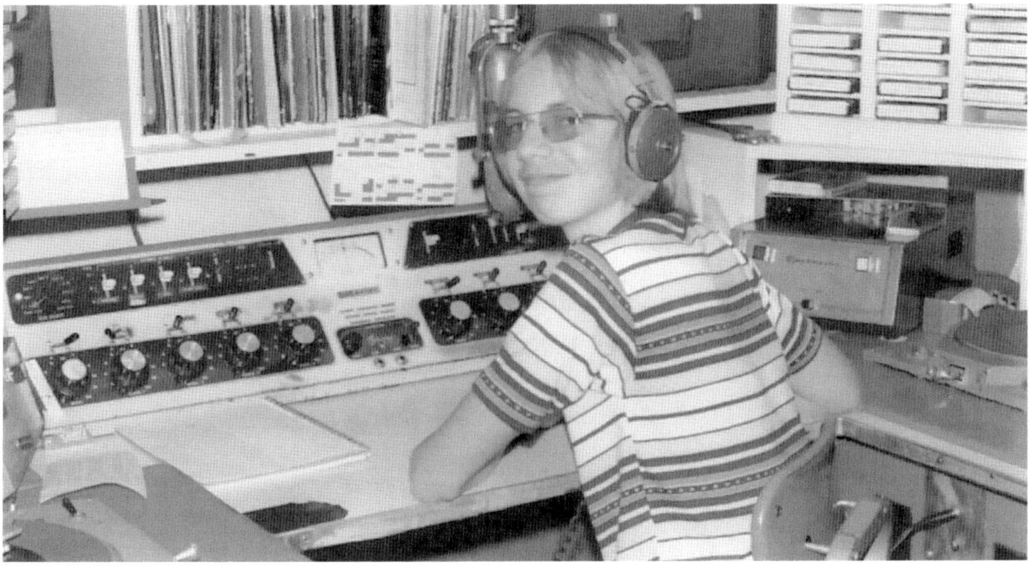

Young Kent Dorsey at WBBO

Prior to the establishment of Washburn & Dorsey Funeral Home, the community already knew Kent Dorsey. He had worked with several radio stations in the area, including WBBO, a local Rutherford County Radio Station in Forest City. Here is a young Dorsey at the controls.

Dorsey had also apprenticed at several funeral homes and, by the 1950s, was ready to transition to the funeral home business, and the community was ready for him. Kent Dorsey bought the Washburn Funeral Service in 1998. Dorsey built a new funeral home and moved into it in 2002. Dorsey summarizes the new Washburn & Dorsey Funeral Home as "a one-man operation" that has some great part-time help. (Kent Dorsey.)

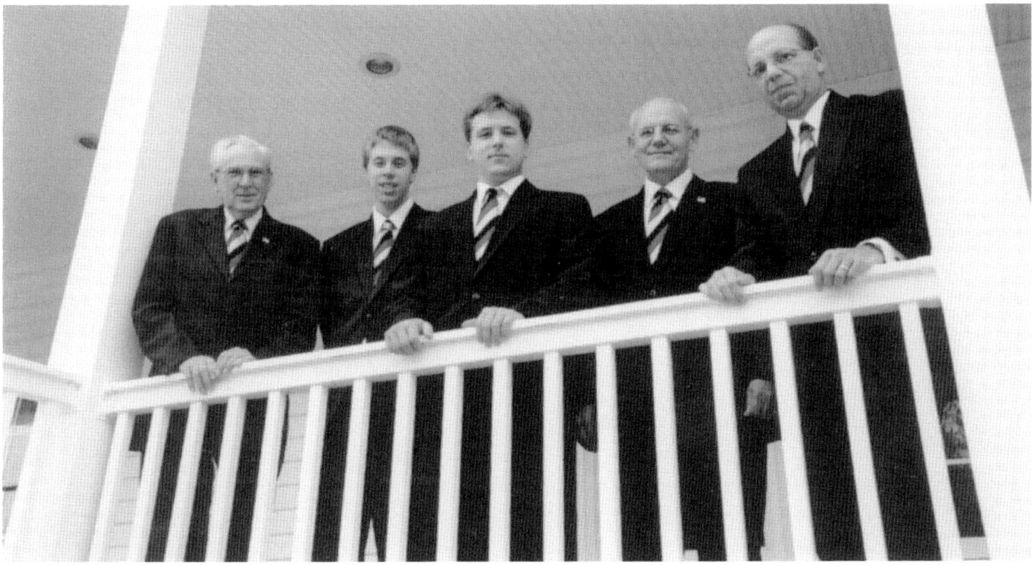

Kent Dorsey and Staff

Dorsey's staff has grown through the years. The 2012 staff of the funeral home includes, from left to right, C.C. Brackett, Bryan Winslow, Matt Wilson, Bob Billingsley, and Dorsey. (Kent Dorsey.)

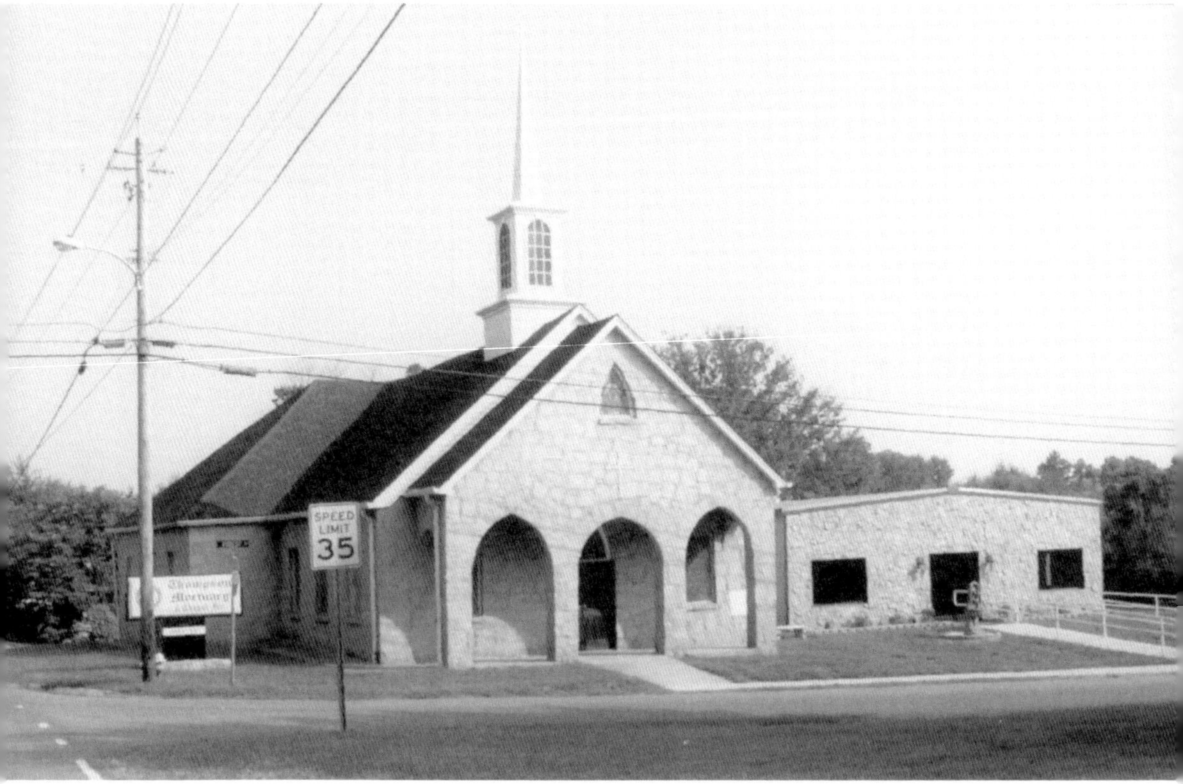

Thompson Brothers Mortuary

In 1935, the brothers Charlie and Gasaway Thompson and their cousin Lester Carpenter founded Thompson Brothers Mortuary. Their establishment not only provided funeral services to African Americans in the area but also helped furnish transportation to the hospital in times of crisis.

This 2004 photograph shows the beautiful, ultra-modern facility available to those who need its services. The owners of the Thompson Mortuary and Chapel still want to serve the area. Their facility is now at the corner of Hardin Road and Forest Street. The design of the mortuary and chapel offers a place of beauty and peace to its visitors. (James M. Walker.)

A.C. and Mary Ellen McKinney (OPPOSITE PAGE)

A.C. and his wife, Mary Ellen McKinney (1928–2011), began the McKinney Funeral Home and Ambulance Service in Cliffside in March 1953. The couple set up their service in Dr. G.O. Moss's former home at 61 North Main Street. They ran the business for 35 years.

In 1965, former employee Horton Landreth became a partner in the business; the name of the business changed from McKinney Funeral Home to McKinney & Landreth Funeral Home. By 1973, a newly constructed brick building was ready for occupancy at 4076 Highway 221A.

In 1988, A.C. McKinney retired; however, he and his wife would often visit and offer their services. Horton Landreth and his wife, Jerene, took over the management of the facility. On August 4, 2004, Steve Carroll, a funeral director since 1996, purchased the well-known funeral home. In 2010, he added Carroll to the name of the landmark brick building, making it the McKinney-Landreth & Carroll Funeral Home. (McKinney-Landreth & Carroll Funeral Home.)

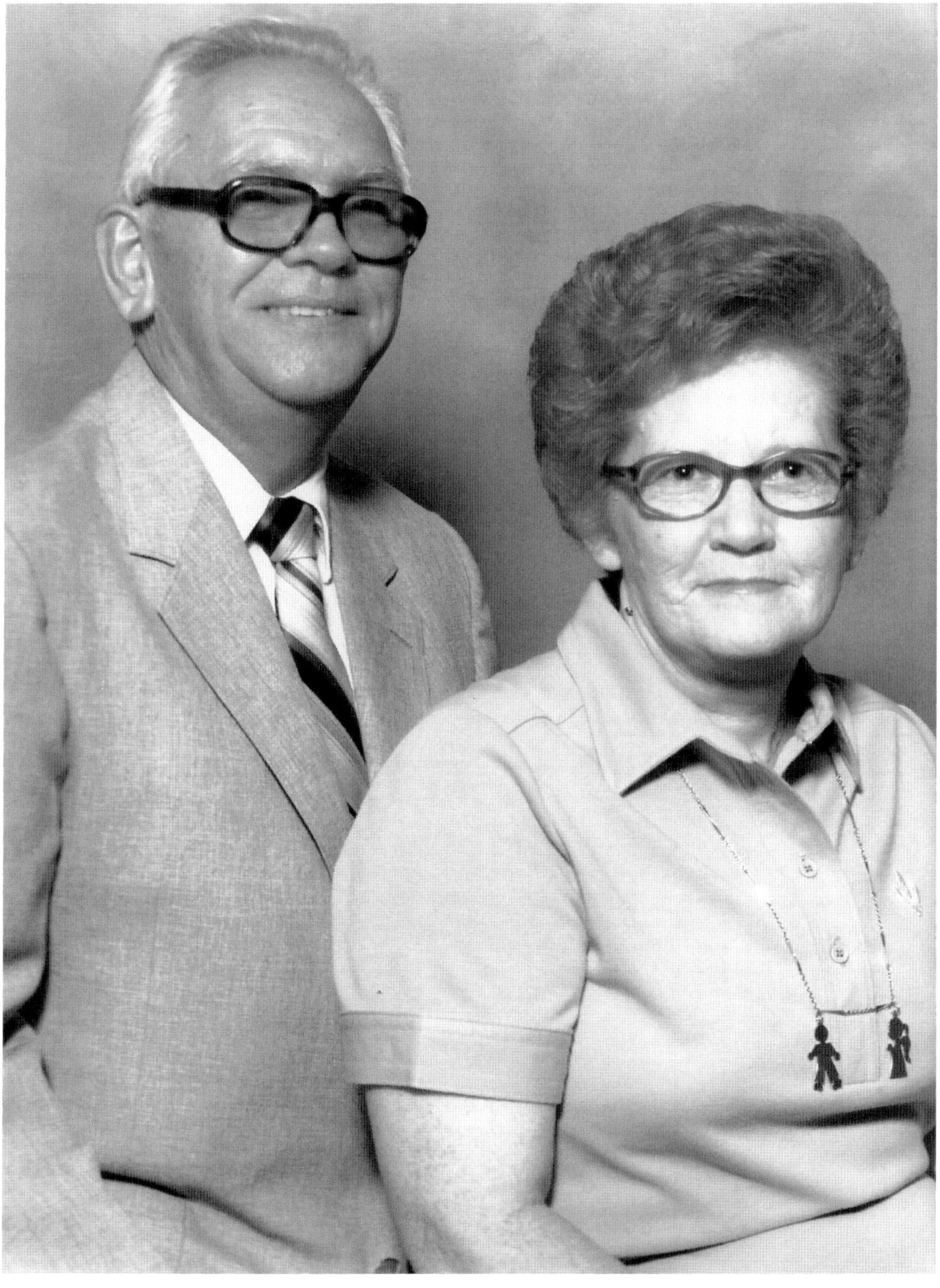

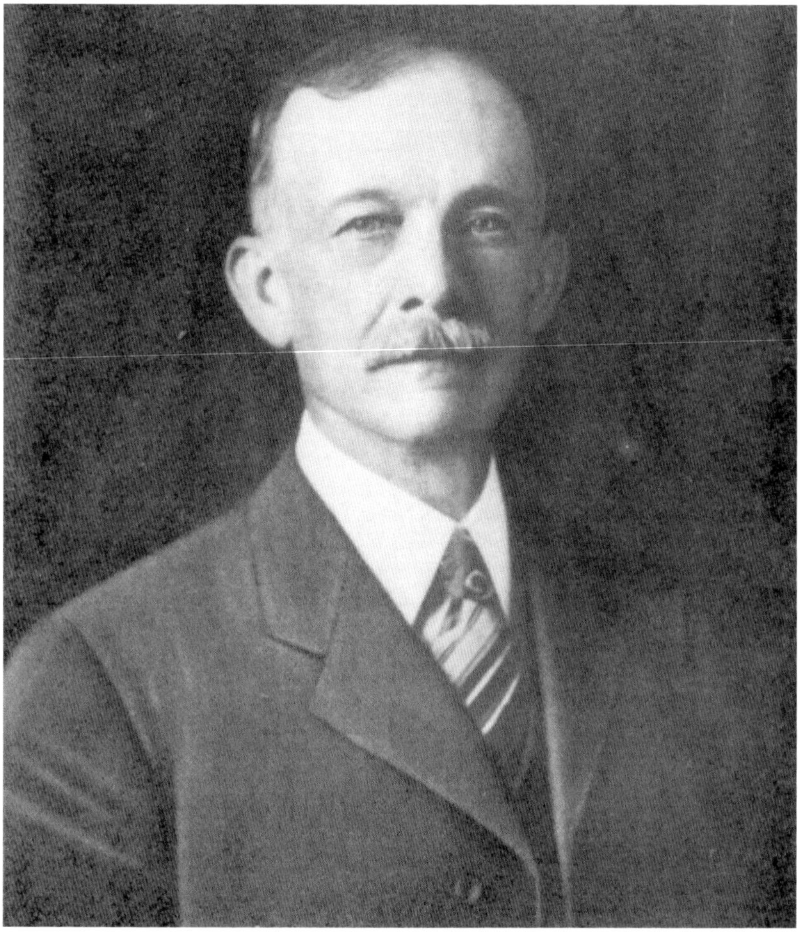

Raleigh Rutherford Haynes

The name of the Rutherford County resident associated most often with textiles and with the use of waterpower in textile production is Raleigh Rutherford Haynes (June 30, 1851–February 9, 1917). In large part, the existence of the Rutherford County towns of Caroleen, Avondale, Henrietta, and Cliffside is because of Haynes's work.

Haynes was the oldest of eight children. He was born in the Ferry Community of Rutherford County in 1851 to Sarah Walker Haynes and Deputy Sheriff Charles H. Haynes (1823–1859), who died when Raleigh was seven. When his father died, Raleigh helped his mother manage the farm. Raleigh learned much about farming and about managing crops and timber from the land; he never had a formal education beyond that of the local county school.

In 1874, Raleigh married Amanda Loretta Carpenter. The couple had eight children before her death in 1890.

As a young man, Raleigh began purchasing land in High Shoals, near the Second Broad River. With some partners, he was able to build a cotton mill in Henrietta with homes for the workers (1887). In 1887, Raleigh served as director of the Henrietta Mills in Henrietta and Caroleen. He helped organize the mills from the beginning of the corporation and helped manage the construction of the houses for the employees. In 1890, Haynes took Litia Kelly as his second wife; she passed in 1892. In 1892, Raleigh, with his associates, purchased the Forest City Cotton Mills, tore down the old facility, and built a new structure. He named the mill after his daughter, Florence. (Hazel Haynes Bridges and Grover C. Haynes Jr.)

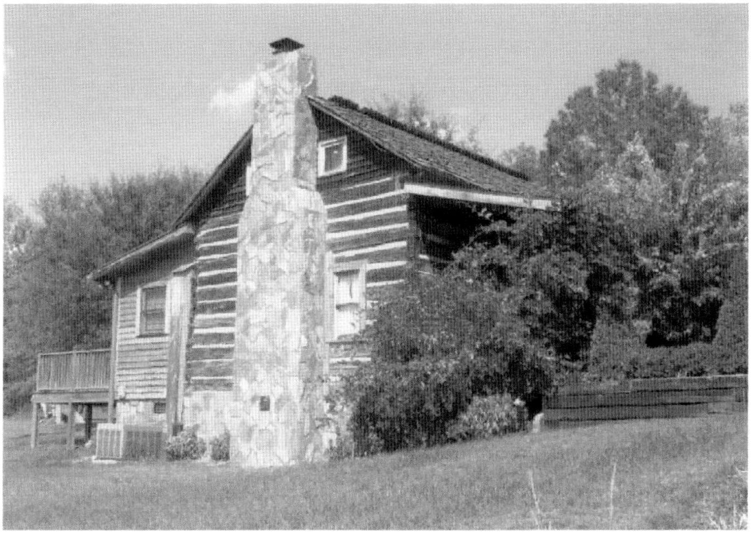

Log Cabin Birthplace of Raleigh Rutherford Haynes
Grover C. Haynes Jr. photographed the log cabin where Raleigh was born after Janice Bridges Swing, Raleigh's great-granddaughter, moved the house to Cliffside Estates. The structure is now on Old Main Street, Cliffside. (Janice Swing.)

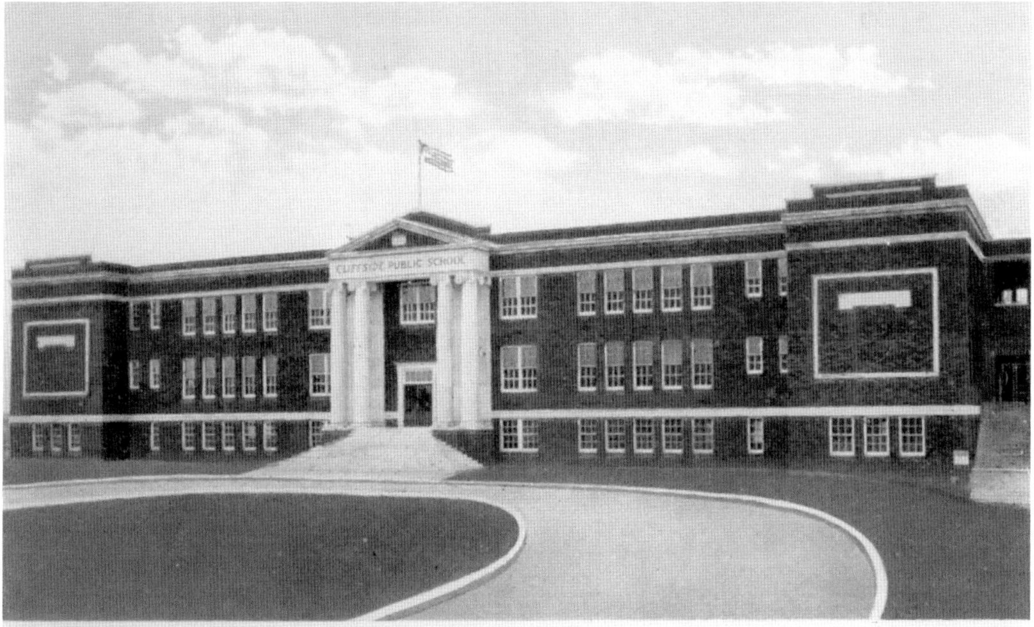

CLIFFSIDE PUBLIC SCHOOL BUILDING, CLIFFSIDE, N. C.

Other Achievements of Raleigh Rutherford Haynes
Haynes and his partners built another mill, Caroleen Mills, in 1895. He built two stores in Henrietta and a second mill at Henrietta: the Avondale Mill. In 1899, he began the construction of Cliffside Mill.

Haynes's dreams, however, extended to more than establishing new mills. He built seven churches, villages near the mills, schools, and many stores. When he died suddenly in Florida in 1917, just before his 66th birthday, more than 3,000 people attended his funeral.

Haynes would have been proud to see the Cliffside school dedicated in 1922. A proponent of education, Haynes had provided classes in the mill itself, over the mill store, and later in a frame building. Louis H. Asbury, who designed the Rutherford County Courthouse and the new Cliffside School, required two million red bricks for the school. Still in use are the 24 classrooms and an auditorium seating more than 800. (Curteich-Chicago "C.T. Art-Colortone" Postcard.)

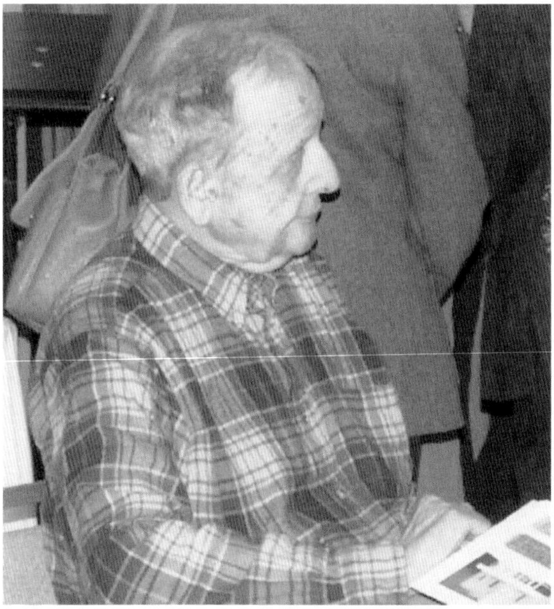

Veteran and Superior Court Judge Hollis Owens Jr.

During World War II, Sgt. Hollis M. Owens Jr. of Weapons Platoon, Company E, 104th Infantry Regiment, 26th Division served in Northern France, the Ardennes, and the Rhineland. On November 19, 1944, Owens received wounds from artillery fire. He earned the Purple Heart, the CIB, the EAME Campaign Medal with three Bronze Stars, and the Good Conduct Medal.

Owens, Raleigh Rutherford Haynes's great-grandson, later received his education at Wofford College and Duke University. Owens distinguished himself as a district judge, a superior court judge, and a state representative. Here, Owens signs a page in *Rutherford County in World War II*, which features his biography. (James M. Walker.)

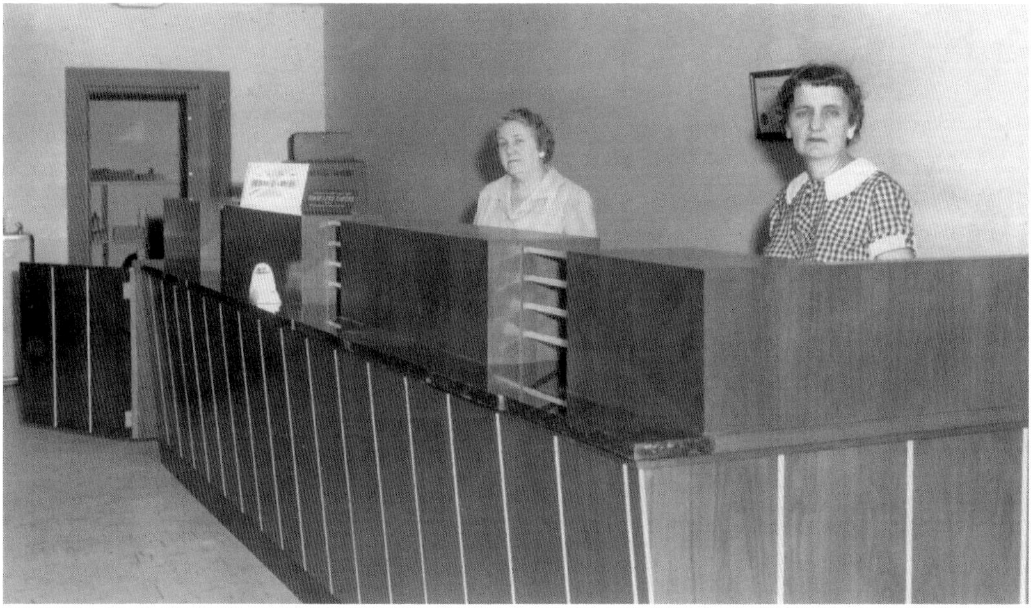

Nelle Pruette Butler Wright

At a time when most women were stay-at-home wives and mothers, Wright had more on her mind for herself and her family. She graduated from Ellenboro High School and attended one year at Gardner-Webb College. She married James Beason Butler after leaving college; they had two daughters: Linda and Sandra. Wright worked in the Queen Anne Mill in Ellenboro and then went to work as a cashier at Tisdale's Grocery. Her next job, an unusual one for a woman at the time, was at Union Trust Company, which later became BB&T. She was in banking for more than 20 years.

Wright stands at her station in the Union Trust Bank in Ellenboro. Standing behind her is another Rutherford County resident, Willie Greene Spurlin (Mrs. Buren Spurlin). (Sandra Butler Weeks and Linda Butler Bridges.)

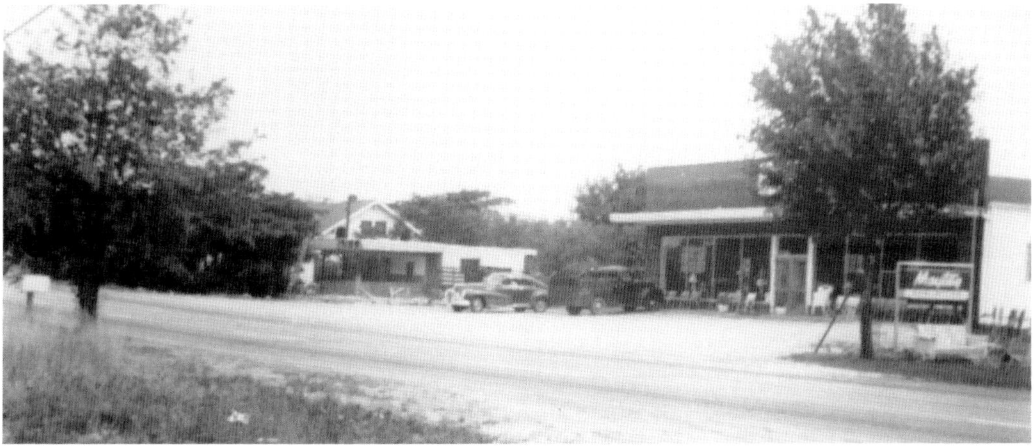

One of Ervin M. Grindstaff's Businesses

More than 60 years ago, Ervin M. Grindstaff founded Grindstaff's Furniture in Forest City. With its timber, skilled labor, and accessible transportation, it is not surprising that Western North Carolina became an ideal location for furniture production, sales, and distribution. Grindstaff's wife, Ruth Price Grindstaff, his son, Boyce, and his daughters, Carolyn Grindstaff Barbee and Barbara Jean Grindstaff Whitehurst, helped with the business. Barbara's later musical career is a part of the chapter on entertainment in this volume. (Boyce Grindstaff.)

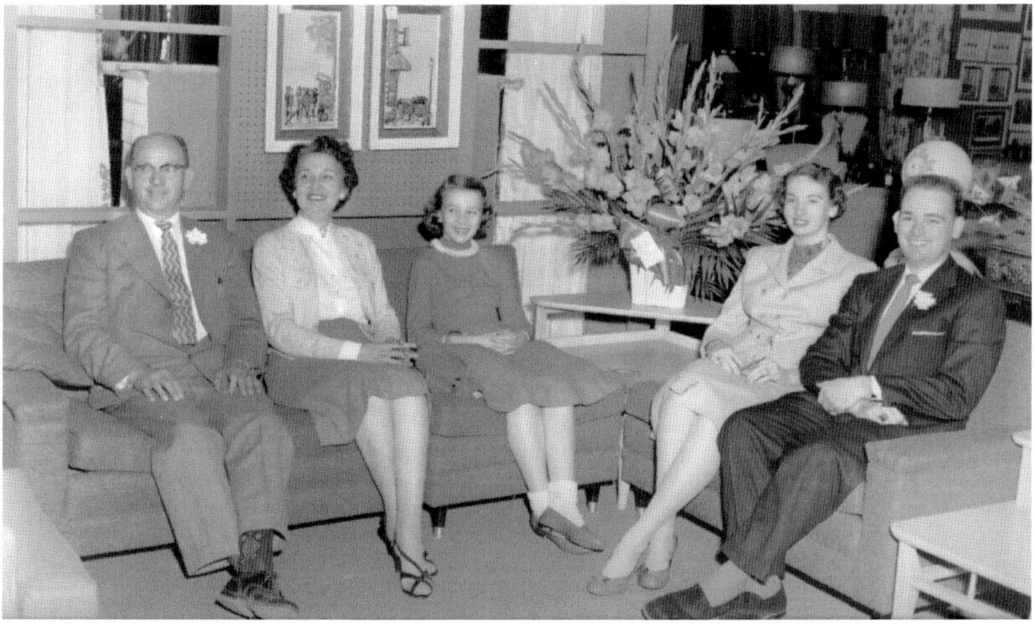

Grindstaff Family

This photograph of the opening of a new addition to Grindstaff's Furniture shows the immediate Grindstaff family in the late 1950s. From left to right are the founder Ervin M. Grindstaff (January 8, 1907–December 25, 1991), Ruth Price Grindstaff (June 10, 1912–January 10, 1983), Barbara Jean Grindstaff Whitehurst, Carolyn Grindstaff Barbee (June 3, 1936–July 30, 2010), and Boyce Grindstaff (husband of Dorothy Smith Grindstaff and the present CEO of Grindstaff's Interiors). (Boyce Grindstaff.)

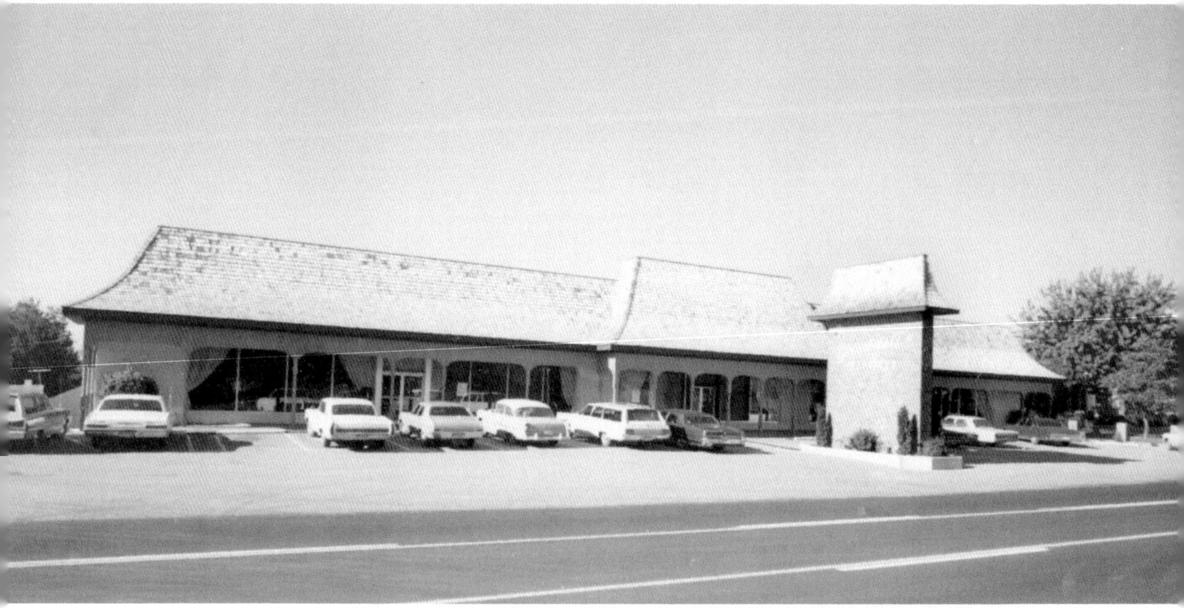

Grindstaff's Furniture in the New Century

Now known as Grindstaff's Interiors, Grindstaff's Furniture has changed dramatically through the years. By 1964, it had the largest display of fine furniture in the Carolinas. CEO Boyce Grindstaff completed improvements to the exterior appearance. Boyce remembers well Forrest Harrill "Smoky" Burgess (February 6, 1927–September 15, 1991), an employee who "sold, delivered, and arranged furniture in our showrooms during that worker's off season from professional baseball." Boyce describes Smoky as one of Grindstaff's all-time best "PR persons." This versatile staff member began working for Grindstaff's in 1954. Smoky believed moving the heavy furniture helped keep him in shape for the upcoming seasons. (Boyce Grindstaff.)

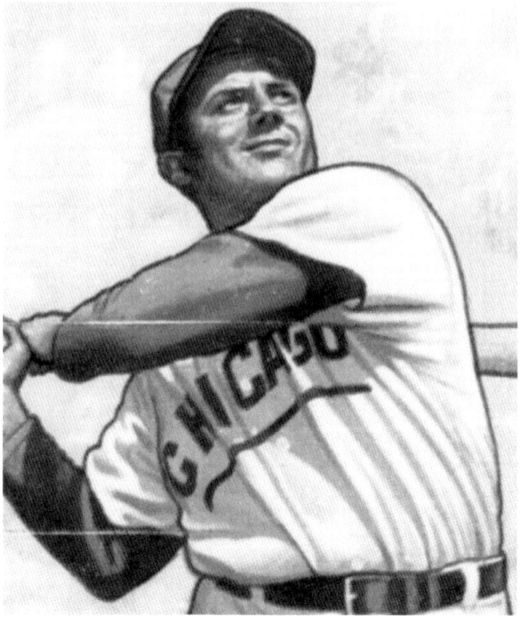

Forrest Harrill "Smoky" Burgess

This rare 1951 Chicago Cubs rookie card (No. 317) by Bowman Company features Forrest Burgess from Rutherford County. Smoky was born in Caroleen. Although he signed with the Cubs in 1944, he missed most of the next two years because of his military obligations. In 1947, he led the batting average in the Tri-State League at .387 and, in 1948, he won the Southern Association batting crown. In 1949 and 1951, Burgess continued with the Cubs. After the 1951 season, he went to the Cincinnati Reds, and two months later, the Philadelphia Phillies drafted him. Smoky served as the starting catcher for the Phillies for the next three years. He had 17 doubles and batted in 36 runs in that season. In his 102 games for the Phillies, he batted .292 in 1953. (Author's collection.)

Smoky Burgess with Phillies, 1953

Burgess was the primary catcher for the Pittsburgh Pirates for four years and later played for the Chicago White Sox. During his career, he hit 126 homers and had a career average of .295. He played in the World Series in 1960. He made the All-Star Team nine times; his last time as an All-Star was because of his record as a pinch hitter.

At the time of his 1967 retirement, Burgess had 145 pinch-hits, a record until 1979. In 2012, 43 years later, his record is still second highest in the nation.

Burgess married Margaret Head from Caroleen, and they had one son, Larry Burgess. Larry remembers his father's work with youth in the community and with the Christian Men's Organization. In addition to his Little League clinics, Smoky was a trustee at Gardner-Webb University.

Smoky died in 1991 at the age of 64. He was laid to rest in Sunset Memorial Park in Forest City. (Larry Burgess.)

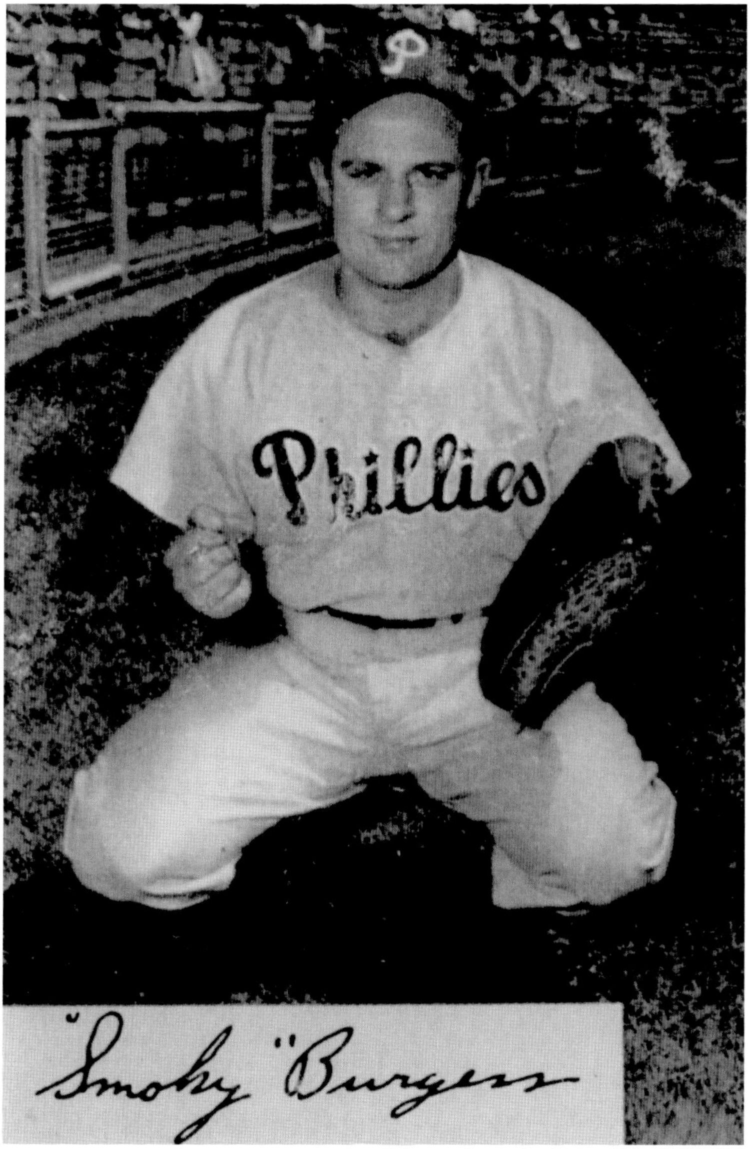

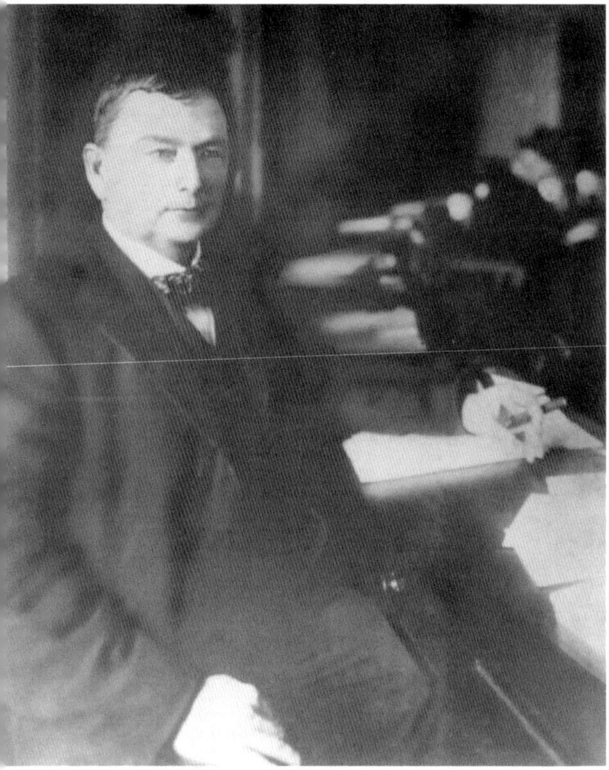

Julius Plato Durham Withrow, "Merchant Prince"

Julius Plato Durham "J.P.D." Withrow (1867–1926) was known as Hollis's "Merchant Prince." His work in Rutherford County preceded that of many other store owners. Withrow was a well-known and well-respected merchant, a state legislator (1937–1943), and family man. He helped the community to realize Hollis School, the Hollis Post Office, and the Hollis Methodist Church. Withrow's first store was in Ellenboro in the late 1890s. His merchandizing fame, however, came from his second general store, located in Hollis. The Withrow Company Store was a general store rich in everything from patent medicine, barrels of candy, tobacco products, sugar, farming equipment, Bibles, and even caskets. Withrow would often take a train to New York to select his merchandise, particularly cloth and sewing machines. He had those items shipped to Lattimore by train; Withrow's full-time wagon drivers would bring the commodities to his store. (Scott Withrow.)

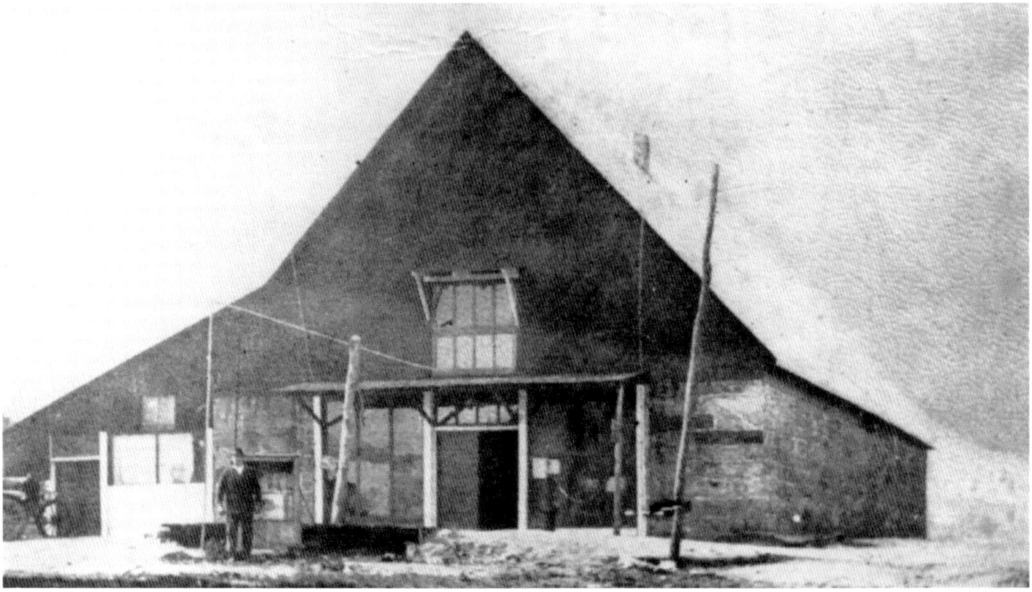

Withrow Company Store

Withrow is pictured in front of his Withrow Company Store. The store operated from 1906 until the 1960s. The rock came from land on Cherry Mountain. Withrow's family, especially his son Grady, helped operate the store. The building is still in use today, however, not as a general store. (Ronald Hester and Vida Hester.)

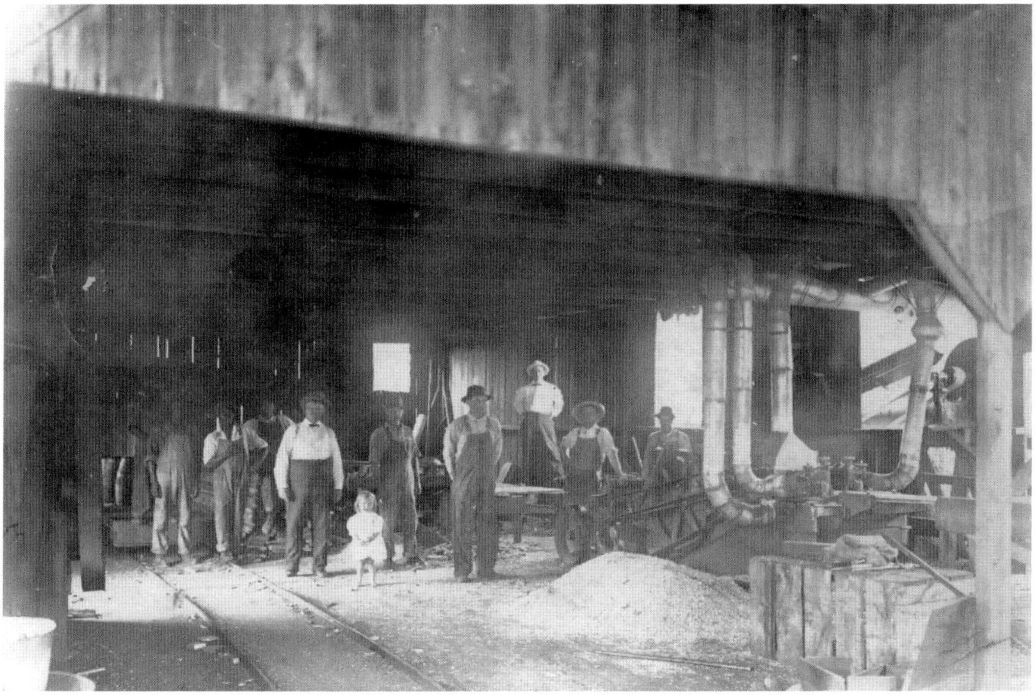

Withrow inside Hollis Gin
Withrow, on the far left in a white shirt and bow tie, is observing the workings inside the one-stand, hand-fed Hollis gin, which is no longer in operation. Withrow encouraged the construction of a school building that was adequate for the Hollis community and also safe and conducive to learning. (Bill Withrow.)

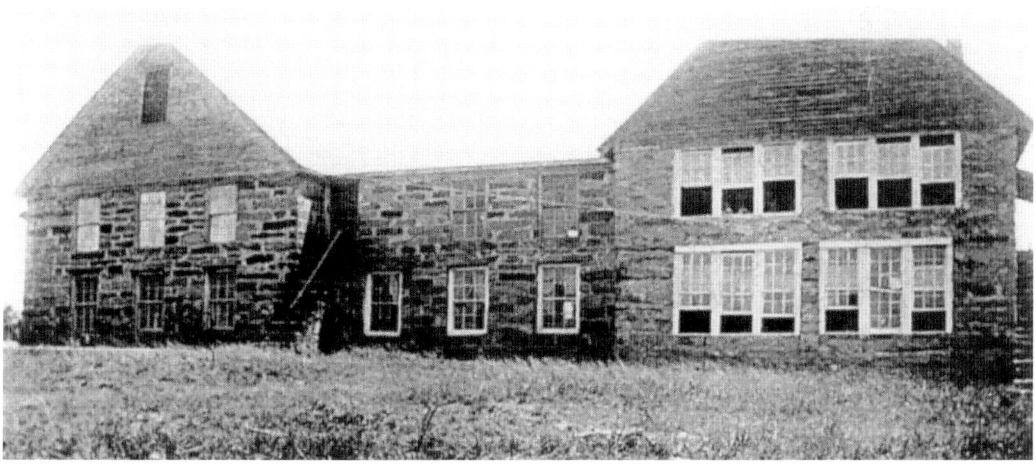

Hollis School
Built in 1905 on Withrow land and primarily with money from Withrow, the school was constructed for $2,400. In 1923, Withrow offered to deed the school property (about seven acres) and the school itself to the board of education in exchange for the addition of four rooms. The four new upstairs rooms, along with an upstairs room in the old part of the school, served high school classes. (Vida Hester and Ronald Hester.)

Withrow's Role in Hollis Methodist Church

The Hollis Methodist Church dates from 1906. After strong winds blew the original wooden church building from its pillars in 1922, the congregation began work on the new building, Even though Withrow was a staunch Baptist, he helped finance the new church. Withrow was operating the Withrow General Store in Hollis at the time. Every time a salesman came through the store, Withrow would ask the vendor to make a contribution to the church and, in return, offered to carve the vendor's company name on one of the rocks for advertisement. Hollis Methodist Church was probably one of the only churches in the nation to advertise snuff and tonics on its walls. Withrow did not live to see the completion in 1927. (Vida Hester and Ronald Hester.)

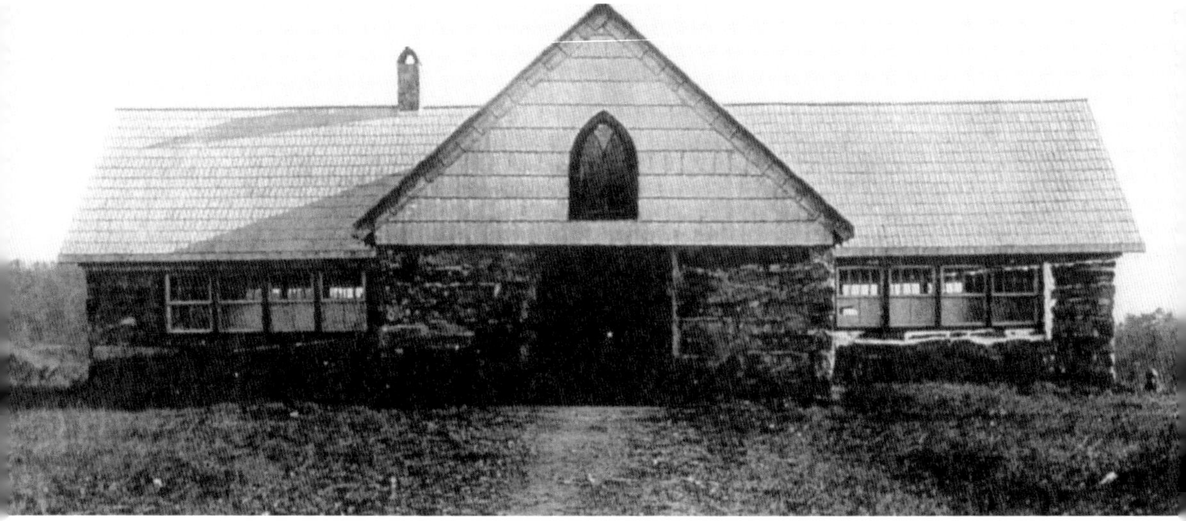

Fola Caroline Wilson McDaniel and William Van McDaniel

(PORTRAITS OPPOSITE PAGE)

Fola (1904–1978) and William (January 20, 1963–April 25, 1972) were active in business with their cotton gins. Reared on a farm on Hollis Road/McKinney Mill Road, William Van McDaniel had an early interest in farming. In 1925, William began working on construction jobs in Florida with Gil Greene. In 1928, William went to work at the cotton gin in Ellenboro; in 1930, he married Fola Caroline Wilson (1904–1978).

Fola and William were the parents of five children: Caroline, Samuel, Robert, Joe, and Mary. William continued to work each fall at the gin from the years 1928 until about 1946. During the rest of the year, he worked in construction and in farming. (William Van McDaniel family.)

William Van McDaniel and the Hopewell Gin

The Lee Robbins family had built the Hopewell Gin about 1928. Victor Cotton Gin in Gaffney later purchased the gin. William Van McDaniel bought it in 1947 and operated the Hopewell Gin until he closed it in 1959. (James M. Walker.)

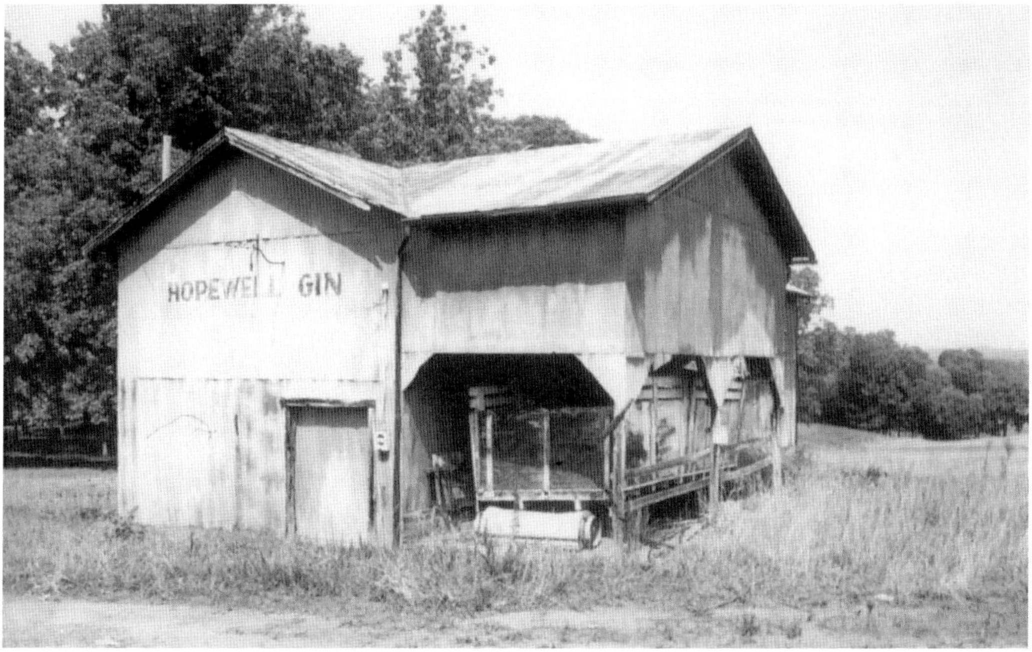

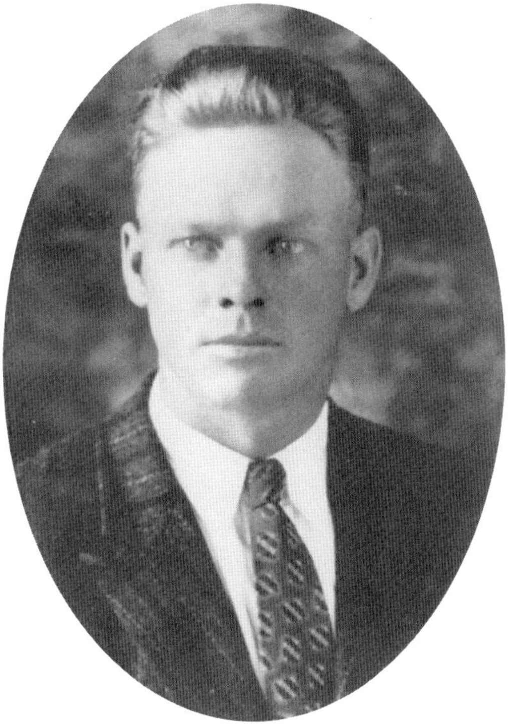

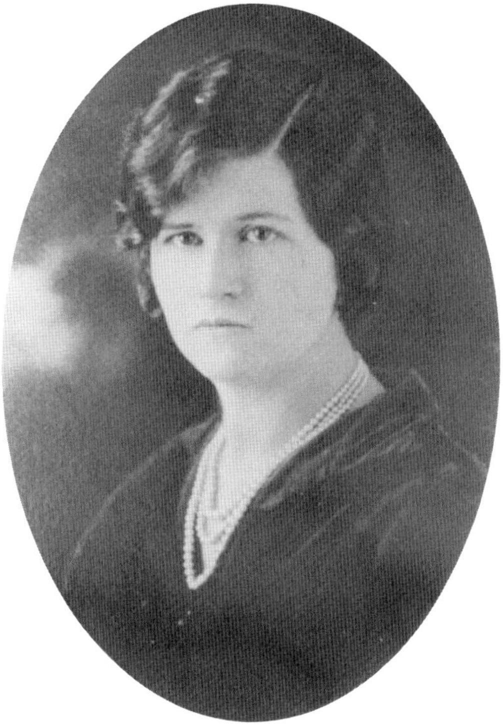

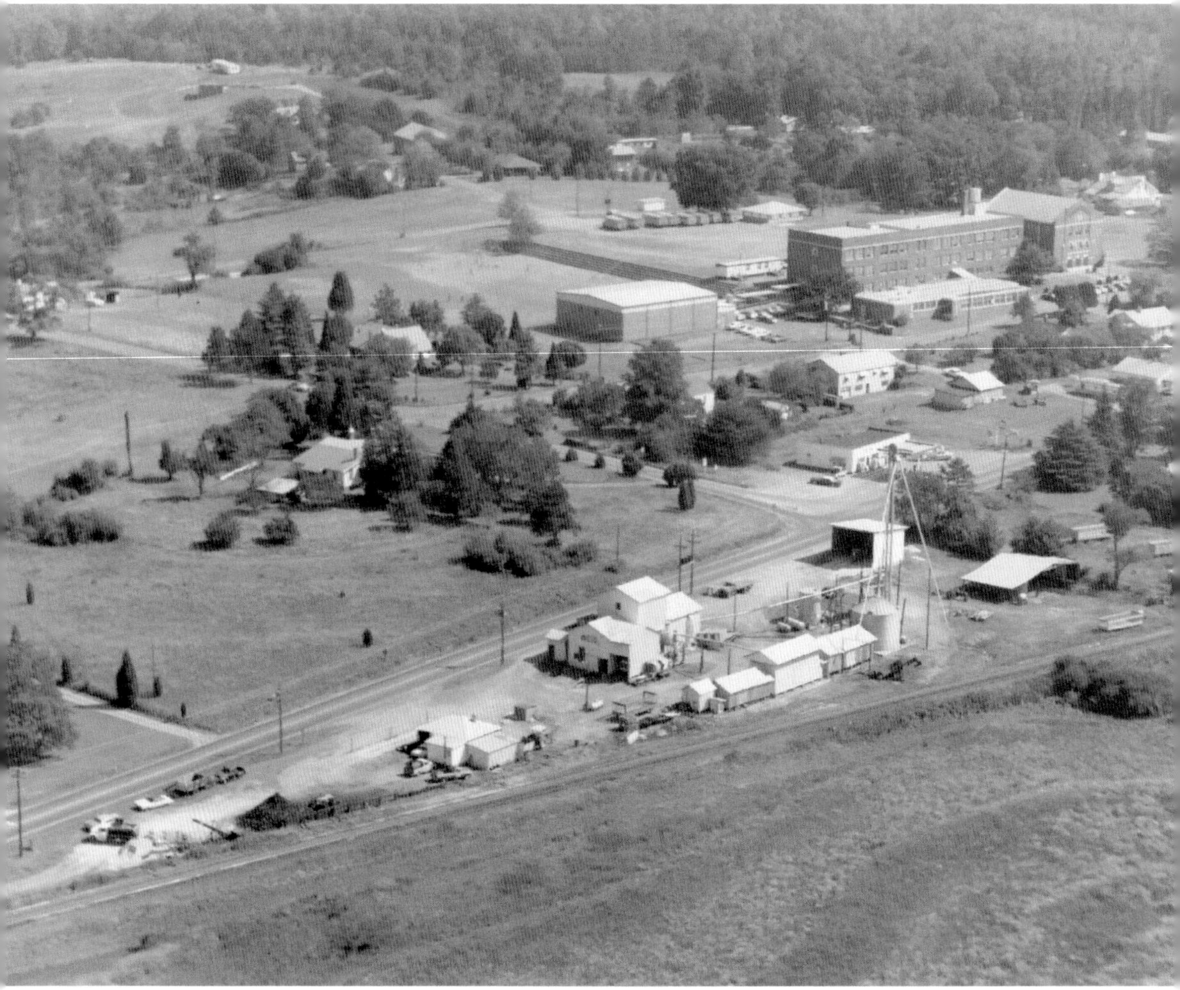

Aerial View of the McDaniel's Colfax Gin in Ellenboro

In 1959, William Van McDaniel bought the Colfax Gin in Ellenboro after Chambers and Turner, Inc., declared bankruptcy and after Lancaster Cotton Oil Company purchased it.

McDaniel operated the Colfax Gin until his death in 1972. After 1972, his sons, Samuel, Robert, and Joe, ran the gin until Samuel's 2010 death; Robert and Joe still work together. William's daughter Mary has been office manager since 1974.

This aerial view has since altered, but the Colfax Gin in the lower left corner is largely unchanged. The Ellenboro School in the background is no more. (Van McDaniel family.)

Zeb Vance Daves, Selma Philbeck Daves, and Ted Michael Daves

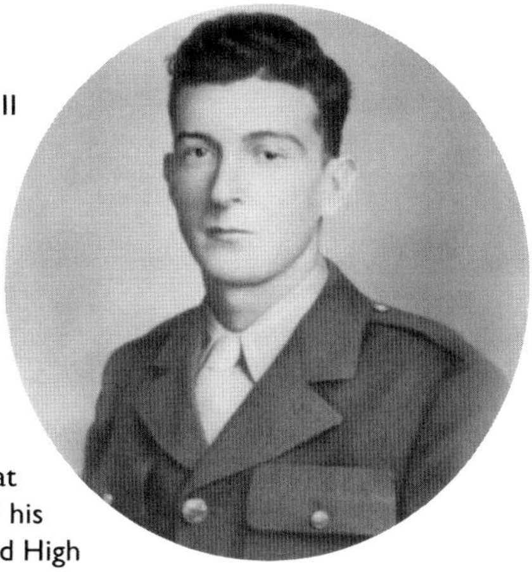

Zeb (November 14, 1919–May 25, 1964), a World War II veteran, served in Hawaii and the Pacific. He and his wife, Selma Philbeck Daves (Bess), of Ellenboro, had one child, Ted Michael Daves (April 15, 1947–September 18, 2012). During the first years of Ted's life, Zeb was a farmer and trucker. He worked the land and harvested timber during the day and, with Selma, he completed long distance truck "runs" at night.

Zeb and Selma began operating Daves's Texaco service station in Mooresboro in 1957. Ted was badly burned in an accident at the station following his eighth-grade year at Ellenboro School. The burns covered about 90 percent of his body. Ted missed his first year (1961–1962) at East Rutherford High School because of the injuries and the surgeries that followed.

Zeb died near the end of Ted's sophomore year. Ted supplemented the family income by driving a school bus on the Bostic route; he loved cars and driving. Ted also worked at their service station with his mother after school (after his bus route), in the summers, and on weekends. Ted remained optimistic and graduated with honors from East Rutherford High School in 1966. He entered Western Carolina University in the fall.

Following graduation from college in 1970, Ted took the prestigious position of test engineer for Nuclear Service and Construction Company, a Virginia company involved with combat ship shock and vibration testing to harden warships against enemy attack. In 1974, Ted earned the appointment of test site manager at the nuclear service test site in Arvonia, Virginia. His work was vital to the nation.

In 1976, Ted (as president) and two partners bought some used equipment in Everett, Washington, and began HI-Test Laboratories, Inc. Under Ted's leadership, HI-Test grew into the largest company in the United States doing underwater shock testing of naval combat vessels; this company eventually bought the original Nuclear Service test site in Arvonia, Virginia. Not only did HI-Test design and conduct unique tests of individualized pieces of shipboard equipment (propulsion systems, missile launchers, control consoles, and so on), but HI-Test also conducted full-scale testing in the Atlantic, Pacific, and Gulf of Mexico of ships for Naval Sea Systems Command. HI-Test also tested experimental Surface Effects Ships and had unique programs involving tests of cruise missiles fired from submarines for NATO.

Ted and his HI-Test Laboratories conducted the testing of the last carrier built for the US Navy: USS *John F. Kennedy* (CV-67, formerly CVA-67), which was the world's largest, conventionally powered carrier. Ted's HI-Test Labs developed the largest vibration table in the world.

In March 1989, the *Exxon Valdez* ran aground in the Prince William Sound; at that time, it was one of the worst human-caused environmental disasters in history. Regulations did not require the double-hull designers to pass any specific strength tests to prove their ability to resist spillage. Ted submitted an unsolicited proposal to the David Taylor Naval Research and Development Center to design and operate such a facility. As a result, he developed and tested many double-hull designs and energy absorbing materials incorporated into modern tankers.

Ted also headed Performance Counts Automotive, which developed and built racing engines. Some of his engines have set world records through the nationally televised *Barrett-Jackson Auto Auction*. In 2000, Ted began operating Sugar Hill Racing, Inc., a NASCAR Late Model Stock Car team. Ted's most recent driver is former National Champion Peyton Sellers of Danville, Virginia.

Ted's marriage to Owana Gwen Bridges of Mooresboro in August 1970 resulted in one daughter, Alecia M. Daves-Johnson. His life was an inspiration to others. He contributed to his nation and world in ways no one else could. He never complained and always found compassion for others. His friends and admirers were many; he passed away September 18, 2012, at age 65. (Selma Philbeck Daves and Alecia Daves-Johnson.)

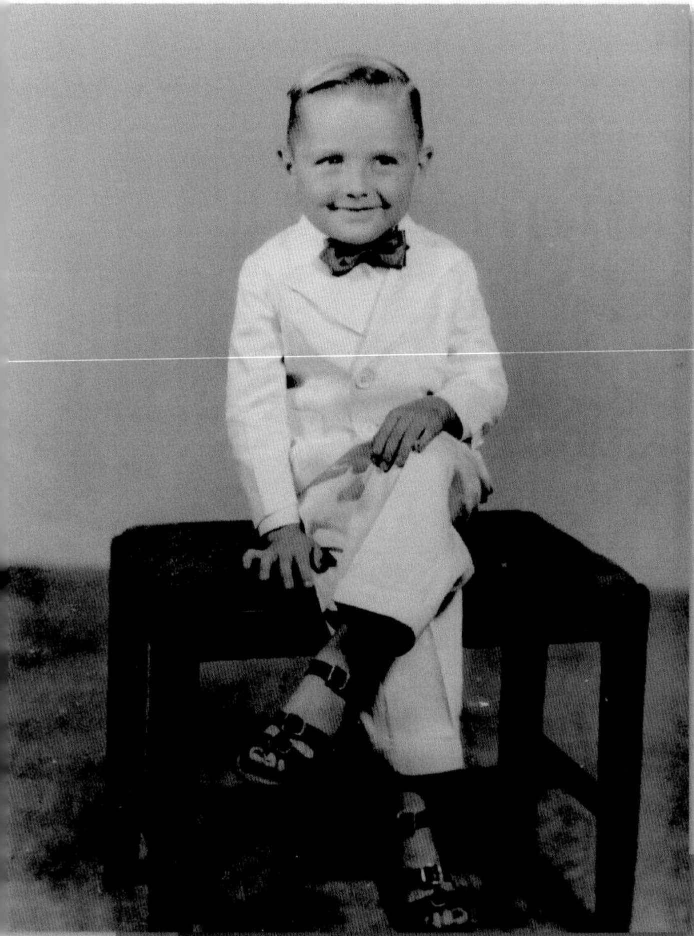

Ted Michael Daves, 1952 Ellenboro School Mascot
This photograph is a favorite of Selma's, Ted's mother. Ted was the mascot of the 1952 graduating class of Ellenboro High School. He was about five years old at the time and had not yet been disfigured by a 1961 fire at his father's service station. Ted's life, his innovations, and his business skills have served as an example to others throughout the past half century. Ted agreed to have his life story included in this volume and handwrote many of the facts about his life from his hospital room just days before his death. (Selma Philbeck Daves Bess.)

Ted Daves, Business Executive, Innovator, and Family Advocate
This photograph shows, from left to right, Ted Michael Daves, his aunt Nell Daves Price Burns, and his uncles Woodrow Daves and Walter Carpenter at a reunion that Ted planned. (Roger Carpenter.)

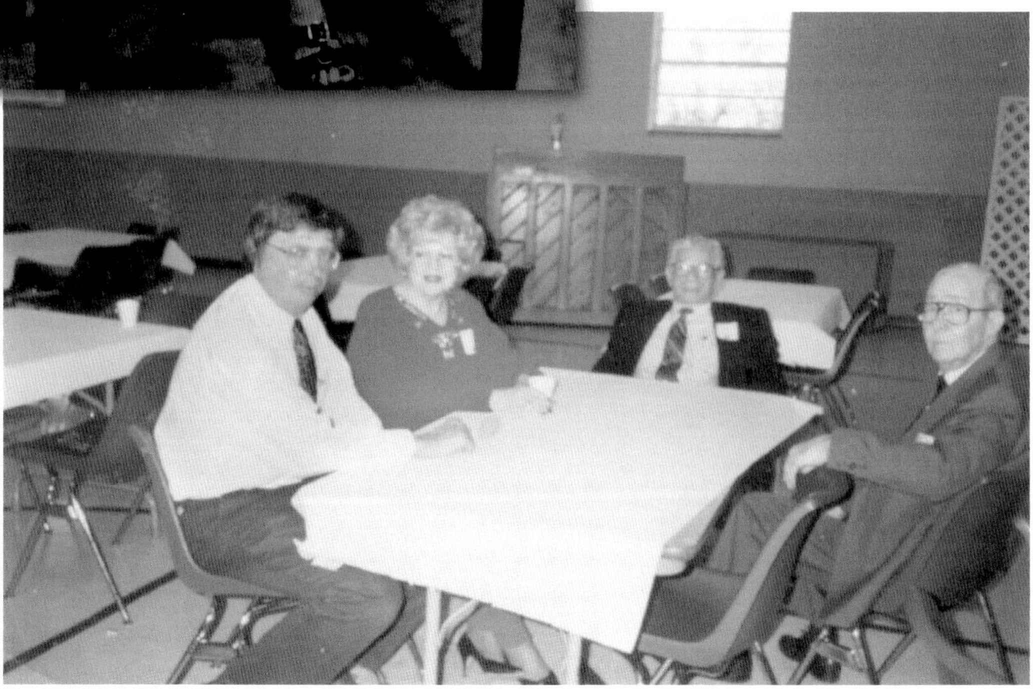

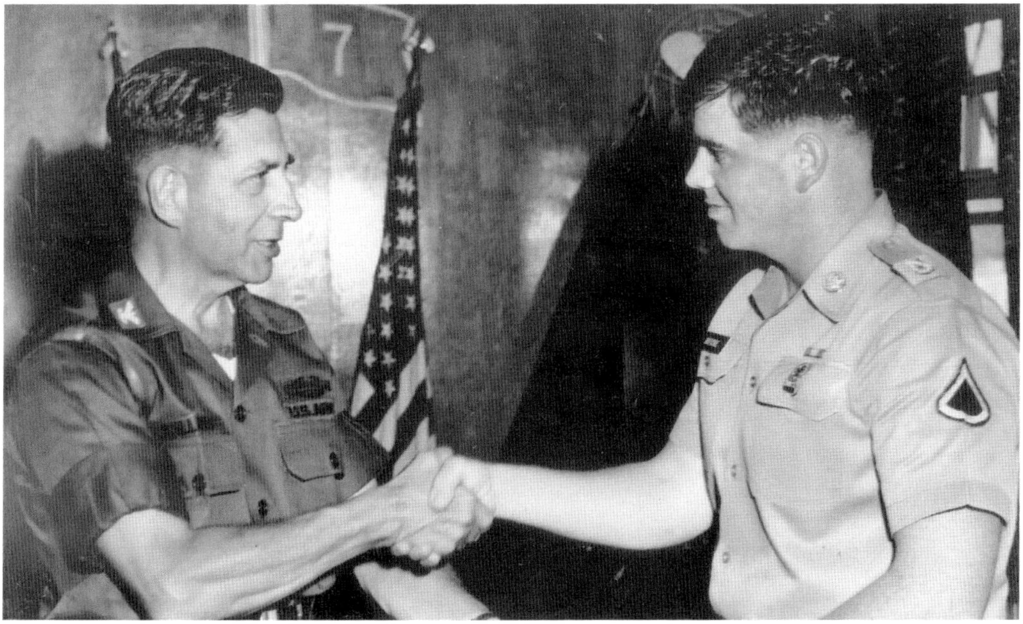

Mike Rhyne, Veteran and Museum Curator

Myron Thomas "Mike" Rhyne was born in Rutherford Hospital in 1946. He attended Ellenboro School and graduated from East Rutherford High School. Rhyne entered the US Army in 1967 and served with distinction. Rhyne is famous throughout the county for his establishment of the Colfax Museum in the restored Ellenboro Depot (below). He envisioned a museum in the Rutherford County area to preserve and communicate the story of the county and its people. The logical place, in his mind, was the 1882 Ellenboro depot. After his military service and after his retirement from work, he was ready to ask for help from Raleigh and from local citizens to realize his dream. He now serves as curator, director, repairman, decorator, and doorkeeper of the facility. Rhyne conducts group tours, especially for school children. In addition, he serves as an Ellenboro alderman. He is very active in the Sons of the American Revolution. He helps also with the annual Fiddler's Convention, local parades, and the Colfax Free Fair. Rhyne and his wife, Pat, volunteer and help wherever there is a need.

Rhyne resides in Ellenboro in the historic home in which he grew up, four houses from where his good friend Ted Daves grew up also. Above, Rhyne, a Vietnam veteran, accepts the award for the Soldier of the Month from his sergeant major. (Above, Mike Rhyne; below, James M. Walker.)

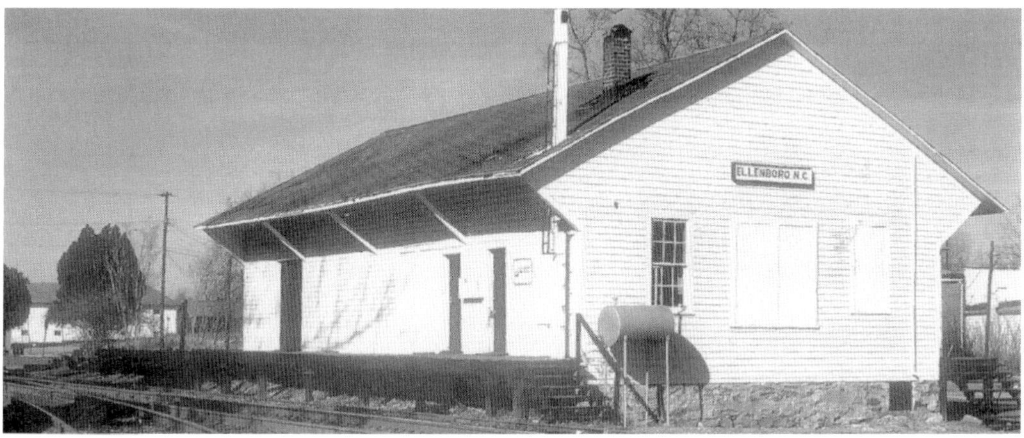

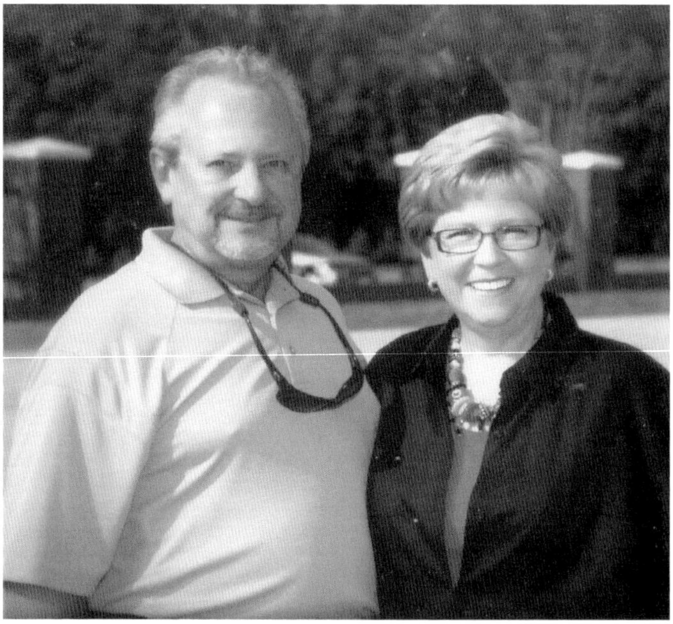

Rutherfordton Mayor Jimmy Dancy and Ginger Dancy
Here, Rutherfordton mayor Jimmy Dancy and his wife, Ginger, appear at a public event. Jimmy Dancy served in the US Army during the Vietnam War era, and his public service continues today. As a mayor, Dancy is an example of a public official who helps to manage the resources of the county. (Jimmy and Ginger Dancy.)

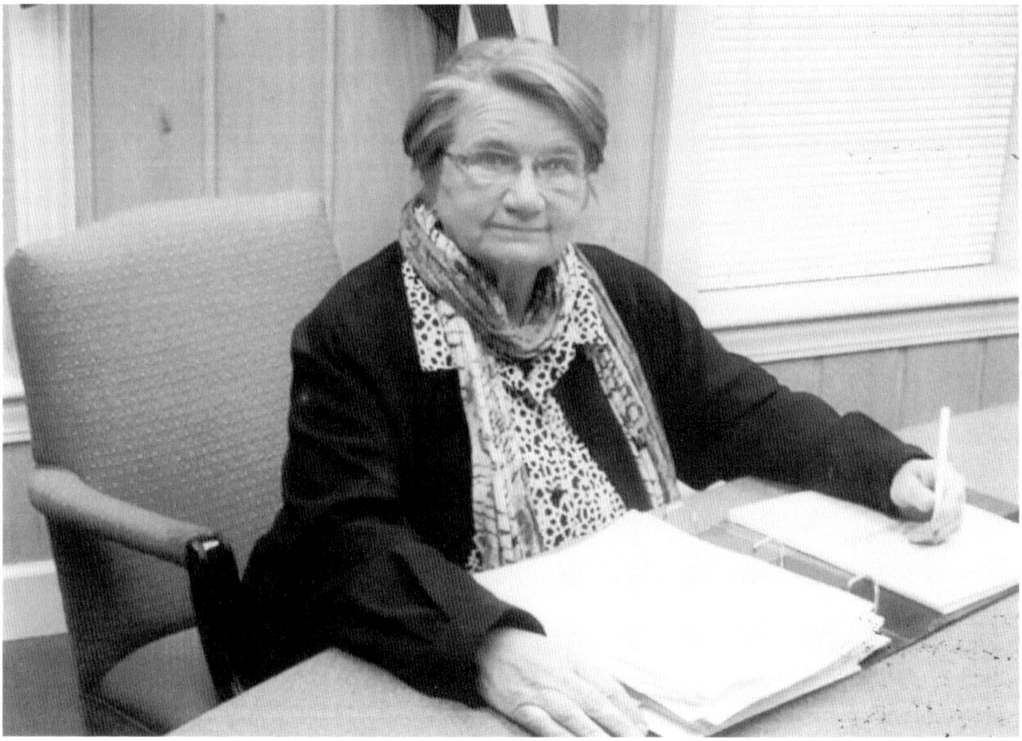

City Manager Danielle Withrow
Withrow has been in the position of city manager of Forest City since 2000. Withrow's length of time as city manager attests to her proficiency and dedication. She earned a baccalaureate from the University of North Carolina at Chapel Hill and a master's in public administration from North Carolina State. (Danielle Withrow.)

CHAPTER FOUR

Communicators

Communication among people can be difficult. When one considers the sparse population within Rutherford County in the past, it is even more evident that communication might have been slow.

Besides word of mouth, newspapers helped convey information. Rutherford County historian Clarence W. Griffin stated that there was an ephemeral nature to the early newspapers in the county. Conveying the news through the written word was especially difficult before the 1940s because newspapers were generally weekly and often transitory. With the advent of World War II, the need for more regular, systematic newspaper communication became even more evident.

Ellenboro was the first town in the county to establish a telephone system for communication. The telephone became an essential way of communicating among the residents and of facilitating the work of the Office of Civil Defense during World War II. The operator who placed the calls before direct dialing became familiar to many users.

In 1947, WBBO, the first radio station in Rutherford County, began broadcasting. Holly Springs Baptist Church bought WBBO and began broadcasting as a gospel station in 1980. There have been many effective communicators in Rutherford County; these important communicators are still remembered.

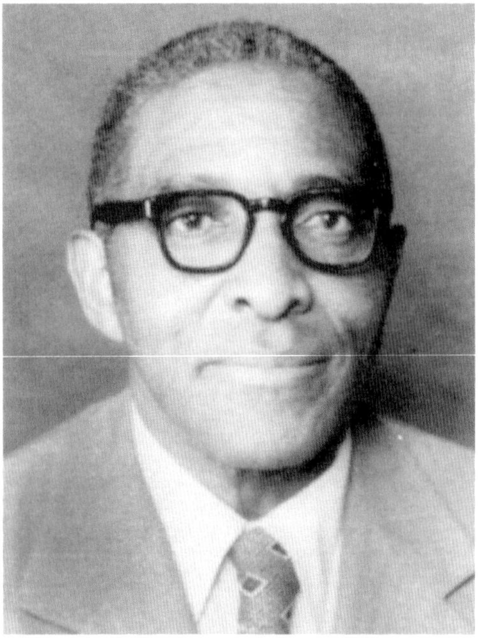

Rev. Dr. M.B. Robinson Sr., Newspaper Founder and Editor
In the 1940s, Rev. Dr. M.B. Robinson established and edited two Rutherford County newspapers designed for African Americans: the *Harris Herald* and the *Star of Zion*. The two were sold throughout the county and in other states. In the still segregated South, Dr. Robinson was an innovator and pacesetter with his much-needed publications. Robinson (1913–1991) had earned his bachelor's of arts (Johnson C. Smith University), his master's in educational administration (North Carolina Agricultural and Technological University), and his doctorate of divinity (Livingstone College). Besides serving as newspaper editor, he worked as a Pullman porter, brick mason, teacher, and past-presiding elder of the AME Zion Church. (Milton Robinson Jr.)

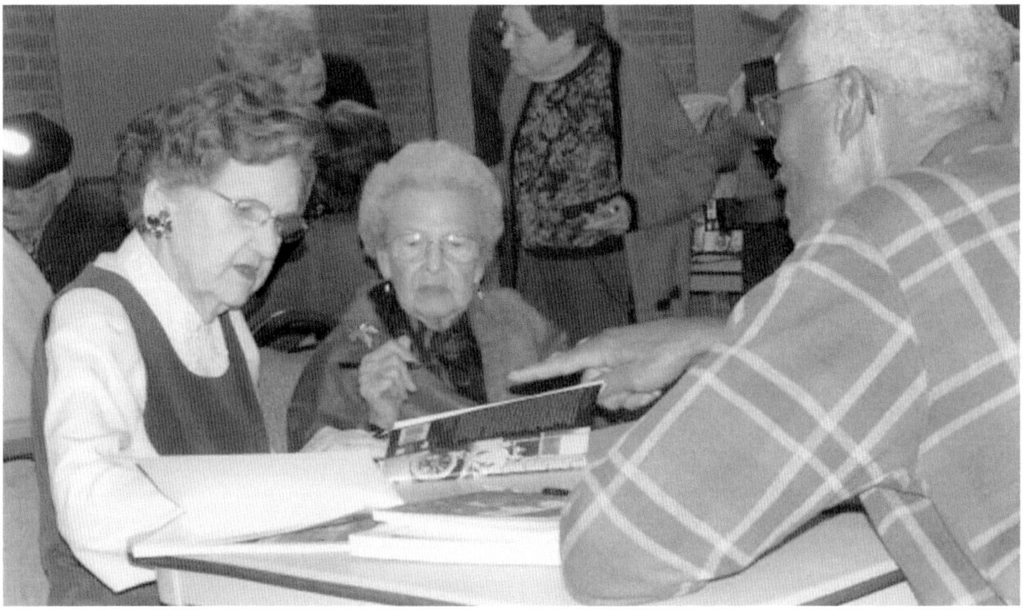

Virginia Blades Biggerstaff Rucker, Writer
A familiar name to those reading the papers in Rutherford County is that of Virginia Blades Biggerstaff Rucker, pictured in the center. Rucker was born in New Bern. After her father, James Blades, died, seven-year-old Rucker and her mother traveled extensively. Rucker entered Salem College at age 14. She and her mother came to Rutherford County to be near her uncle who had tuberculosis. They lived in Rutherfordton, where she met Bill Biggerstaff, and they married. They had two children. The family was able to travel some with him while he served in World War II. Mae Blanton (left) and veteran Milton Robinson (right) discuss with Rucker the book *Forest City* by Anita Price Davis and James M. Walker. (Garrett Byers and Virginia Blades Biggerstaff Rucker.)

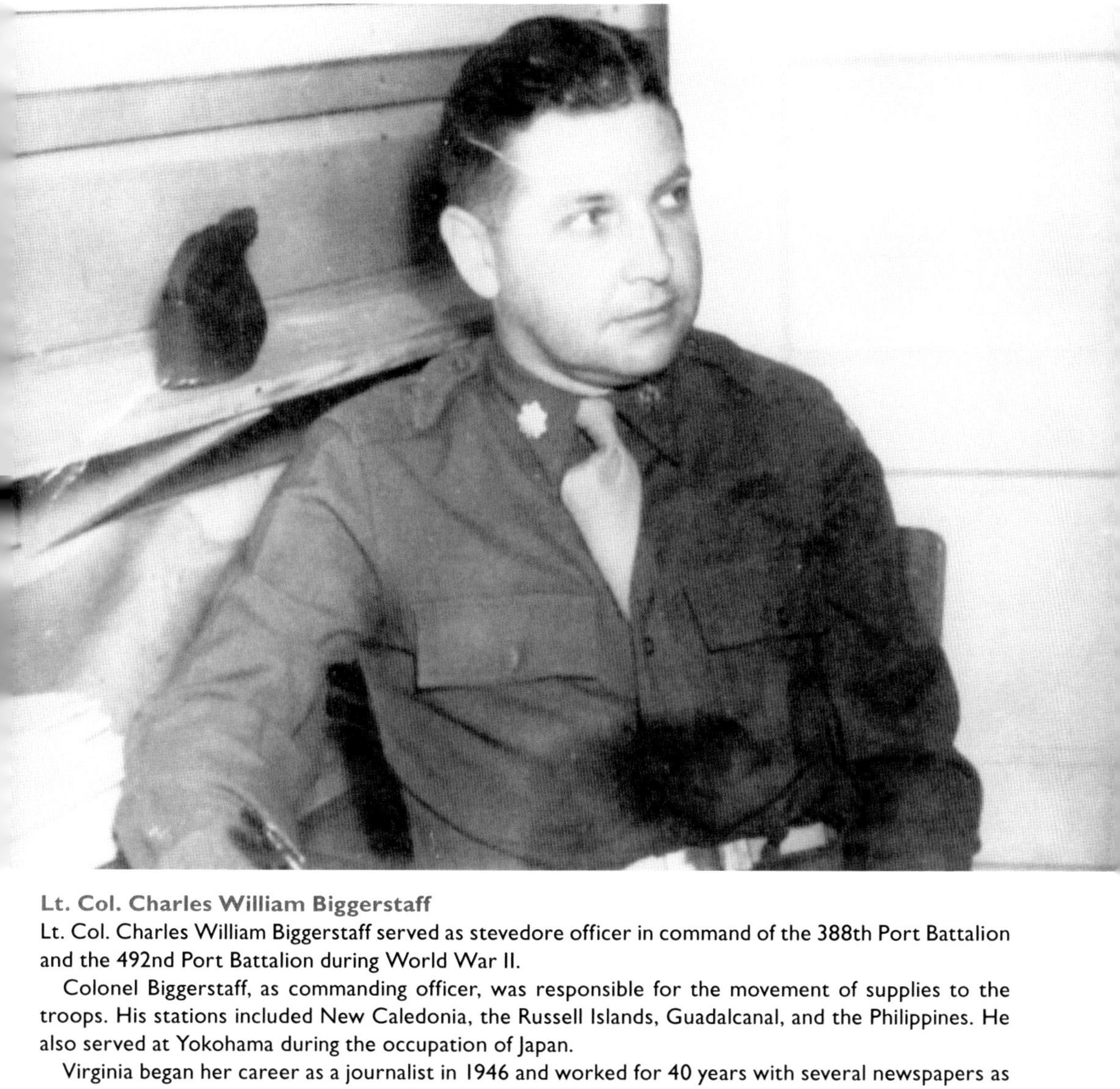

Lt. Col. Charles William Biggerstaff

Lt. Col. Charles William Biggerstaff served as stevedore officer in command of the 388th Port Battalion and the 492nd Port Battalion during World War II.

Colonel Biggerstaff, as commanding officer, was responsible for the movement of supplies to the troops. His stations included New Caledonia, the Russell Islands, Guadalcanal, and the Philippines. He also served at Yokohama during the occupation of Japan.

Virginia began her career as a journalist in 1946 and worked for 40 years with several newspapers as writer, reporter, and associate editor. After the death of Bill Biggerstaff, she married Albert Rucker; she worked under the names of Virginia Biggerstaff and Virginia Rucker.

Virginia Rucker (left) served as president of the North Carolina Press Women. She was the first woman to receive the Kiwanis Club Special Cup Award. Beautiful, intelligent 96-year-old Virginia Rucker is still active. She declares happily that her life has been good. (Virginia Biggerstaff Rucker.)

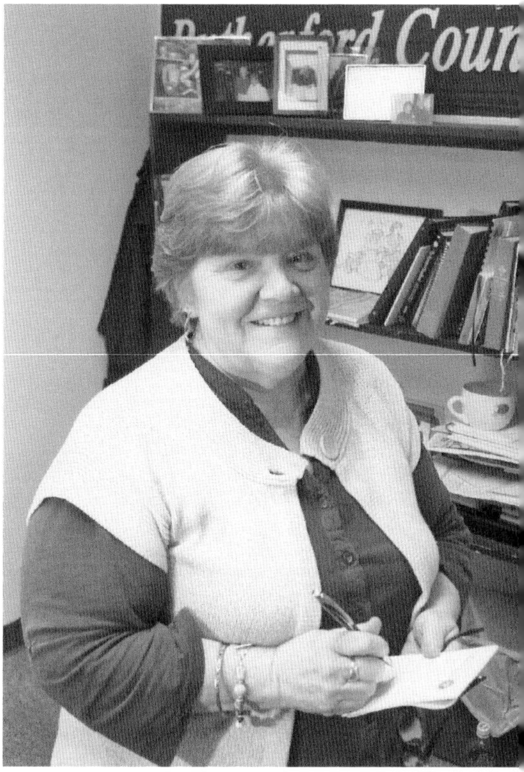

Jean Gordon, *Daily Courier* Features and Arts Editor
Jean Gordon had been a student at Isothermal Community College and knew the county well. She brought her enthusiasm and her knowledge with her to the newspaper offices. Gordon is the daughter of the late Irene Crawford Gordon and Edgar Gordon. At only 18 years old, she began her newspaper work in 1970 as a typesetter at the *Rutherford County News*. By 1972, she had become news editor and then editor in 1986. When Forest City Publishing bought the *Rutherford County News*, Gordon went to the *Daily Courier*, where she has served as features and arts editor. (Garrett Byers.)

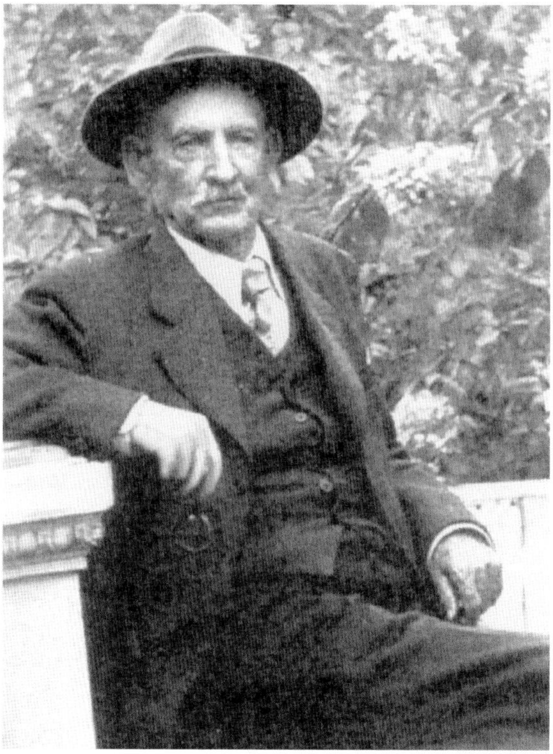

William E. "Will" McArthur
Photographer William E. "Will" McArthur (1859–1956) with his camera was a familiar sight in the county. His work was recognizable to the readers of the Rutherford County newspapers and to those who purchased local postcards. He was the uncle of W.H. "Bill" McArthur of McArthur's Tin Shop in Forest City and was one of the earliest photographers in the county. Postcard companies relied on his sharp, clear, glass-plate negatives to depict accurately the Rutherford County area. (W.H. McArthur and William E. McArthur.)

Clarence W. Griffin

Pictured here are writer and editor Griffin (with telephone) and banker J. Worth Morgan, who worked with Farmers Bank and Trust and with Union Trust Company. They made the first direct-dialed call between Forest City and Rutherfordton on the new direct-dial telephone. At the age of 21, Griffin began working with the *Courier.* In 1941, Griffin and C.E. Alcock established the *Spindale Sun.* Griffin had a deep devotion for the community. He served in the general assembly (1933–1935), helped establish the Western North Carolina Weekly Press Association, and served as its president and secretary for some time. He was the historian of the North Carolina Press Association from 1938 until his death in 1958. He was a member of nearly every county civic group and still found time to write such books as *The History of Old Tryon and Rutherford Counties* (1730–1936) and *History of Rutherford County* (1937–1951). Griffin was at his desk at the *Forest City Daily Courier* when he suffered a fatal heart attack on a cold winter day in 1958. (Bob Morgan.)

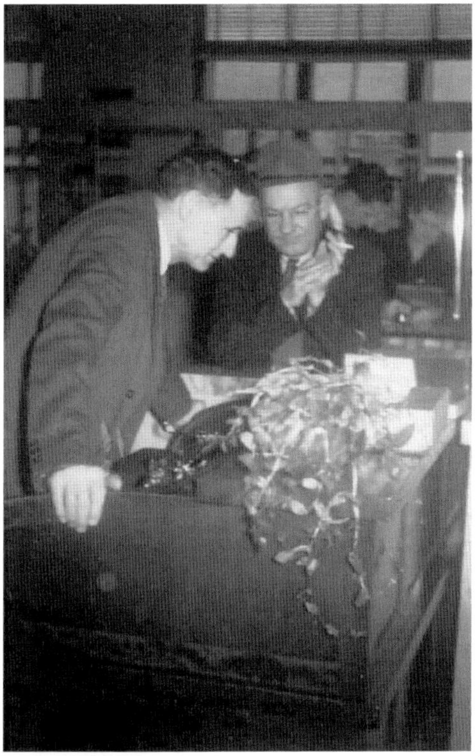

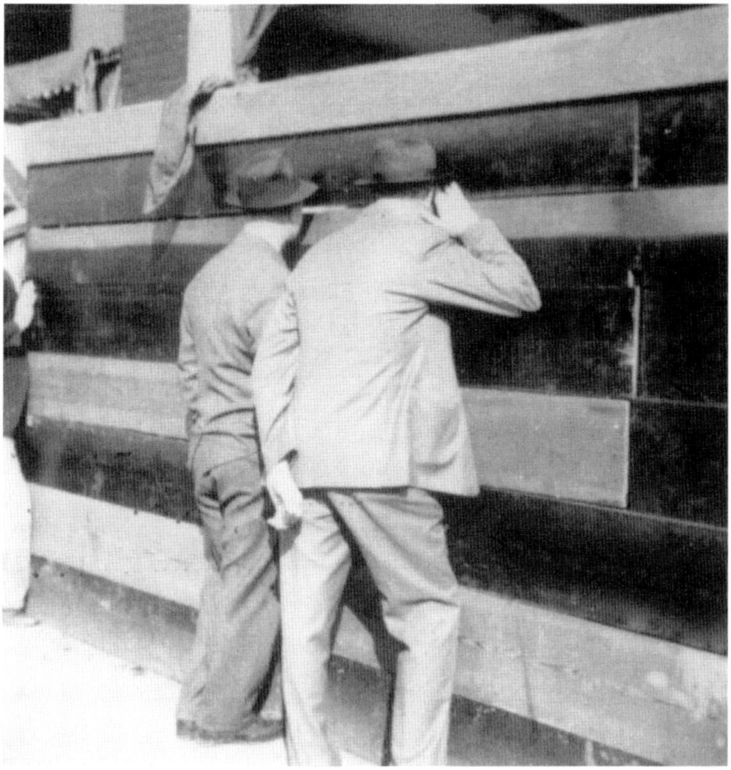

Griffin outside Smith's Drugs

This photograph shows Griffin (left) staying abreast of happenings in the area when he was not at his desk. He and his friend J. Worth Morgan check on the progress of the construction of Smith's Drugstore in Forest City. (Dr. W.L. Stallings and Betty Jo Carpenter.)

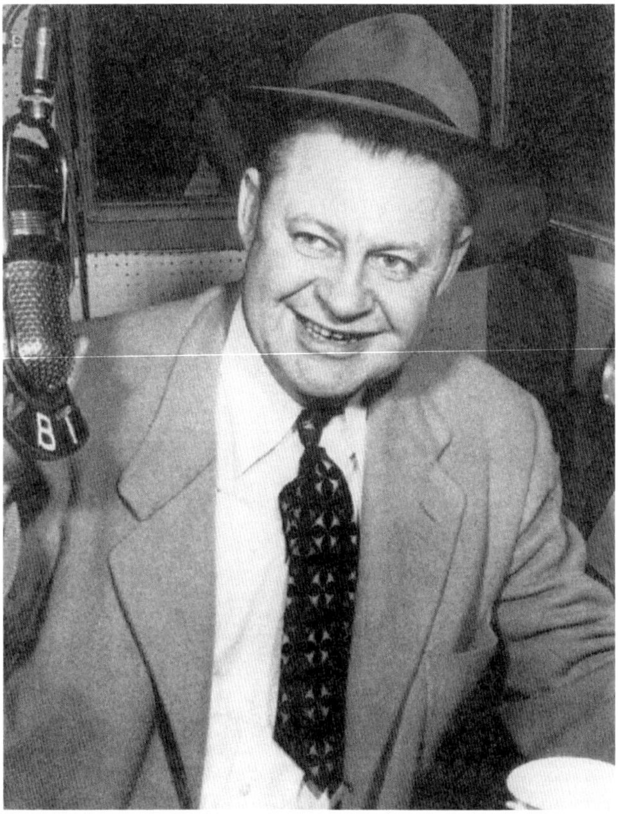

Grady Cole of WBT in Charlotte

On April 10, 1922, the US Department of Commerce issued a license for the first commercial radio station in the Southeast. The license went to WBT in Charlotte, North Carolina. Grady Cole (pictured here) began working with WBT in 1929. His voice became a recognizable one to many people in Rutherford County.

Nell Daves Price (Burns) reported that when she visited her soldier husband at Camp Breckinridge in Kentucky in 1943, she could not find Grady Cole on the radio. She felt that she and husband, Arthur Price, were too far from home when she could not hear Cole's familiar voice. (WBT, Charlotte.)

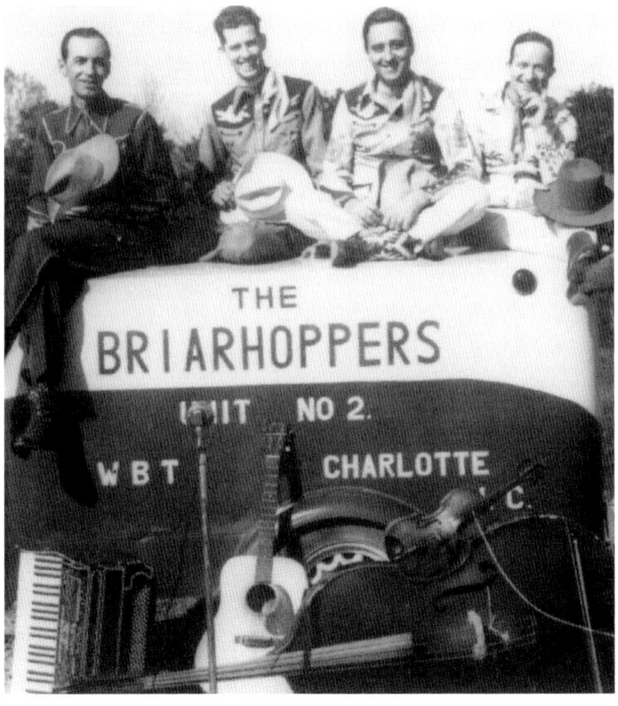

The Briarhoppers, with Claude Casey

A bluegrass musical group called The Briarhoppers began its career in 1935 on WBT in Charlotte. Claude Casey, a member of the Briarhoppers, moved to Rutherford County in the 1950s and appeared regularly at Ed Price's Capri Park in Ellenboro.

WBT/WBTV became the employer of another Rutherford County native: Reno Bailey. Both Claude Casey and Reno Bailey appear later in this volume, pages 96 and 82, respectively.

Although the members of The Briarhoppers changed at times, Claude Casey was a regular in the group and frequently served as the announcer. In the photograph here, Claude Casey is the third from left. (Carolyn Grindstaff Barbee.)

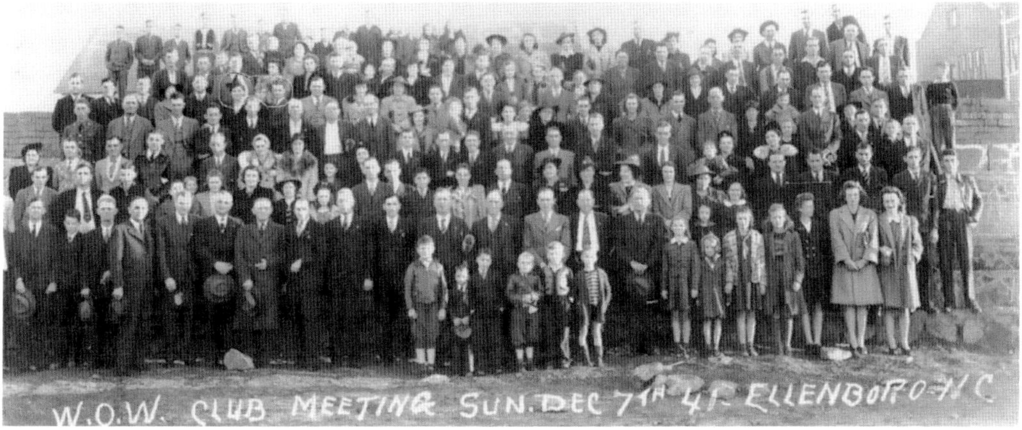

Jerrell Bedford

Jerrell Bedford wanted to be a professional baseball player, but in his words, "Just after my 12th birthday in 1948, the Lord let me know that baseball was not a part of the plan for my life." In November 1948, Bedford became paralyzed from the waist down from polio. He was hospitalized for nine months. Job prospects for a handicapped person were limited at that time. Bedford became interested in "ham" radio and secured a license. He had some friends (Hoyle Lovelace and Gerard Thompson Becknell) in broadcasting and believed he could work in radio; however, it would take him a while before he could try his hand at broadcasting.

After his graduation from Ellenboro High School, Bedford attended Duke University and talked the "prettiest girl in the world" into marrying him. He tried door-to-door sales and working with textile engraving. While listening to a radio station one day, he learned of a contest for a scholarship to broadcasting school. Bedford entered and won. When Becknell and Lovelace started WAGY, Bedford went to work for them as announcer, copywriter, and jack-of-all-trades. His name on the air was "Pappy." When WAGY changed hands, Bedford worked for WGMA in Spindale and for WSPA-TV in Spartanburg, South Carolina. He spent 38 years in the broadcast industry. He met and got to know such people as Ronnie Milsap, Dolly Parton, Billy Walker, and Bill Anderson.

This image dates from December 7, 1941. Bedford (1936–) and his parents (fifth row, with a drawn circle around them) gathered after church with other members of the Woodmen of the World Insurance Company on the Ellenboro School grounds for a photograph. What they did not know at the time was that the Japanese had bombed Pearl Harbor or what would happen to Jerrell in seven years. (Jerrell Bedford.)

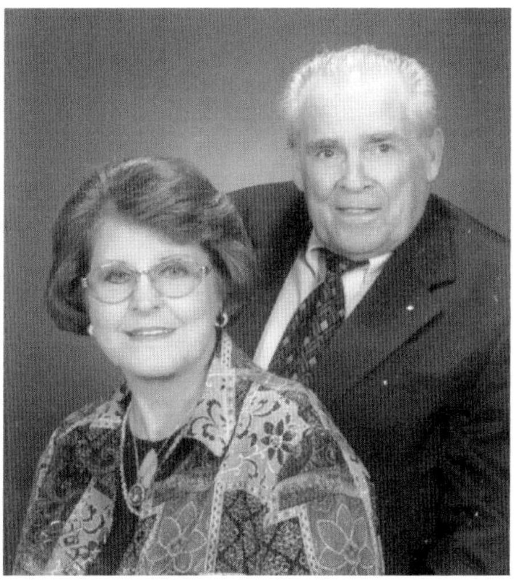

Jerrell Bedford and Pat Bedford

Jerrell and his wife, Pat, have two sons and four grandchildren. Married for more than half a century, they still reside in Rutherford County. They are both active in Oak Grove Methodist Church, and Pat volunteers regularly for hospice. (Pat Bedford.)

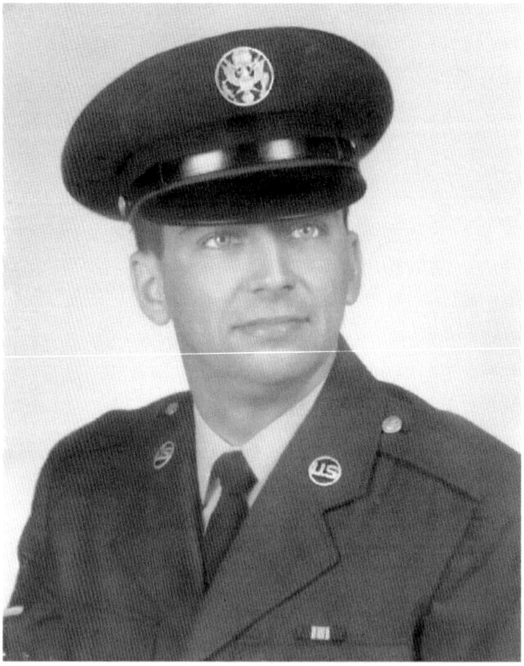

James "Jim" Harold Bishop
Bishop, a Caroleen native, entered the US Air Force on July 30, 1968, and served until July 20, 1974. Bishop completed his basic training at Lackland Air Force Base in San Antonio, Texas, and took further training at Keesler Air Force Base in Biloxi, Mississippi. His specialty title was "chaplain services," a job that compares to the civilian job of church secretary. Bishop received a special commendation from the chaplain for his performance. Bishop's job location was at Warner-Robbins Air Force Base in Georgia. His final assignment was to Elmendorf Air Force Base in Anchorage, Alaska. Bishop earned the National Defense Service Medal, the Good Conduct Medal, and an Honorable Discharge. He earned the Airman of the Month and received the Marksmanship Award. (James Harold Bishop.)

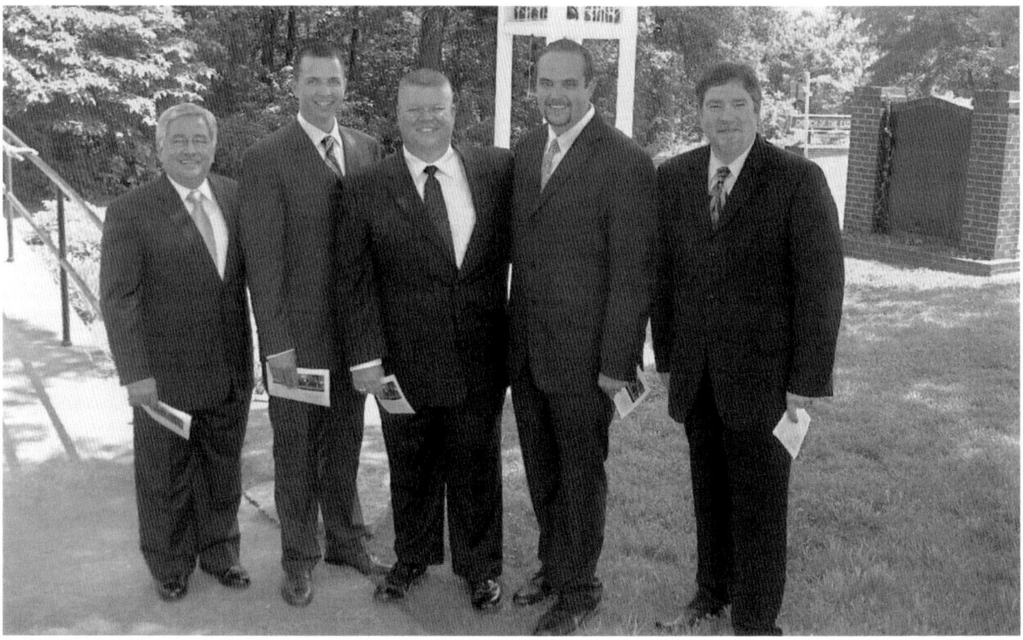

Jim Bishop, a Veteran, Broadcaster, and Singer
Bishop is best known today in Rutherford County as a radio broadcaster and as a member of the gospel group In His Glory that performs regularly. The 2012 members are, from left to right, Jim Bishop (baritone), Thad Harrill (lead), Howard Gordon (bass), Michael Henderson (tenor), and David Roach (pianist). Through the radio station WCAB, Jim enters many homes in Rutherford County with his community service announcements, a daily radio show, interviews, and gospel music. In His Glory is a source of inspiration and pleasure to listeners. (Jim Bishop and Lou Gilliam.)

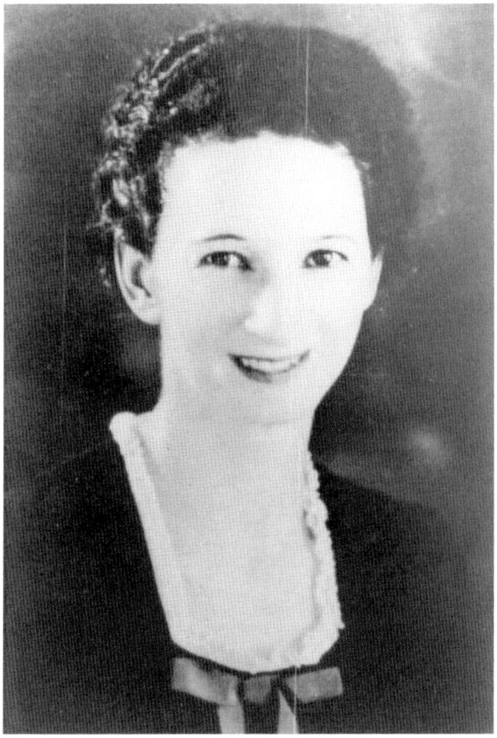

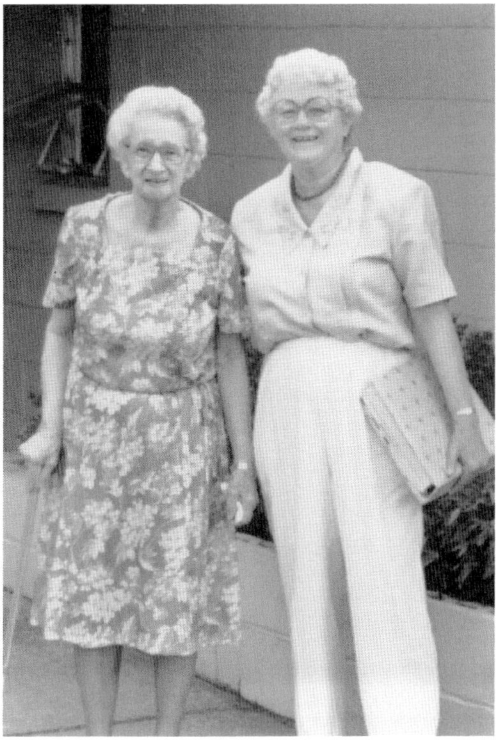

Merle Price, Rutherford County Poet and Writer
Price was a poet who spoke to and for the local residents. She was the youngest of nine children on the Price homeplace in Sandy Mush. At a time in history when many local women did not pursue a higher education, Price (August 20, 1910–June 30, 1992) attended Limestone College from 1928 through 1932 and graduated with a bachelor of arts degree in English. She served on the staff of the school newspaper (the *Lantern*) and as editor of the Limestone annual (the *Calciid*). Merle Price earned also her master of arts in English degree from Appalachian State Teachers College.

In 1929, she and her sister Winifred "Winnie" Price Bayon published a book titled *Reminiscence and Other Poems*. Winnie prepared the illustrations for the volume. Winnie Price was only 19 at the time. Price and her sister Selma "Polly Anna" authored an advice column for the local papers. Their work also occasionally appeared in the *Charlotte Observer*.

Price served as a teacher, librarian, and residence counselor at Converse College and Spartanburg Methodist College. Banner Press of Emory University published two of Price's books: *The Heart Has Its Daybreak* (1930) and *Splendid Rumor* (1950). Archibald Rutledge, the first South Carolina Poet Laureate (1934 to 1973), endorsed Price's *Splendid Rumor*; on the book jacket, he calls Merle Price "one of the clearest and most distinctive voices in the whole field of modern poetry." He authored the foreword in *The Heart Has Its Daybreak*. In the second photograph, Price (left) appears with Rebecca Harrill Thompson (right). (Jane Thompson Gurley.)

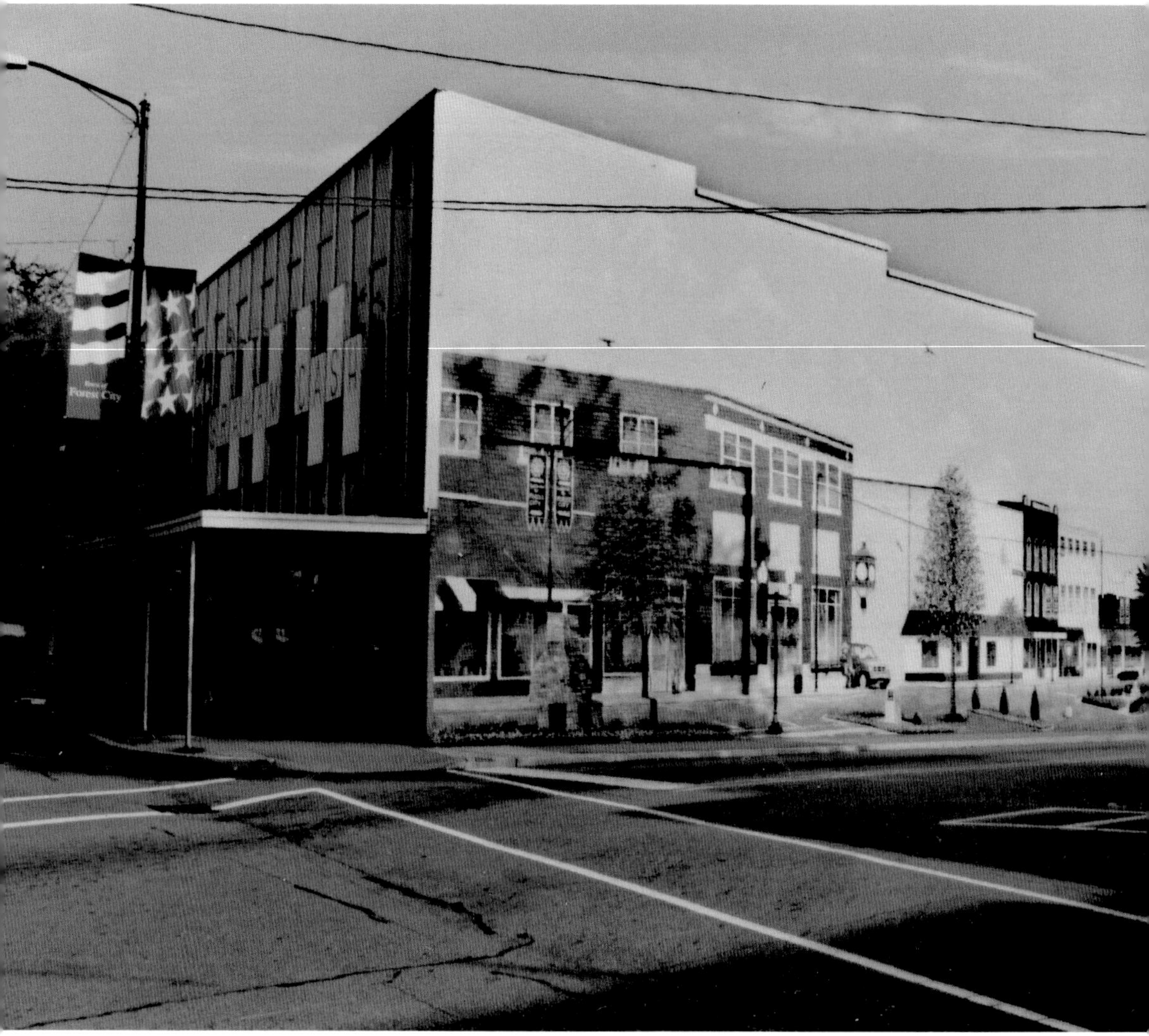

Clive Haynes's Main Street Mural

One of the first things one sees when traveling west on Main Street in Forest City is a mural on the side of Graham Cash Company. This mural is the work of Clive Haynes. Rutherford County resident Haynes (1953–) has chosen his murals as his own unique way to communicate with others. Clive's personal story is unique, also.

Clive's father, Eddie Yates Haynes, lived in the Duncan's Creek Community until he entered the military and served in the Pacific and in England. While Eddie was in Liverpool, he met Lilly Roberts, his future bride. The couple had three children: Steven, Clive, and Irene. Clive studied art and music in Italy at Harrow Art College and Oxbridge Tech. In 1973, Clive was a musician and singer in an Italian band (Goblin) in Rome. After painting two murals in England, Clive bought a shoe shop and decorated the inside with his own work. He knew he had found his passion. In 1986, Clive left his parents in England and came to North Carolina to do what he enjoyed most: painting murals. To date, Clive has completed over 100 paintings. (James M. Walker and Clive Haynes.)

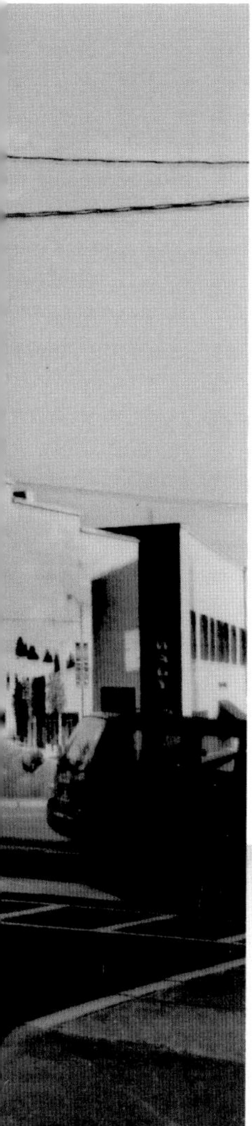

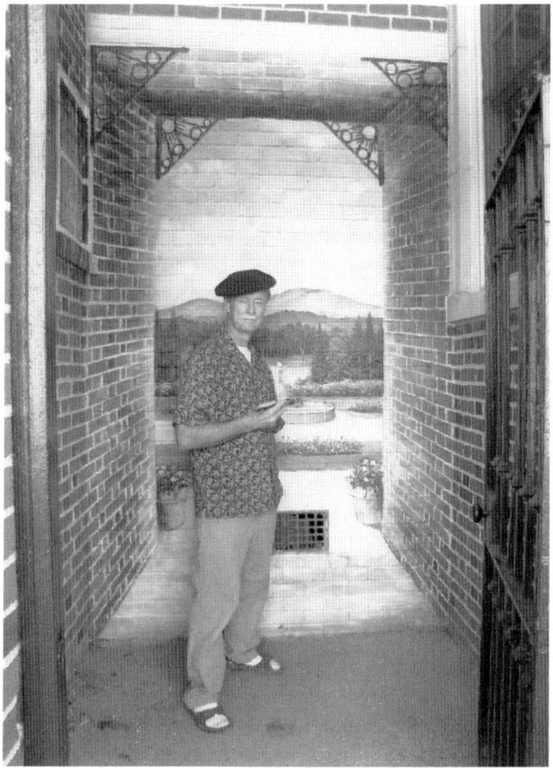

Clive Haynes's Mural in Smith's Drugs
This unique mural in Smith's Drugs shows Main Street in Forest City from some time ago. Clive's murals live in the Rutherford County Farm Museum, Chimney Rock Park, Rutherford County Hospital, Valdese, Spartanburg, Kings Mountain, and elsewhere. At left, Haynes works on the town hall mural. (Clive Haynes.)

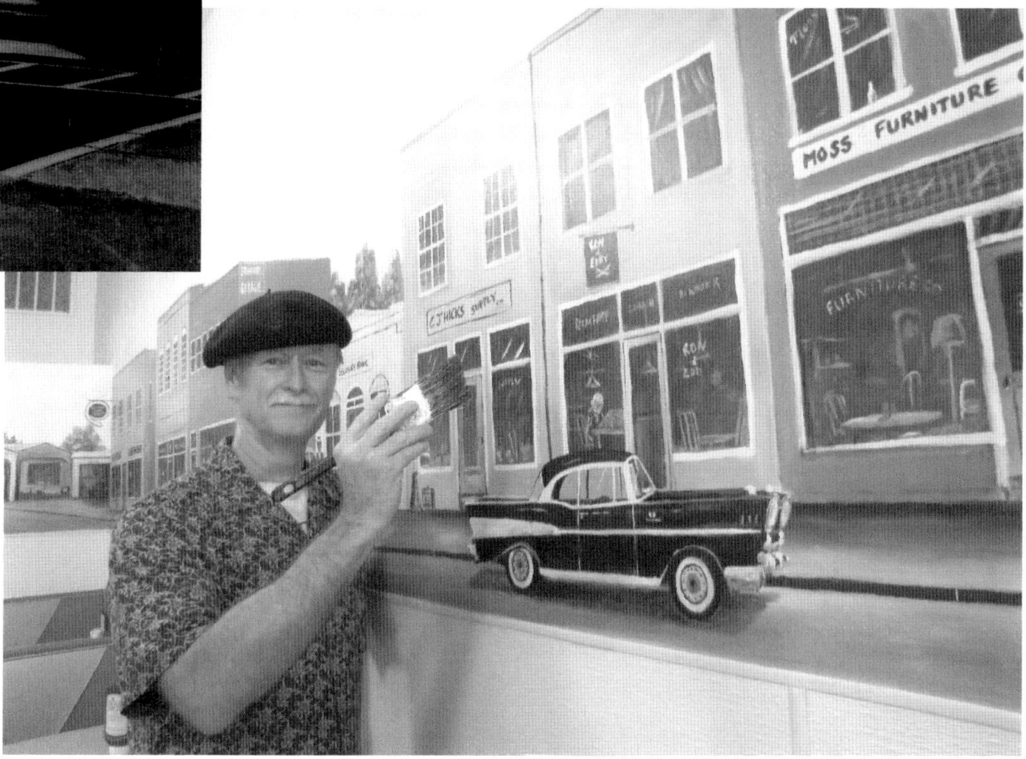

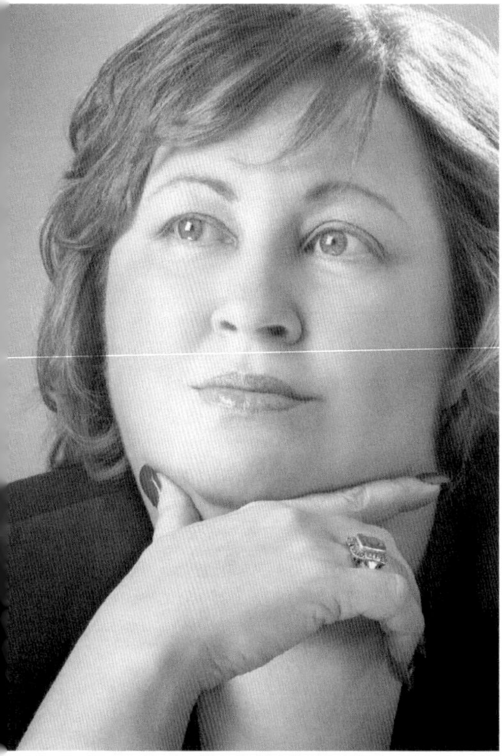

Daydreaming Author Kay Hooper

Rutherford County resident Hooper is a *New York Times* best-selling author. Her work includes more than 70 novels. She saw her first romance novel in print when she was only 22. Hooper was born in California in 1958 while her military father was stationed at an Air Force base there. Kay, her younger sister and brother, and her parents moved back to Rutherford County after his service was complete. Hooper is an East Rutherford High School graduate. She enrolled at Isothermal Community College as a business major after her high school graduation. When she found that business was not her "calling," she changed her major to literature and history.

Hooper asked for a typewriter for Christmas and promptly began writing a romance novel. Dell Publishing Company published Hooper's first novel, *Lady Thief*, a Regency romance. More than 70 novels, primarily suspense and romance, have followed this first one. Despite her busy writing schedule of more than one book a year, Hooper gives back to her community. She endorses the Community Pet Center of Rutherford County, located at 578 Laurel Hill Drive, Rutherfordton, and provides a foster home for some of the animals. Hooper and her sister Linda Hooper Parks are owners of Fireside Books (below) in Forest City, North Carolina. They schedule many events that serve the local community. (Linda Hooper Parks.)

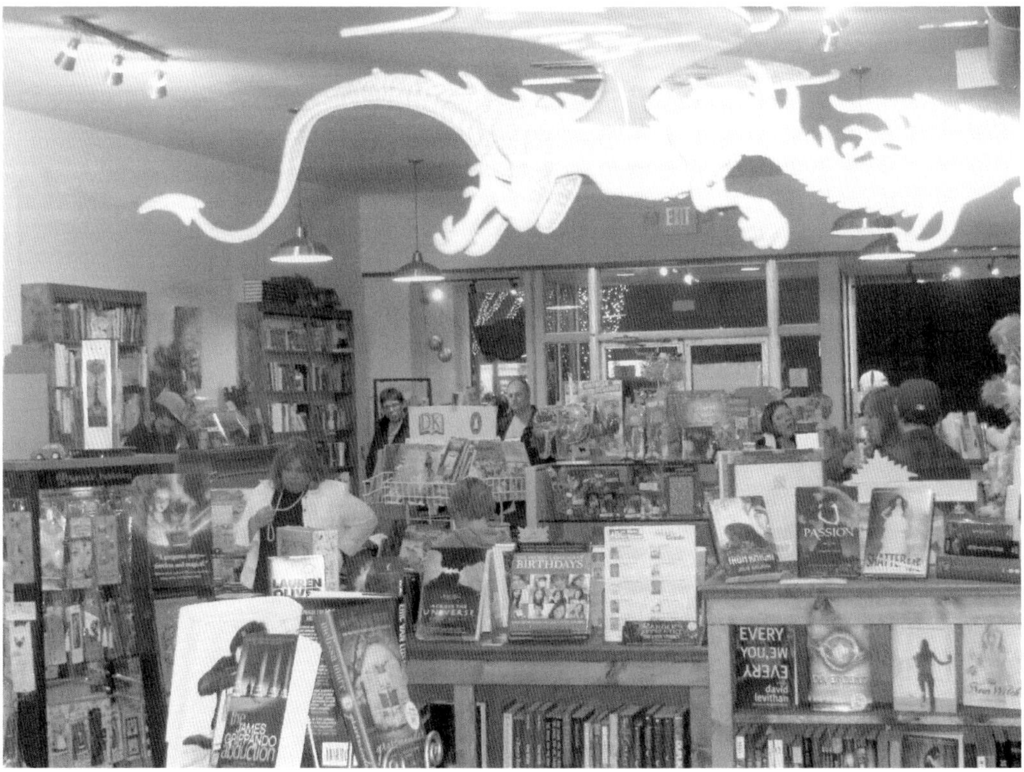

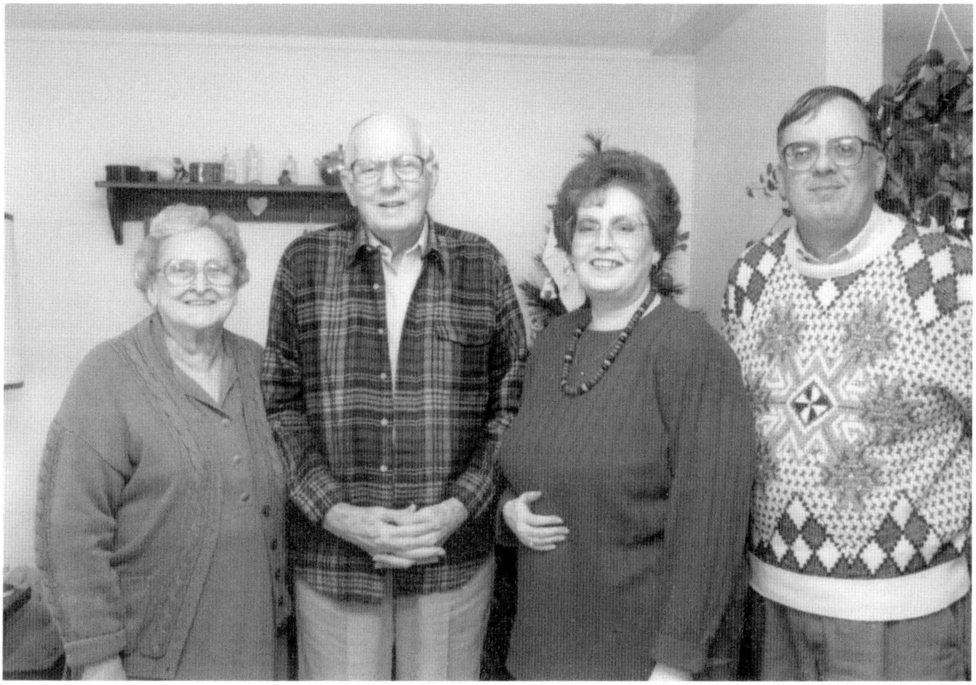

Photographer and Historian James M. Walker
Walker (January 10, 1949–December 5, 2008, on right) was a Rutherford County native, historian, and photographer. He attended Ellenboro School and graduated from East Rutherford High School in 1967. He majored in history at the University of North Carolina at Chapel Hill (1967–1970).

Jim was an active member of Bethel Baptist Church all his life. He attended their morning exercise class and was an assistant teacher of the pastor's sanctuary Sunday school class. A retired county educator of 31 years, Jim, also known as "Mr. Picture," had begun taking photographs of trains near his home when he was seven. As a professional photographer, his work enhances more than 10 volumes. Pictured in 1995 are, from left to right, Nell Culbreth Walker (mother), father James Maze "Doc" Walker, James's sister Anna Walker Greenway, and James. "Doc," Nell, and James are buried in the Bethel Baptist Church Cemetery in Ellenboro. Anna is an Asheville resident. (Anna Walker Greenway.)

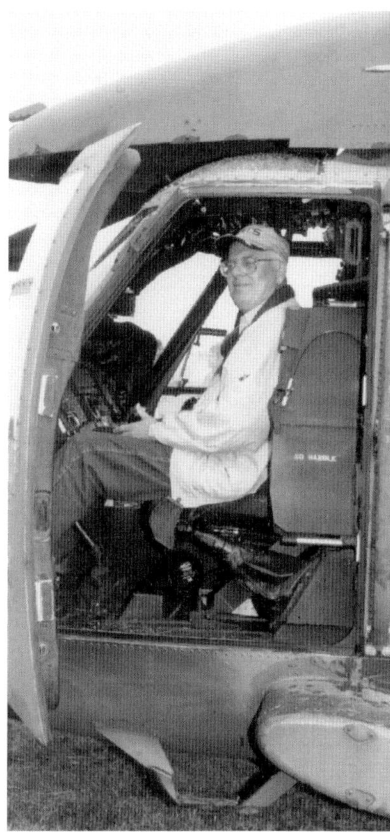

Walker in Helicopter
Photographs of Walker are often difficult to find because he was usually on the other side of the camera. Here is a rare photograph of Jim as he sits in the cockpit of a helicopter. His unexpected death left many people shocked and grieving.

A fitting tribute for him came at the end of his memorial service. As the last Amen was uttered, a train began blowing its whistle loudly before it reached the church, as it passed the church, and for some time afterward. All those who knew Jim and his love of trains were deeply moved by the sound. (Anna Walker Greenway.)

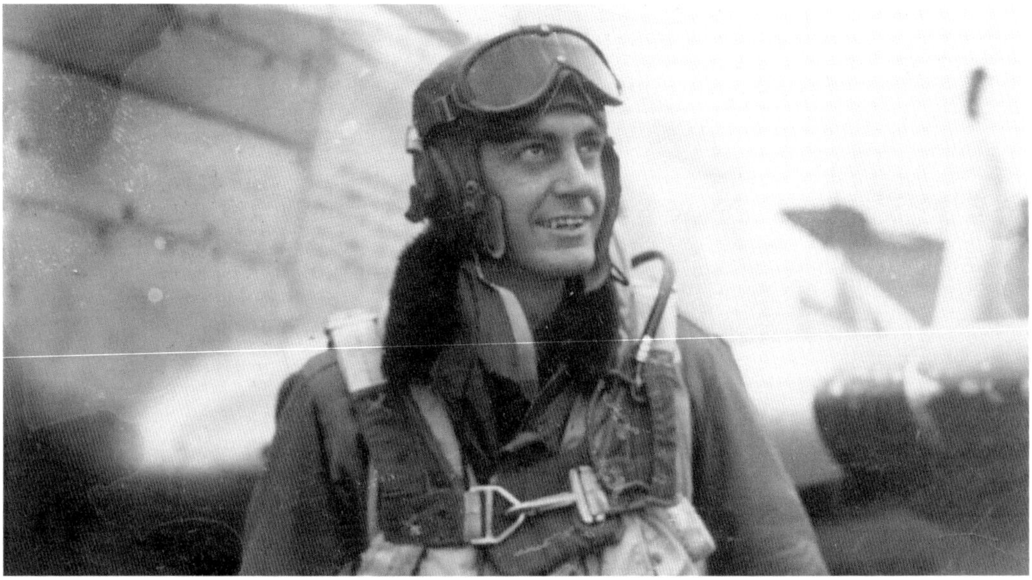

1st Lt. Robert Watkins, Rutherford County Photographer and Public Servant
During World War II, First Lieutenant Watkins flew a P-51 Mustang with the 358th Fighter Squadron, 355th Fighter Group, Eighth Air Force based at Steeple Mordan near Cambridge, England. Watkins flew 60 missions over occupied Europe in his plane named "Kitten." He received credit for one possible kill and three damaged enemy aircraft. After his honorable discharge from the Air Force, Watkins began an apprenticeship with Forest City photographer J.T. Gilbert, on the south side of the square. Gilbert's studio was over Ivey Drum's Restaurant, formally named Ivey's Restaurant. In 1959, Watkins moved his studio to his home at 114 Webb Street. Fifty-three years after relocating, Watkins still makes photographs. One can usually find him with camera in hand at all-important county events. Watkins volunteers for the American Cancer Society. He was Relay for Life Crusade chair (1981–1996) and serves on the State Board of Directors of the American Cancer Society. (Robert Watkins.)

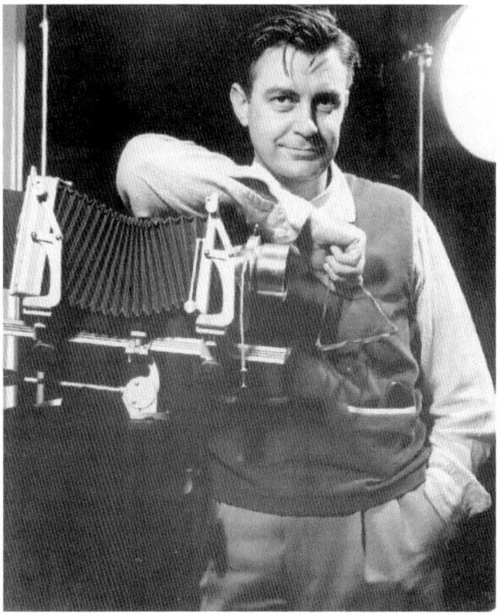

Watkins with Camera
Most area residents recall seeing Watkins with his camera as he recorded significant events for them. Watkins, in fact, photographed the author's wedding at the Burns family home in Ellenboro in 1962. (Robert Watkins.)

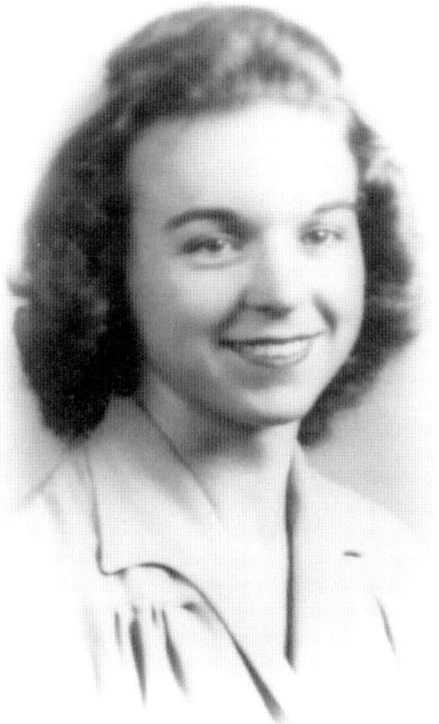

Evelyn "Polly" Hamrick Mauney
During World War II, Mauney had communication duties that were crucial to the area and the nation. Evelyn usually made the morning call to A.B. Bushong, the air raid warden for the Office of Civil Defense. The code words Evelyn used when she called Bushong's home were "Bacon 28." A typical call might be, "Bacon 28 reporting. Sighted three planes, flying low, two engines, flying east from the north." Nighttime was more serene with the blackouts. Hamrick married Ivey Ray Mauney (page 17). (I. Ray Mauney.)

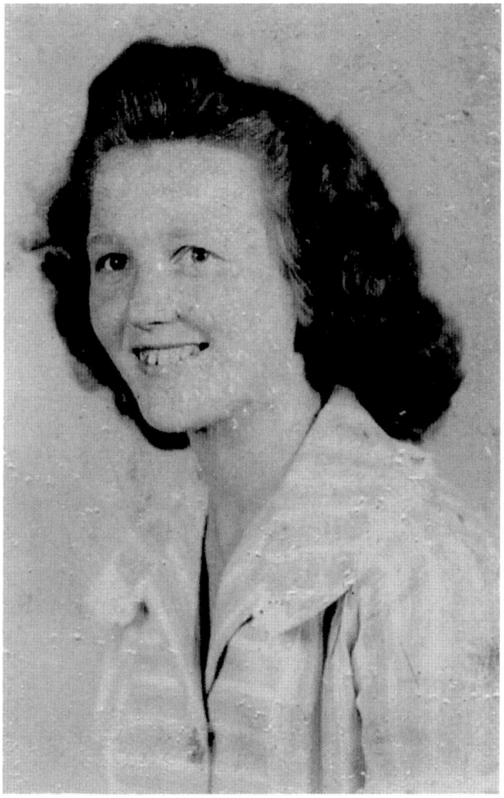

Communicator
Callie Waters Whitener (Wright)
Hollis High School graduate Callie Waters Whitener Wright's duty during World War II was serving as a telephone operator. She remembered the many excited voices of those who were returning to the states and were asking for her help in phoning family and friends to share the news. She also remembered some of the sad voices of people trying to notify others of injuries and deaths. (Callie Waters Whitener Wright.)

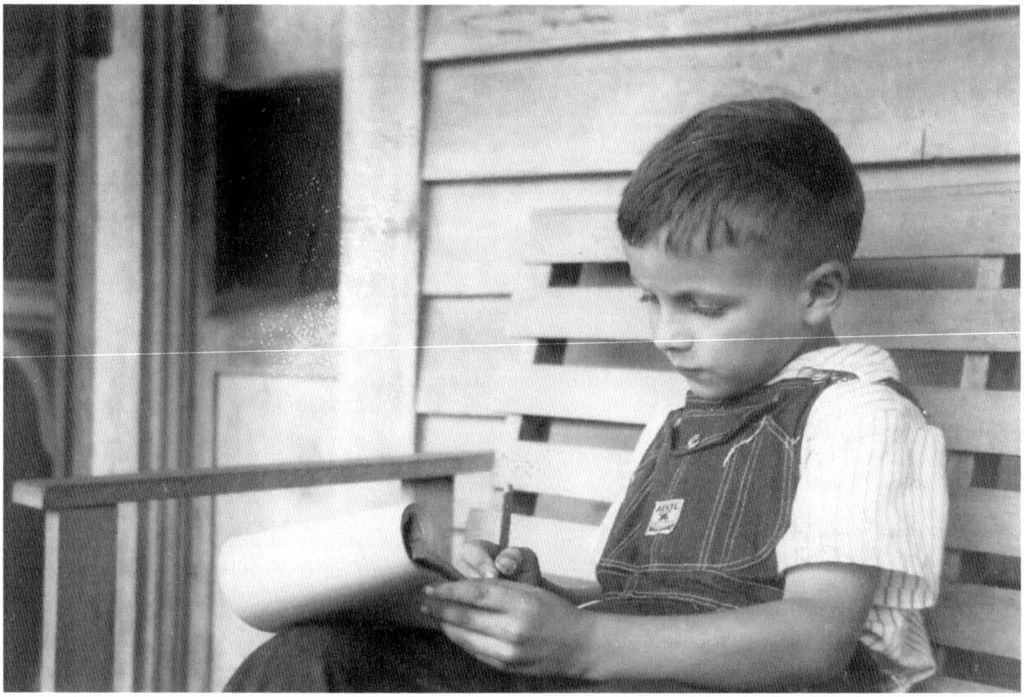

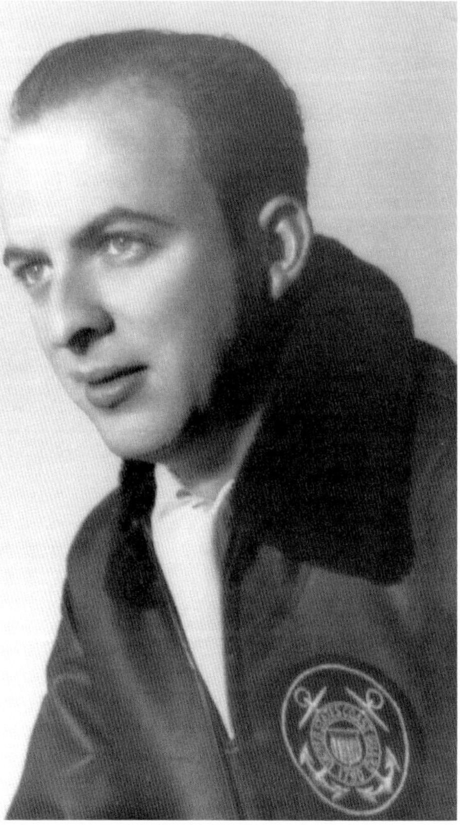

Young Reno Bailey (1935–)
This early photograph shows a young Reno Bailey doing what he has always loved: writing and communicating. Reno, the son of Ruby Fraser Bailey and Byron Bailey, is on the porch of their Cliffside home, which was beside what would be the McKinney Funeral Home. Later, at Cliffside High School, Reno explored the media arts and was on the staffs of both the yearbook and the school newspaper. He and Earl Owensby (see pages 122 and 123) shared a love of movies; they tried to show movies in a chicken coop. After graduation from Cliffside High in 1953, Reno went to the University of North Carolina at Chapel Hill. (Reno Bailey.)

Bailey in Coast Guard Uniform
In 1954, Bailey withdrew from the University of North Carolina at Chapel Hill and joined the US Coast Guard. He served as a radioman and saw service in the Pacific. After his military career, Reno reentered the University of North Carolina at Chapel Hill. In 1962, he graduated with a major in radio, television, and movies. He immediately went to work with the Jefferson Standard Broadcasting Company, which included WBT and WBTV. With WBTV, he created commercials. (Reno Bailey.)

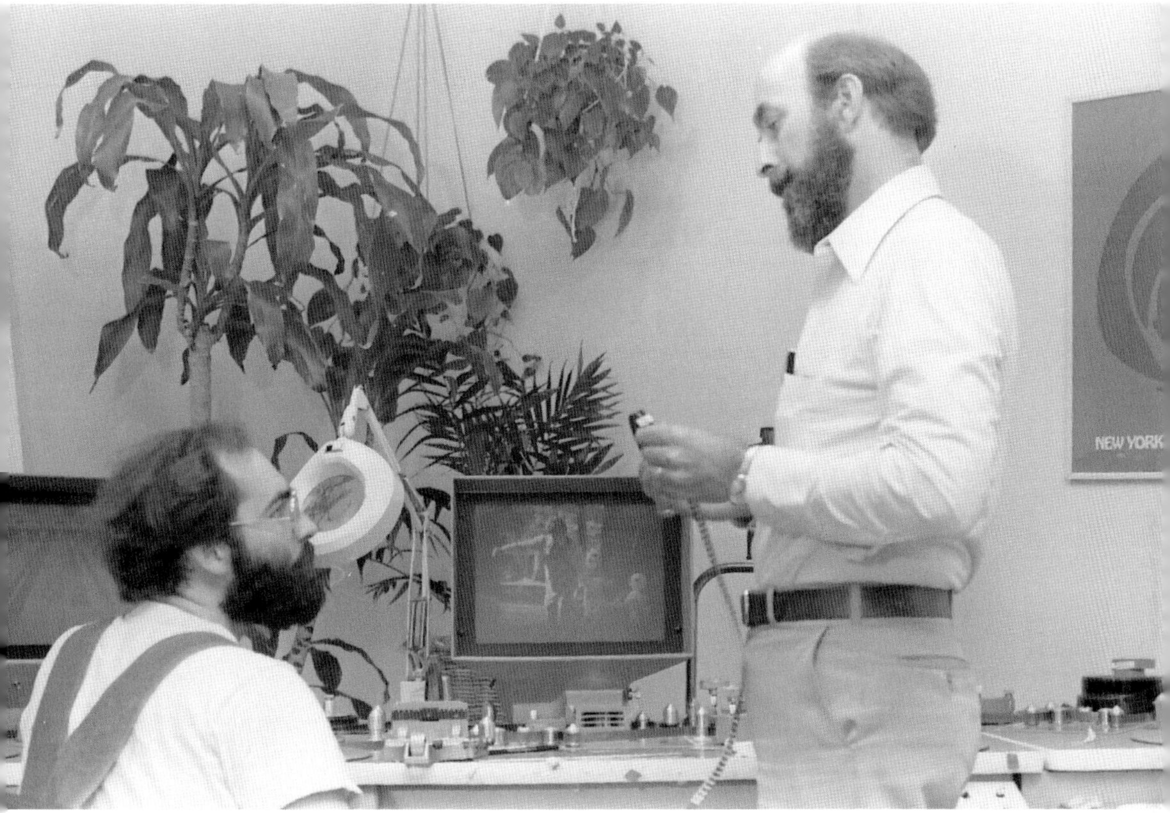

Bailey, Jefferson Productions Employee

In addition to announcing, "Channel 3, WBTV, Charlotte," between certain shows, Bailey became film production manager for Jefferson Productions. In this photograph, film production manager Reno Bailey (right) and editor Barry Stillwell (left) assess the progress of an editing job. By 1964, Bailey began to assume acting roles on WBT and WBTV. He was Irving Glick on *The Belmont Tunnel*, Kelton B. Goodfellow on *The Yellowjacket*, and a tap dancer on WBTV's *Morning Show*. His other roles are no longer on record.

Five years after serving at WBT-FM, Bailey became "publicity supervisor/director" of creative services of WBTV. He also held the positions of film production supervisor for Jefferson Films and of operations manager.

From the early 1980s until his retirement in 2001, Reno Bailey served as software developer and computer consultant. He was able to use this knowledge to create two websites: *Remember Cliffside* and *BT Memories*. The community honored him with an award for his services in October 2012. Reno Bailey has found time also to write two books, *Cliffside: Portrait of a Carolina Mill Town* for Arcadia Publishing and *Faces & Places of Old Cliffside*. His website, *Remember Cliffside*, remains popular and current. (Reno Bailey.)

Tony Earley, *New York Times* Best-selling Author

This is a recent photograph of Earley, a *New York Times* best-selling author. Currently, he is a Vanderbilt creative writing professor. Tony Earley's 1962 birth to his military parents, who were living in Texas at the time, is, according to him, the only "blot" on having spent his entire youth in Rutherford County, North Carolina. The Earley family moved back from Texas to Rutherford County within 18 months after Tony's birth; Earley's writings reflect his Rutherford County childhood.

Tony Earley studied English at Warren Wilson College. Upon his 1983 graduation, he secured a job at the *Thermal Belt News Journal* in Columbus, North Carolina. He moved from that paper to the *Daily Courier* in Forest City; he worked at the *Courier* as sports editor and feature writer.

Tony covered the council meetings for the town of Ellenboro when he worked for the *Courier*. As had James M. Walker (page 79) and Mike Rhyne (page 65), Tony Earley found a fascination with the trains, the railroad, and the depot of the town. He included Ellenboro as Aliceville in his *Jim the Boy*, which was on the *New York Times* Best-seller List. *The Blue Star* was a follow-up to *Jim the Boy*.

Tony enjoys featuring Rutherford County, North Carolina, in his writings even though he is no longer a resident of the state. *Here We Are in Paradise* (1994) was his first book; most of the stories in the volume have North Carolina as a setting as do the stories in *Somehow Form a Family* (2001). As a professor, he is quick to tell his students that writing is difficult! (Vanderbilt University.)

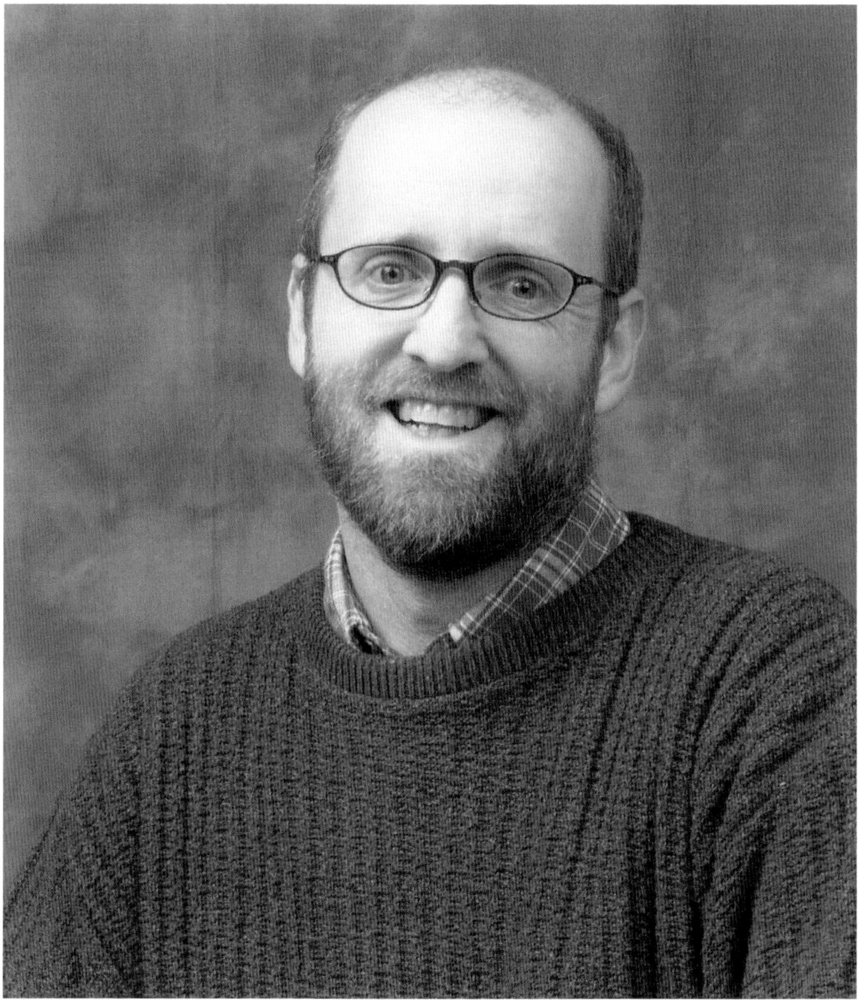

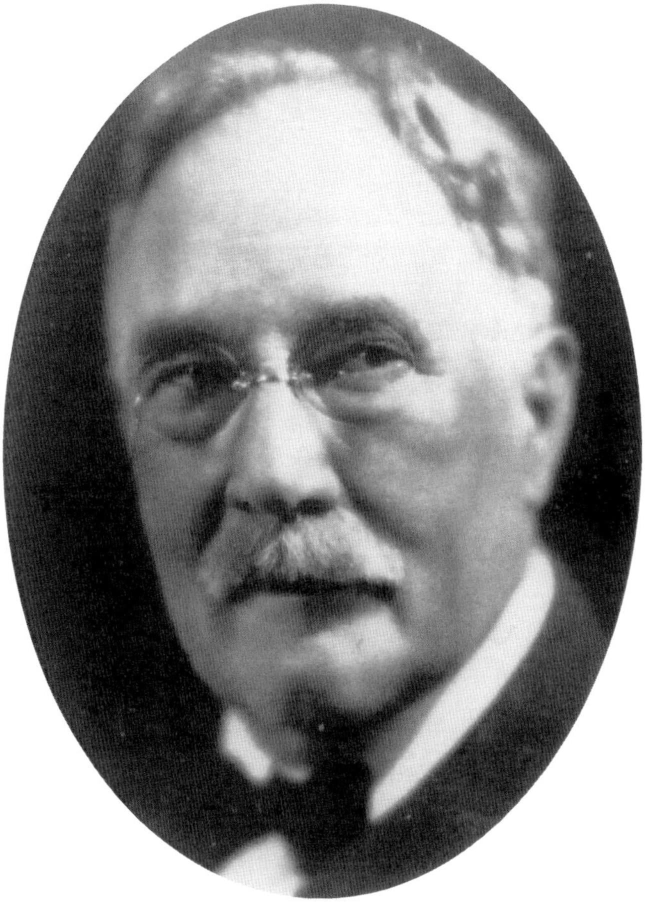

Textile Executive Simpson Bobo Tanner Sr.
Tanner (December 8, 1954–July 3, 1924) helped establish several textile mills and helped bring about the incorporation of the town of Spindale on August 21, 1923. Known as a leading textile manufacturer of Rutherford County, he was a manager of cotton mills and a pioneer in building them in the county. Clarence W. Griffin links Tanner's name "with every worthwhile movement within the [textile] industry."

In 1923, 28-year-old Tanner, a graduate of the University of North Carolina at Chapel Hill, met the striking actress Mildred Miller. After a brief courtship, the two married. By 1927, Bobo, Millie, Kate, and Bobo III were residing in the new Lake Lure Inn. Bobo had invested heavily in the Lake Lure project; unfortunately with the crash of the stock market in 1929, he lost heavily. Millie and Bobo moved to Rutherfordton and rented a main street home near what would become a prestigious hospital. In 1931, Bobo and Millie launched the Doncaster Collar and Shirt Company. The name Doncaster came from a place in England where Millie and Bobo spent some time on their honeymoon. Millie suggested the manufacture of the shirtwaist dress and the hiring of fashion consultants; the use of the clean lines of a fine dress shirt became important also. Direct sales, elegant apparel, consultants, and private appointments were the watchwords of the company. Bobo, Millie, and their sons Jimmy, Mike, and Bobo III built the Doncaster Collar and Shirt Company into a business with international recognition. At the time of Tanner's death, he was president of the Spencer, Spindale, Stonecutter, and Sunlight Mills and Horn Company in Spindale; president of the Cleghorn Mill of Rutherfordton; and president of the Green River Manufacturing Company of Tuxedo. Tanner was involved also in various other companies. (Tanner Corporation.)

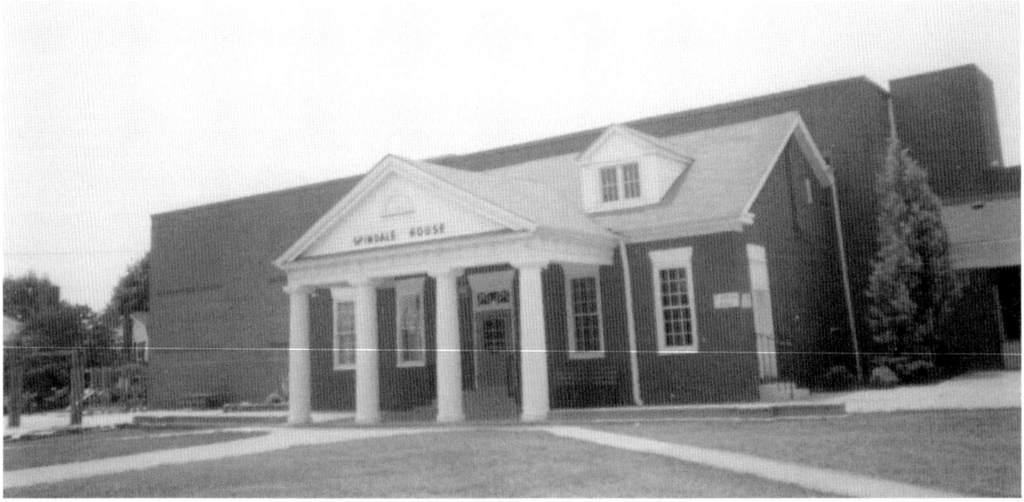

Spindale House

On February 22, 1925, shortly after the death of Jesse Spencer Tanner, Simpson Bobo Tanner Sr., Lola Spencer Tanner, their family, and the community established the Spindale House as a memorial to the Tanners, especially Jesse. The facility would serve as a local recreation center. (James M. Walker.)

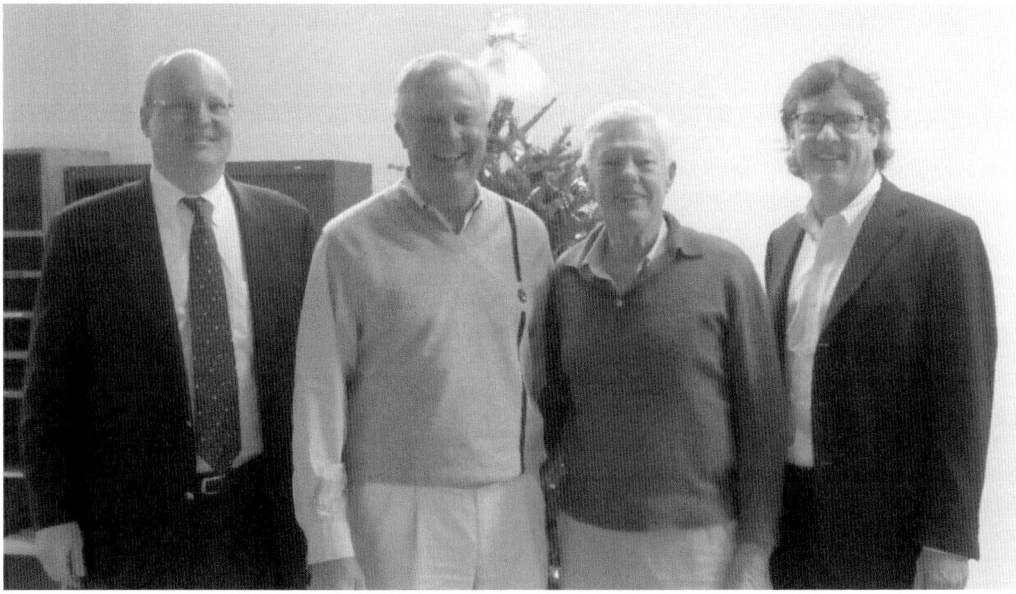

Members of the Tanner Family

This 2012 photograph shows some members of the Tanner family. From left to right are Bobo Tanner, Mike Tanner, Jimmy Tanner, and CEO Pell Tanner.

Pell began serving Doncaster in the 1980s. He is serving today (2012) as a CEO of the family business. Pell is the son of Jimmy Tanner and the grandson of Bobo Tanner Jr. Pell grew up in Rutherfordton and knew from the time he was in seventh grade that he wanted to enter Doncaster for his life's work. His love of foreign cultures, his travels abroad, his education at the University of North Carolina, and his devotion to the family business have served him and the company well. His work at Doncaster is more than merely a job. (Doncaster.)

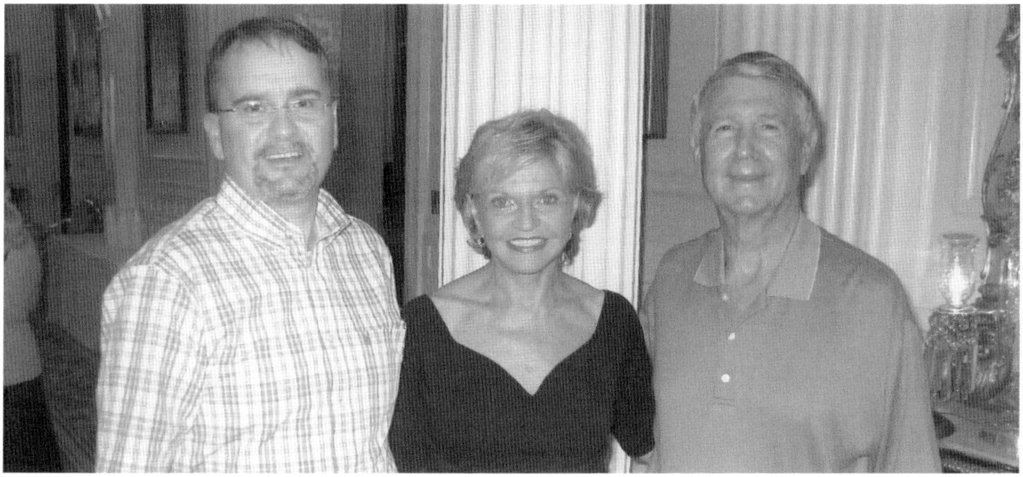

Robin Lattimore, Gov. Beverly Eaves Perdue, and Robert Eaves
Historian Robin Lattimore (left) stands here with Gov. Beverly Eaves Perdue (2009–2013) of North Carolina and her husband, Robert Eaves. Lattimore is an award-winning journalist and author of more than 20 books of local, state, and regional history. He has received the North Carolina History Book Award, the Henry Timrod Southern Culture Award, the North Carolina Baptist State Convention History Award, and five writing awards from the North Carolina Press Association. In 2009, the North Carolina Society of Historians named him the North Carolina Historian of the Year. Lattimore was the chief historian for the UNC-TV original documentary *Gold Fever and the Bechtler Mint*. Lattimore has been a repeat guest on UNC-TV's *North Carolina Now* news program and has appeared on WRAL-TV's *Tarheel Traveler*. He has been interviewed for many radio programs, including *All Things Considered*, and featured on National Public Radio.

Today (2013), Lattimore serves as an official historian of Rutherford County, president of the Rutherford County Historical Society, and chair of the Rutherford County Library Board. He holds an associate of arts degree in journalism. He earned the bachelor of science degree in historical research from Appalachian State University in 1991. While at Appalachian, Lattimore completed an internship with the curator's office at Biltmore Estate in Asheville. He was named a National Presidential Scholar in 1988. Lattimore is currently the student research coordinator at Thomas Jefferson Classical Academy in Henrietta, North Carolina. Below, Lattimore stands on the front porch of historic Snee Farm House, near Charleston, South Carolina. (Above, Robin Lattimore; below, Lesley M. Bush.)

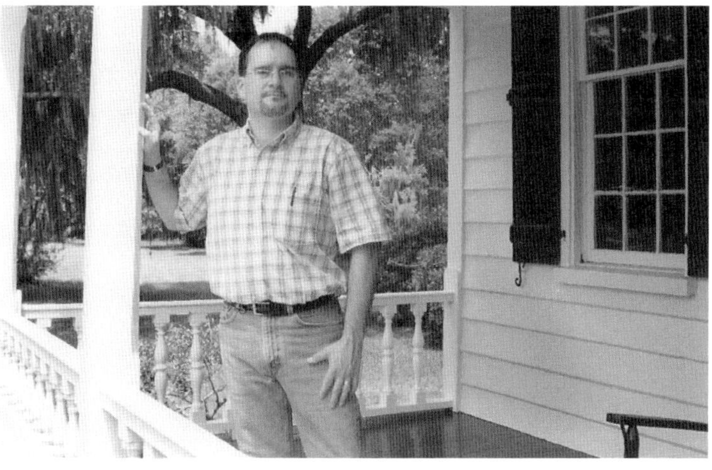

Earl Owensby and his Studio

Named for its founder, Earl Owensby Studios is the largest independent studio in the Southeast; it produced 41 films. Most residents of Rutherford County remember its documentary *Rutherford County Line* (1987), later called *Damon's Law.* Owensby was both a producer and main actor in the film that tells of Sheriff Damon Huskey's search for the person that killed three law enforcement officers (pages 123–124 in this volume) in the county.

Owensby (former Cliffside resident) and the Earl Owensby Studio near Shelby have been profiled by major media that includes magazines (*GQ* and *Esquire*), newspapers (*Variety* and *LA Times*), and broadcasts (*David Letterman, ET, 20/20,* and *60 Minutes*). Owensby has received induction into the North Carolina Hall of Fame and recognition as No. 15 of the Top 100 People in North Carolina in 100 years. Owensby autographed his photograph, above, for 15-year-old Robbie Davis in 1987. Robbie was thrilled with the photograph of the star of *Rutherford County Line*, which had also included Robbie's grandmother Nell Daves Price Burns.

On October 1, 1936, the *Forest City Daily Courier* printed the following notice: "Mr. and Mrs. Tom Owensby [of Cliffside] have adopted into their home a little one-year-old boy—Earl." Owensby said he felt the whole town of Cliffside had adopted him. He disclosed that he had been born out of wedlock to a father who died while transporting moonshine down a mountain in Tennessee. His mother had two other children; she gave Earl away because his legs were "ill-formed," and he would be expensive.

Earl worked around the Cliffside theater. He brought ice water to the cashier, popped corn, and ran the movie projector; he worked in the mill and set up bubble gum machines around town. He bought a Cadillac before he could drive. Earl enlisted in the Marines and worked for a supply company before his film career took off. (Above, Earl Owensby; below, Allen Oren and Earl Owensby.)

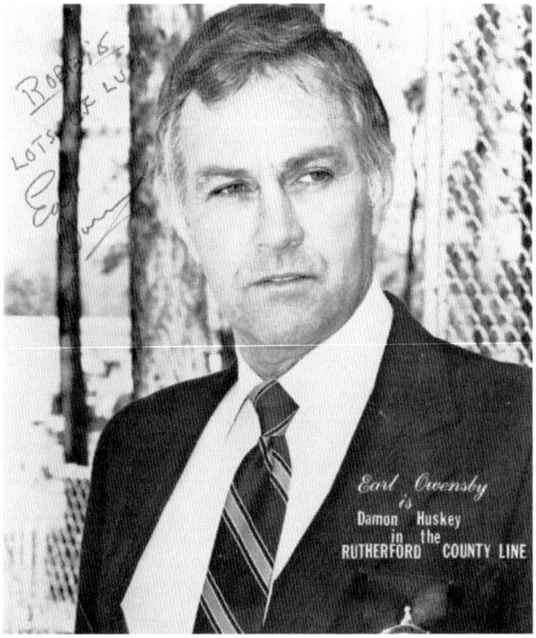

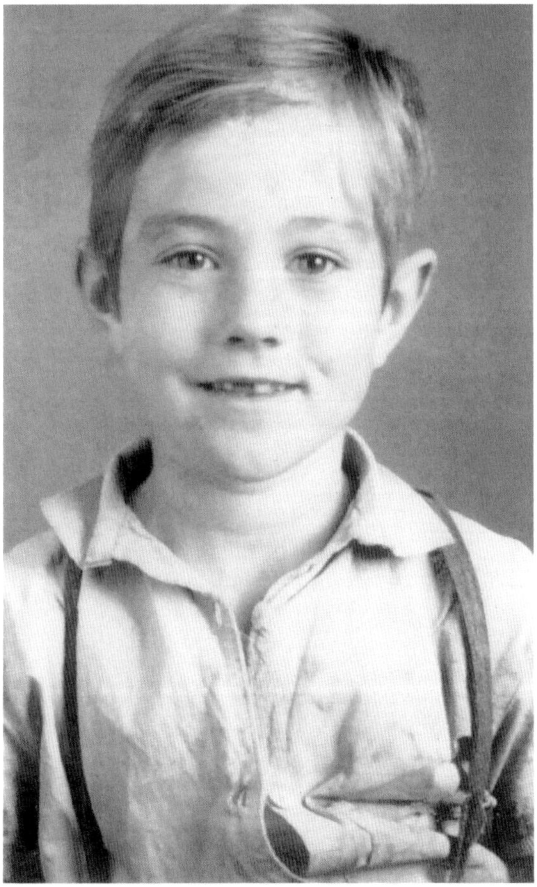

CHAPTER FIVE

Entertainers

Rutherford County has always been a productive county. Its people have worked hard, but they have recognized also the importance of relaxation to ensure their own good emotional health and that of others.

Events at the local churches and activities at the local schools helped to provide certain spiritual services and some necessary social contacts. Special occasions included "singings," baptisms, worship services, baseball games, bazaars, revivals, fall festivals, and fairs.

At times, even the physical features of Rutherford County provided relaxation for the citizenry. Visiting Chimney Rock Park, swimming and boating at Lake Lure and Sunshine Lake, and enjoying the scenic beauty of a mountain drive were some of the county's features afforded to visitors.

Sometimes entertainment was as simple as telling family stories on the front porch after a day in the field or factory. These stories usually improved with each telling; with the passage of time, the original event was not easily recognizable—even to those who were present when it had occurred.

In many homes, singing around the piano, picking a banjo, or strumming a guitar in the parlor brought satisfaction to the listeners and to the performers. Even harmonizing around the fireplace or in the kitchen could relax a family.

The next few pages will give the reader a glimpse of the pleasures afforded by and for those in the county after the work was done for the day or the season.

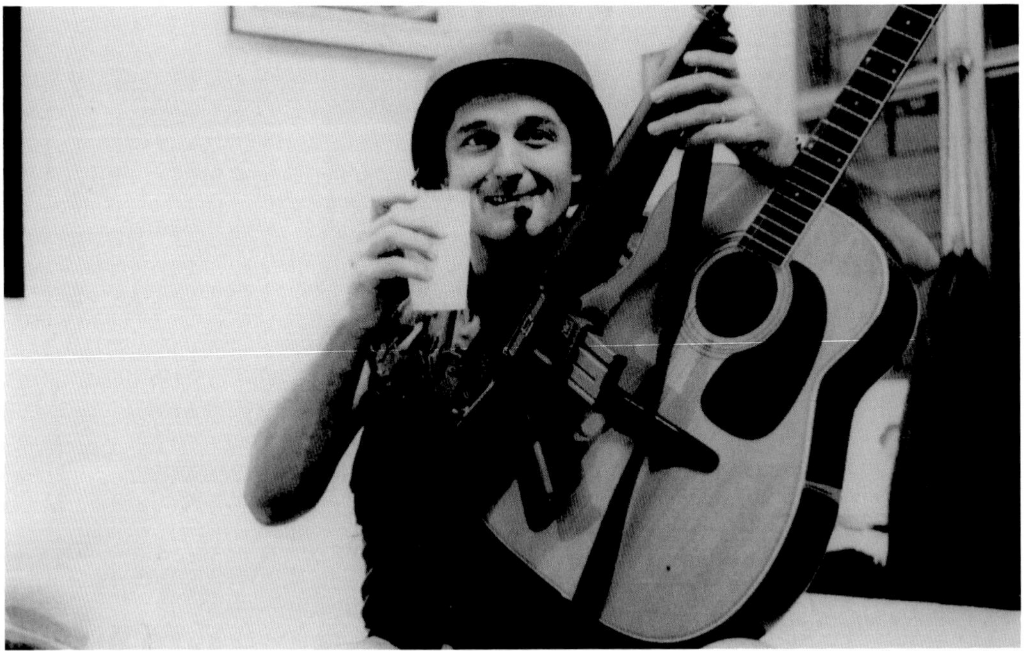

Cliffside Native Jerry Norville with Guitar
In the above photograph, Norville is in "the ultimate warrior" pose while off-duty in Vietnam in 1961. He asks the question, "Is there anyone from Cliffside (Rutherford County) who does not play country music?"

Norville was born on September 19, 1935, at 5 Church Street in Cliffside. He enlisted in the Air Force in 1951 and completed basic training at Lackland Air Force Base in San Antonio, Texas. Before his discharge, Norville would earn many military awards in both his enlisted and his officer status; even the Republic of Vietnam recognized his service and presented him with some awards for distinguished service. Norville also earned the master of science degree. Despite his arduous and important activities, he did find some time for relaxation. (Jerry Norville.)

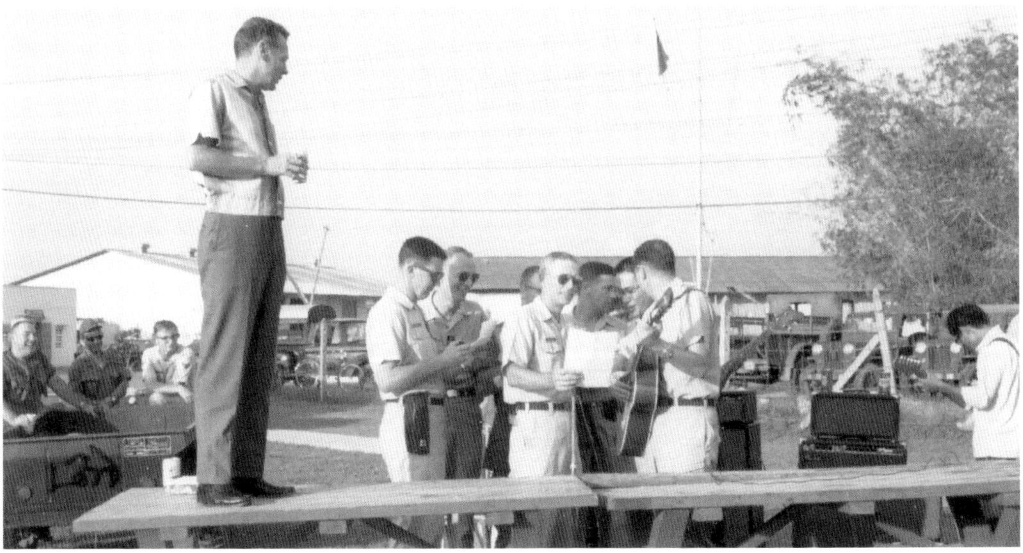

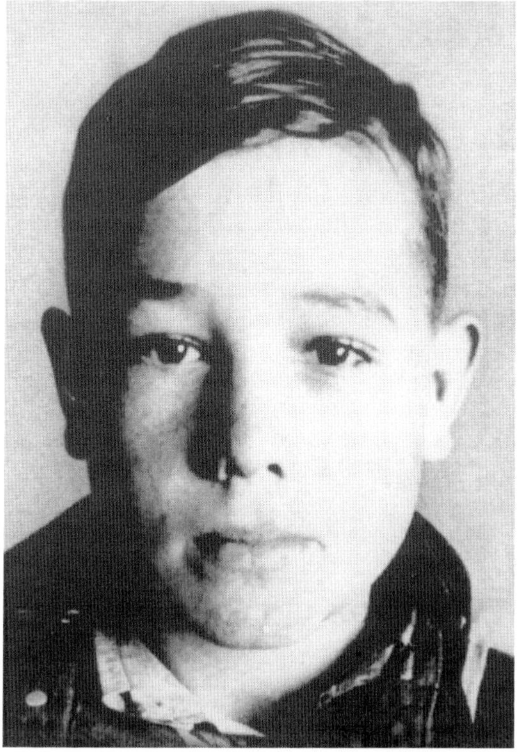

Earl Scruggs's First Public Performance

An unidentified 1970 advertisement shows a boyhood photograph of Earl Scruggs. Scruggs (January 6, 1924–March 29, 2012) developed his own style of playing the banjo. His easily recognizable recordings include "Foggy Mountain Breakdown," "The Ballad of Jed Clampett" for the television program *The Beverly Hillbillies*, the themes for *Green Acres* and *Petticoat Junction*, and the escape theme for *Bonnie and Clyde*. Music ran in Earl's family. His mother, Lula Ruppe Scruggs, played the organ and his two older sisters Eula Mae and Ruby played the banjo and the guitar. Earl's brothers Junie and Horace played the banjo and guitar. Earl's father was George Elam Scruggs, a farmer and bookkeeper who played the fiddle and banjo. About the same time as the death of Earl's father, four-year-old Earl began playing the banjo and the guitar. Earl used a two-finger style and spent most of his time on the banjo; he was self-taught. At the age of 10, he began to use three-finger picking—"Scruggs-style picking." (Anthony Scruggs.)

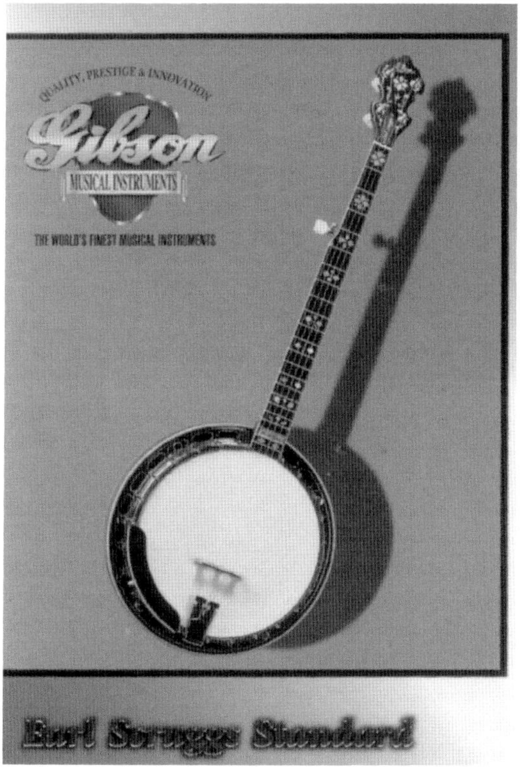

The Earl Scruggs Guitar

In 1984, Gibson Strings introduced the Earl Scruggs Standard Guitar, a re-creation of Earl Scruggs's guitar at that point in time. Later, Scruggs worked with Gibson craftsmen for the return of the "double-cut peghead design." This card indicates the guitar style. Scruggs received entrance into the Country Music Hall of Fame in 1985. In 1991, Bill Monroe, Lester Flatt, and Scruggs became members of the International Bluegrass Music Association's Hall of Honor. Scruggs died of natural causes on March 29, 2012, in a Nashville hospital. He was 88. (Gibson Strings & Accessories, Card Series 1, 49 of 50.)

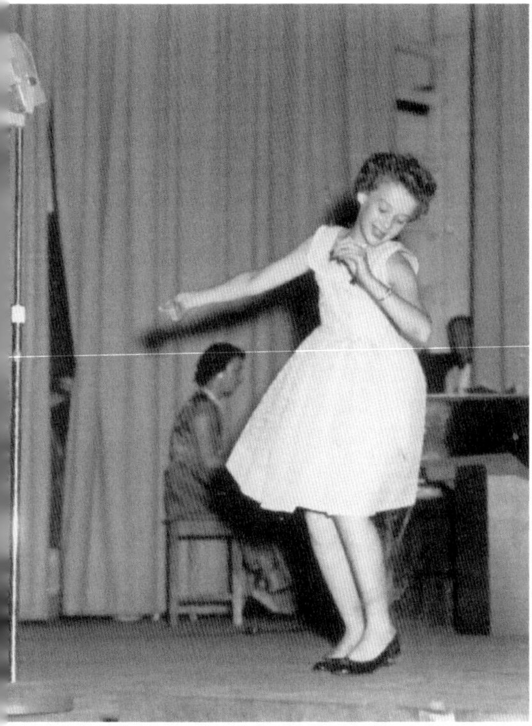

Barbara Grindstaff in Local Competition
In this photograph, local singer Barbara is performing at a 1950s Cool Springs High School Talent Show in Forest City. Barbara's sister Carolyn Grindstaff (Barbee) plays the accompaniment for her. Barbara Grindstaff was born in Cleveland Memorial Hospital in Shelby in 1949. Her father, Ervin M. Grindstaff (page 55), was the owner of Grindstaff's Furniture Store (later Grindstaff's Interiors) in Forest City. Barbara began competing in local talent shows at the age of 10. She appeared on the national *Ted Mack Original Amateur Hour* and became a regular on the *George Hamilton IV* television show; she performed frequently on *The Arthur Smith Talent Show* on WBTV. (Carolyn Grindstaff Barbee.)

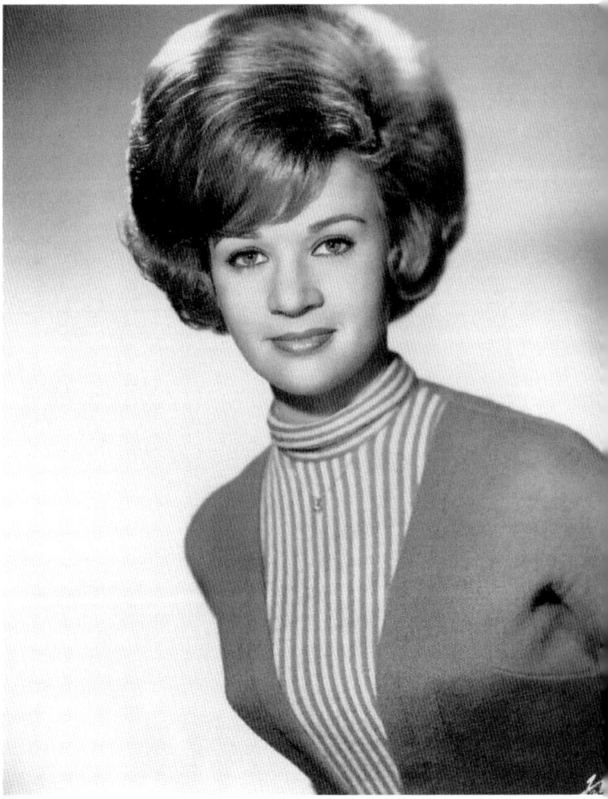

Publicity Photograph of Bobbi Staff
Barbara adopted the stage name "Bobbi Staff" while she was recording for RCA in the 1960s. With 26 other Americans, Grindstaff represented the United States in a 1957 tour of Europe. She performed abroad in the summer of 1958. Barbara took national honors in the United Nations Oratorical Contest. In 1961, she graduated from Cool Springs High School. Barbara recorded 16 songs for RCA; Chet Atkins produced 13 of these. Grindstaff married Jerry Whitehurst, who was the pianist for the television show *Hee Haw* and who played at the Grand Ole Opry. They had a son and a daughter. Barbara had her own daytime television show before her retirement. Barbara currently resides in Tennessee. (Carolyn Grindstaff Barbee.)

Ben Humphries at Bluegrass Music Festival

In the photograph here, Cliffside resident Ben Humphries (left) pauses for a few moments with his honored guests at the annual Snuffy Jenkins Old-time and Bluegrass Music Festival. This photograph shows, from left to right, (sitting) Ben Humphries, Dewitt "Snuffy" Jenkins, Grandpa Jones, and two bluegrass fans (one seated at the far right and one kneeling). The Snuffy Jenkins Old-time and Bluegrass Music Festival was an annual event promoted by Ben Humphries and hosted on his property for many years to honor Dewitt Snuffy Jenkins; later, the event included others.

Internationally known Dewitt Snuffy Jenkins (October 27, 1908–April 29, 1990) was the last of seven (some sources say ten) children born into the Jenkins family in Harris, Rutherford County, North Carolina. Dewitt followed the musical pathway pursued by many of his family members. These music lovers and musicians included Dewitt's brother Charlie Verl Jenkins (September 18, 1901–May 2, 1969) and two of his nephews Harry Hoke Jenkins (August 4, 1917–July 22, 1967) and Oren Mack Jenkins (October 21, 1932–October 5, 1984).

Dewitt Jenkins began playing the fiddle by plucking the instrument. He later switched to guitar and still later to a homemade banjo that he and his brother Verl made together. When he was 19 years old, he bought his first banjo.

Dewitt observed the techniques and styles of local banjo players. Most of the area performers used a style known as the Broad River style. The name Broad River style comes from a geographic feature of the area—the Broad River—and refers to the use of two fingers on a five-string banjo.

Jenkins also began watching intently the three-finger style that Smith Hammett and Rex Brooks used; he soon developed the three-finger style further. Trischka in his *Bluegrass Unlimited* quotes Don Reno as saying, "There was other fellas that played with three fingers before Snuffy [Dewitt], but he was the first one who ever put it together."

Dewitt Jenkins earned the nickname "Snuffy" because of one of his comedy acts in the 1930s. Dewitt pretended he had a runny nose and kept sniffing and wiping his nose on his sleeve. His friends began to call him Snuffy. The nickname stuck. (Ben Humphries.)

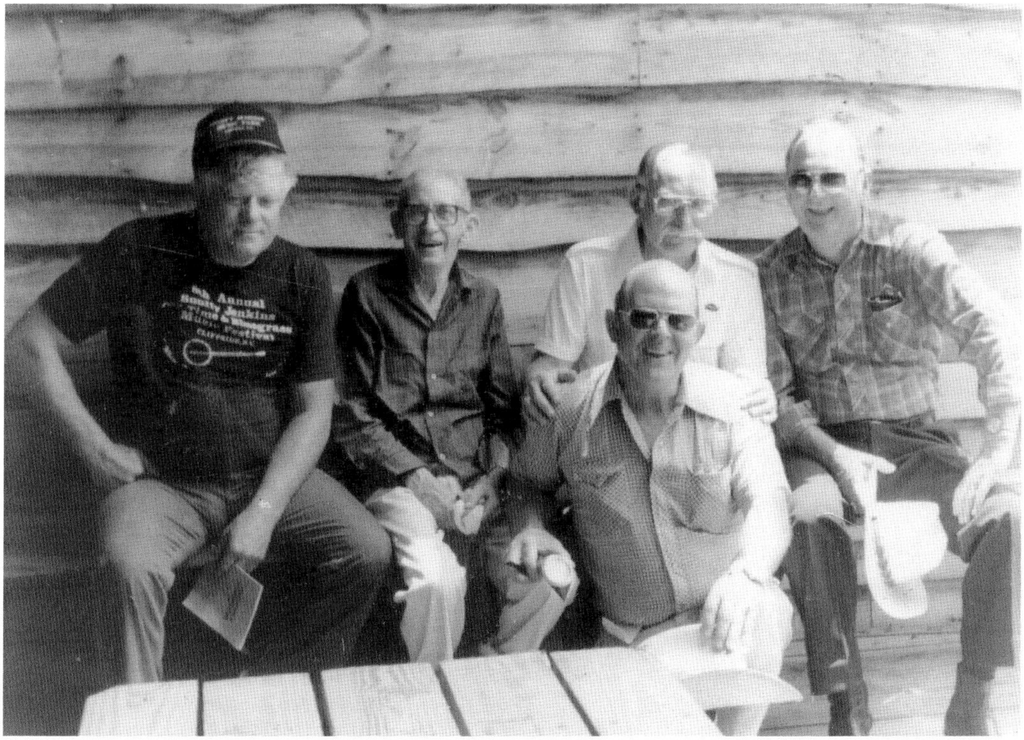

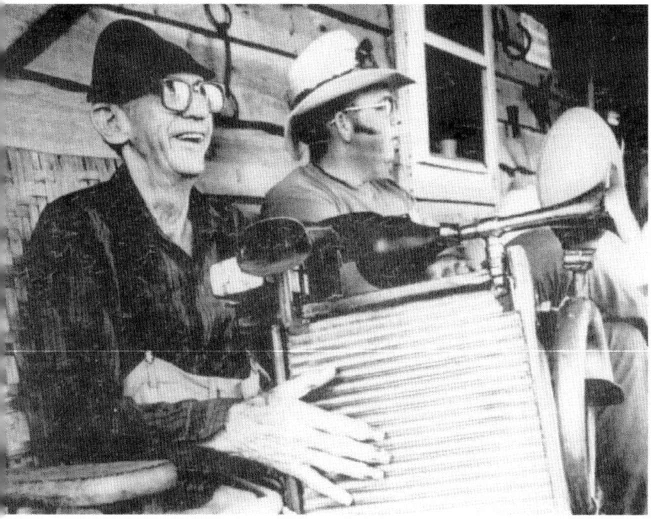

Snuffy Jenkins
Wearing his customary pointed hat and holding a washboard, his musical instrument during some performances, Snuffy Jenkins (left) relaxes with some unidentified bluegrass fans at the home place of Ben Humphries in Cliffside. The man seated at the far right may be Merle Watson, the son of Doc Watson and a performer also. During his lifetime, Jenkins won the coveted International Bluegrass Music Award. Other significant recognitions include induction into the Blue Ridge Music Hall of Fame and the Jean Laney Harris Folk Heritage Awards; Phillip Jenkins, Snuffy's great-nephew, accepted the Blue Ridge Music Hall of Fame Award for his great-uncle. (Ben Humphries.)

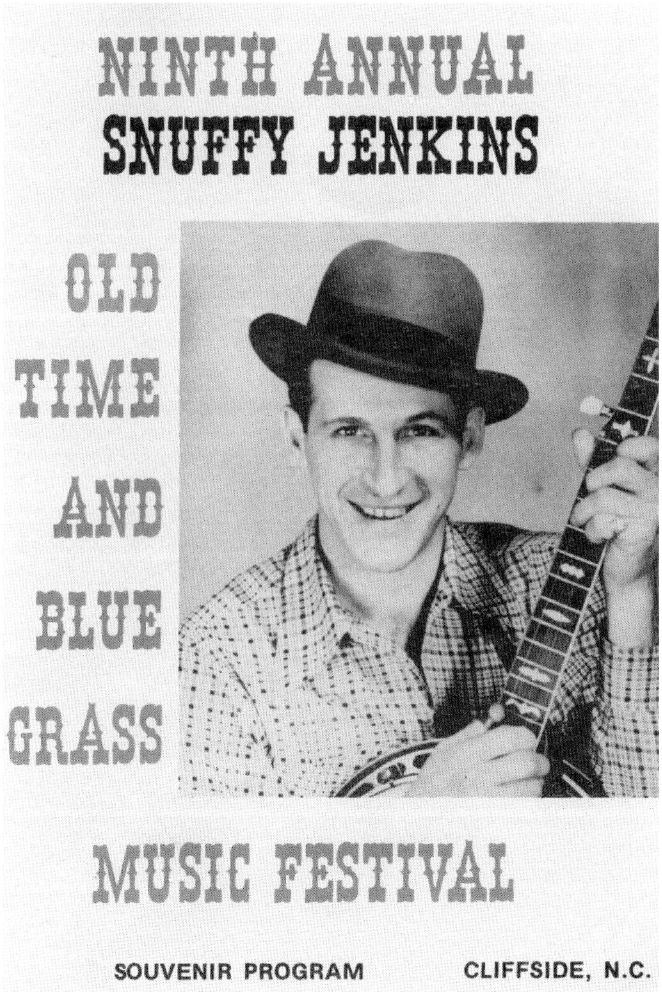

Harry Hoke Jenkins, "A Jenkins Boy"
Hoke (August 4, 1917–July 22, 1967) was the brother of Oren Jenkins and the nephew of Snuffy Jenkins. Hoke, according to Ben Humphries, "took to a five-string banjo like Karo took to molasses." During his short life of only 50 years, Hoke became a recognizable bluegrass musician. He worked with the Morris Brothers. He recorded with Jim and Jesse McReynolds. After the bombing of Pearl Harbor, Hoke left his music career to serve his country. After he returned from the military, he resumed his career in music. Hoke and the Smoky Mountaineers performed in 1949 after Hoke's return from service. By 1967, one of the nation's best banjo players was gone. The 1984 annual Snuffy Jenkins Old-time and Bluegrass Musical Festival honored Hoke also. This photograph of Hoke Jenkins shows him with his favorite instrument. Upon his death, Hoke left his gold-plated five-string banjo to his brother Oren. (Ben Humphries.)

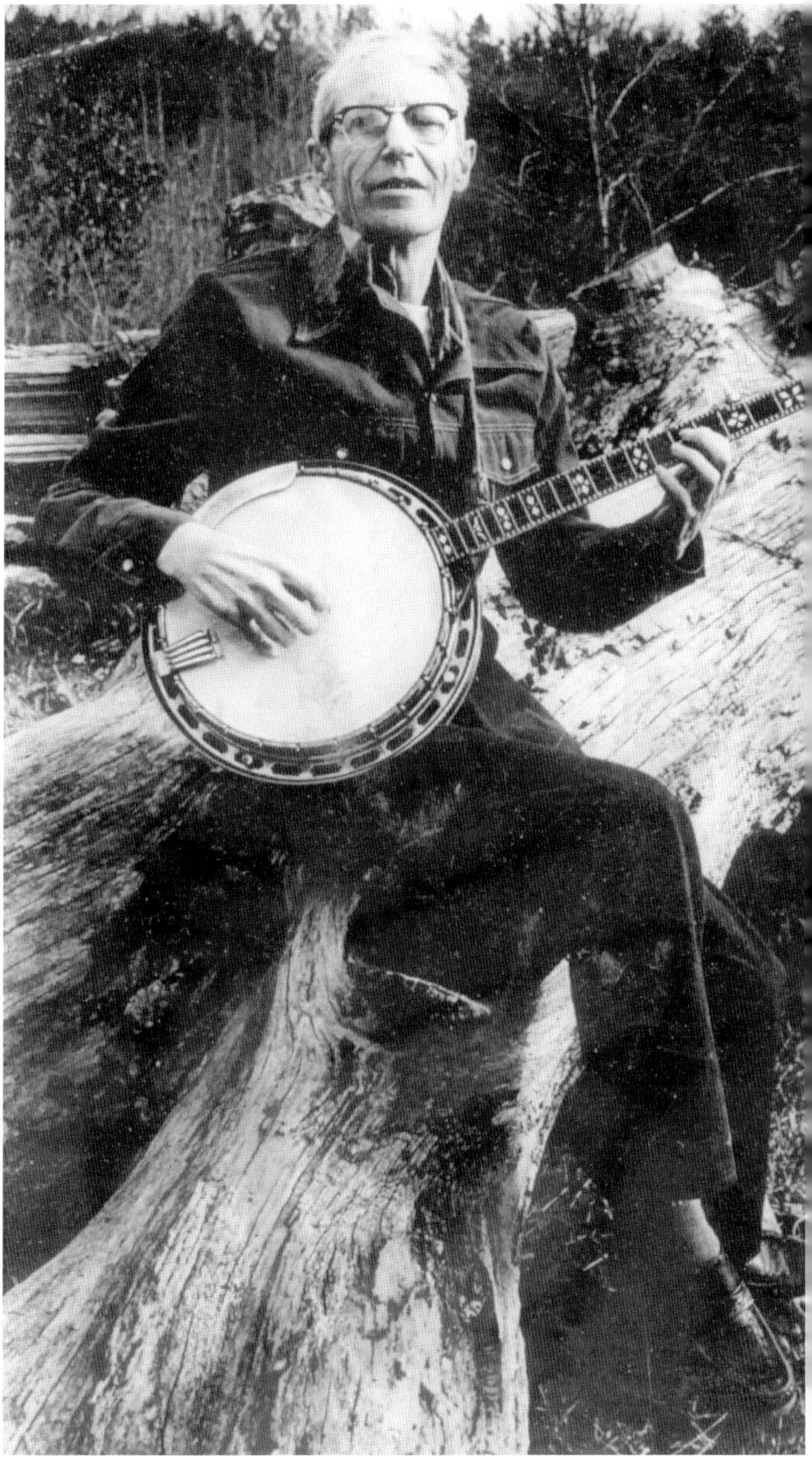

Oren Jenkins
Oren Jenkins (October 21, 1932–October 5, 1984) was Snuffy Jenkins's nephew and Hoke's brother. Family stories note that Oren could play the banjo before he could tie his shoes. He passed this love to his son Phillip. Oren holds the gold-plated Gibson banjo left to him by his brother and is seated on a tree stump of the Jenkins home where Hoke and Oren grew up. Humphries observes that Oren was "as fine a banjo player as can be found." When Oren was only about 16, Jesse McReynolds of the bluegrass brothers Jim and Jesse McReynolds wanted Oren to play banjo for some recordings that he and Jim were making in Nashville. The reputation of the "Jenkins boys" was continuing.

Former Rutherford County deputy Ben Humphries and his wife, June Humphries, of Island Ford Road in Cliffside, were instrumental in organizing, hosting, and promoting the annual Snuffy Jenkins Old-time and Bluegrass Music Festival, beginning in 1975. They held the event at the Snuffy Jenkins Music Park, and the attendance was outstanding. The celebration of the Snuffy Jenkins Old-time and Bluegrass Music Festival is still a part of the Rutherford County community. (Ben Humphries.)

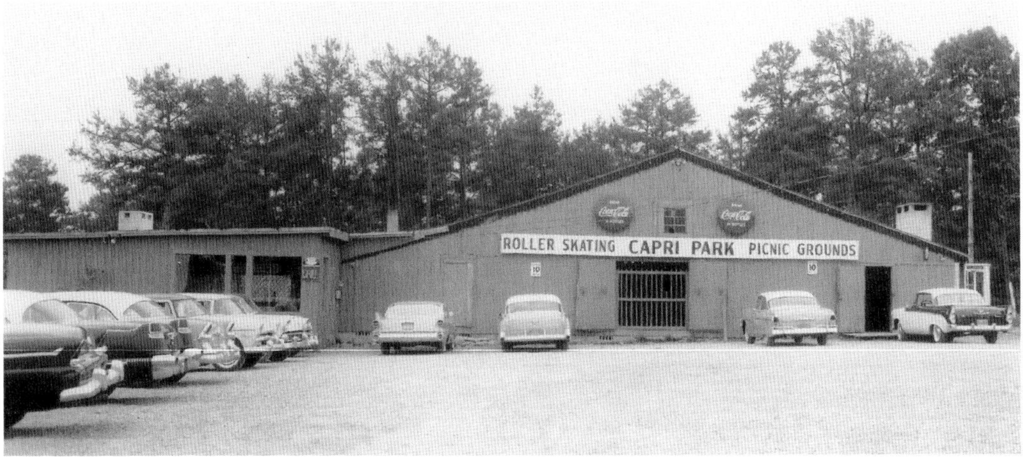

Capri Park and Ed Price

In the mid-1950s, Edward Rollins Price (1913–2004) had the innovative idea to build Capri Park, an entertainment facility east of Ellenboro. The facility would host roller-skating through the week, include square dancing on Saturday nights, and feature the musician and actor Claude Casey to play, sing, and call the dances. Some of the local preachers expressed concern about the opening of Capri Park, but the park proved itself "above board" and a wholesome place for young people to frequent. This photograph of Capri Park shows Ed Price's 1956 Dodge on the far right. (Mike Rhyne.)

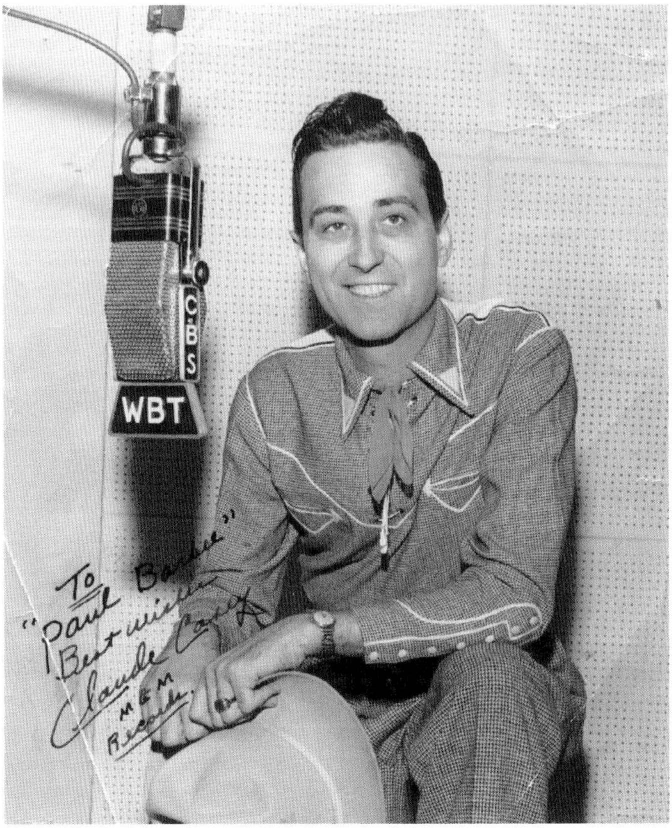

Performer Claude Casey and Rutherford County

Claude Casey (September 13, 1912–June 24, 1999) moved into the Park House that Ed Price had built for the Caseys beside Capri Park, where Casey would play, sing, and call square dances. The county residents were familiar with Casey before his move to Ellenboro. He had worked with WBT for 12 years, had been the lead singer and the emcee for the Briarhoppers on WBT, had recorded for the RCA and MGM labels, and had founded and would found WJES-AM and EKSX-FM, respectively. Casey appeared in 10 movies, the first with Dale Evans. After Casey's days at the house at 217 Capri Park Drive were over, Casey moved back to South Carolina, and Ed Price moved into the house that the Caseys had occupied. (Carolyn Grindstaff Barbee.)

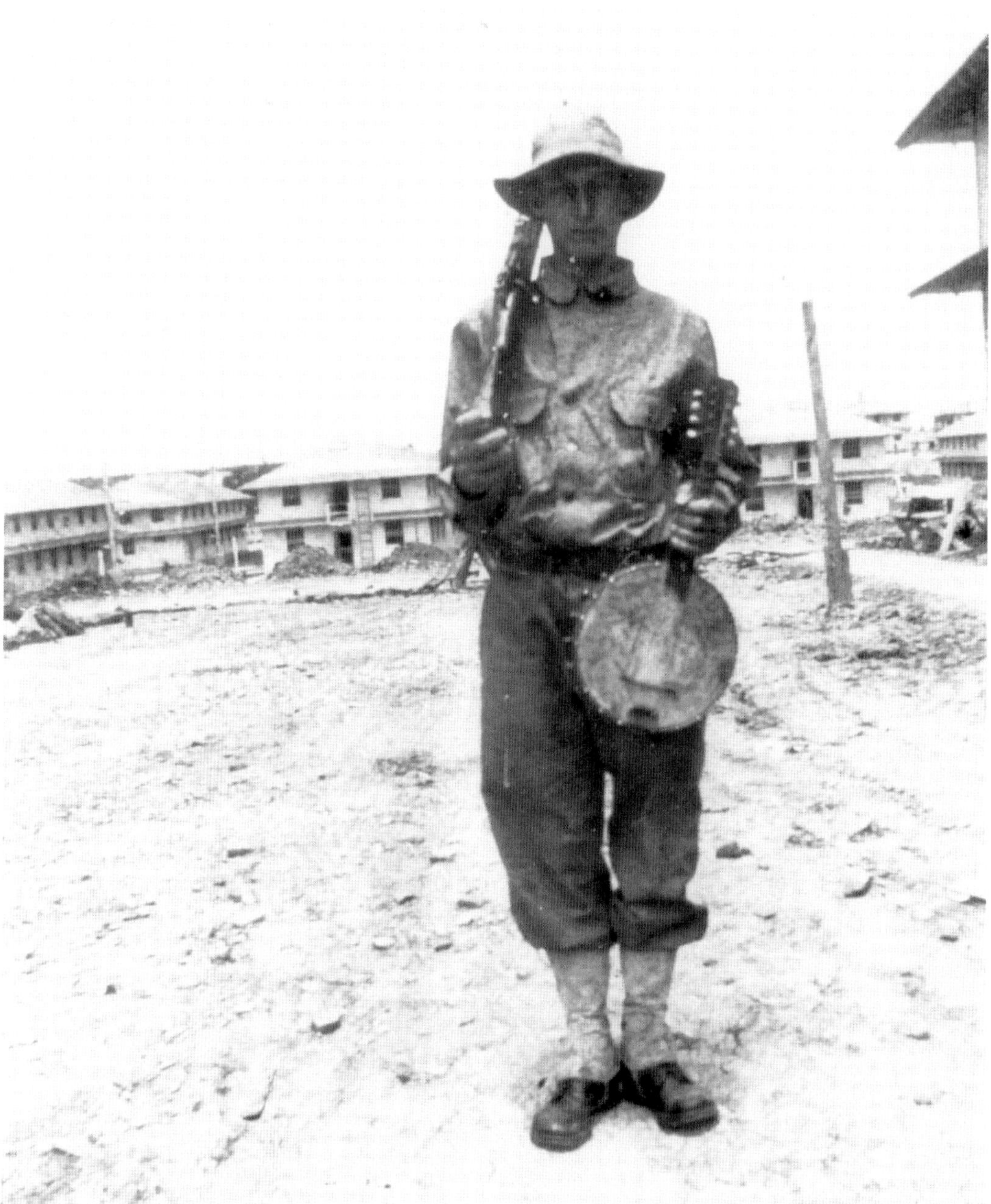

Vernon Joseph Lowery with Banjo

In the accompanying photograph, Vernon Joseph Lowery (June 9, 1921–January 28, 1943) holds a banjo. During his military service in World War II, Lowery sent this photograph home to his brother Bud. The banjo Vernon holds was a gift from a fellow Army buddy. Sadly, Lowery never came home to use the banjo. Lowery was one of the 149 Rutherford County men who died in World War II. Lowery died in action in the Guadalcanal combat zone. His parents, Perry Daniel Lowery and Dora Revels Lowery, did not receive word of his death for one month. Vernon had been in the US Army only one year when he lost his life. He is buried in the Holly Springs Baptist Cemetery. (Billy Seay.)

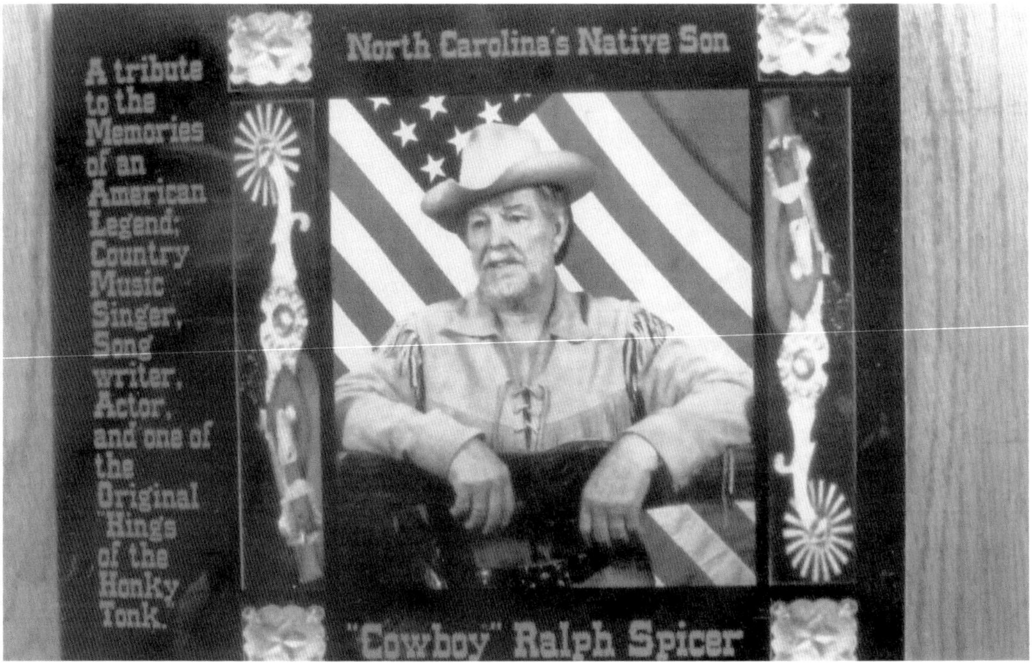

Ralph Spicer, Native Son (ABOVE)
Rutherford County resident "Cowboy" Ralph Spicer was born in Wilkes County on November 27, 1926. *North Carolina's Native Son* is his biography. Spicer's family history is traceable to Willie Spicer, the judge for the gunfight at the O.K. Corral. Two of Spicer's best friends—country singers, composers, and recording artists Hank Williams and Lefty Frizzell—gave Ralph his nickname, "Cowboy." Spicer had two aims for his biography: truth and "a party on every page." It includes Spicer's experiences as a rodeo rider, as a performer with Hank Williams, and as both a singer and accompanist for 26.5 years with Lefty Frizzell ("If You've Got the Money, Honey, I've Got the Time") before settling in Rutherford County. He credits his wife, Mamie Johnson Spicer, for many of his accomplishments. (Ralph Spicer.)

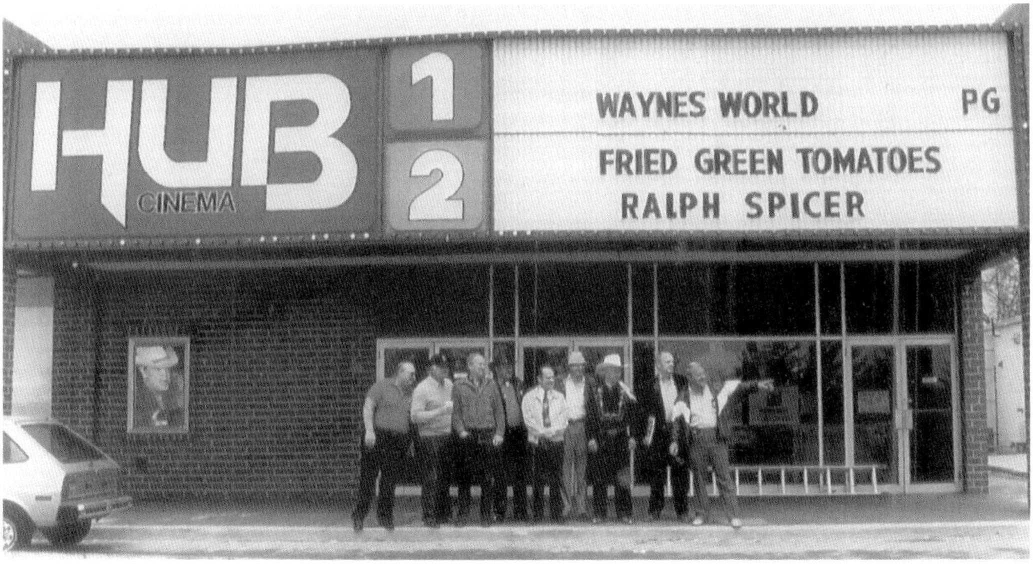

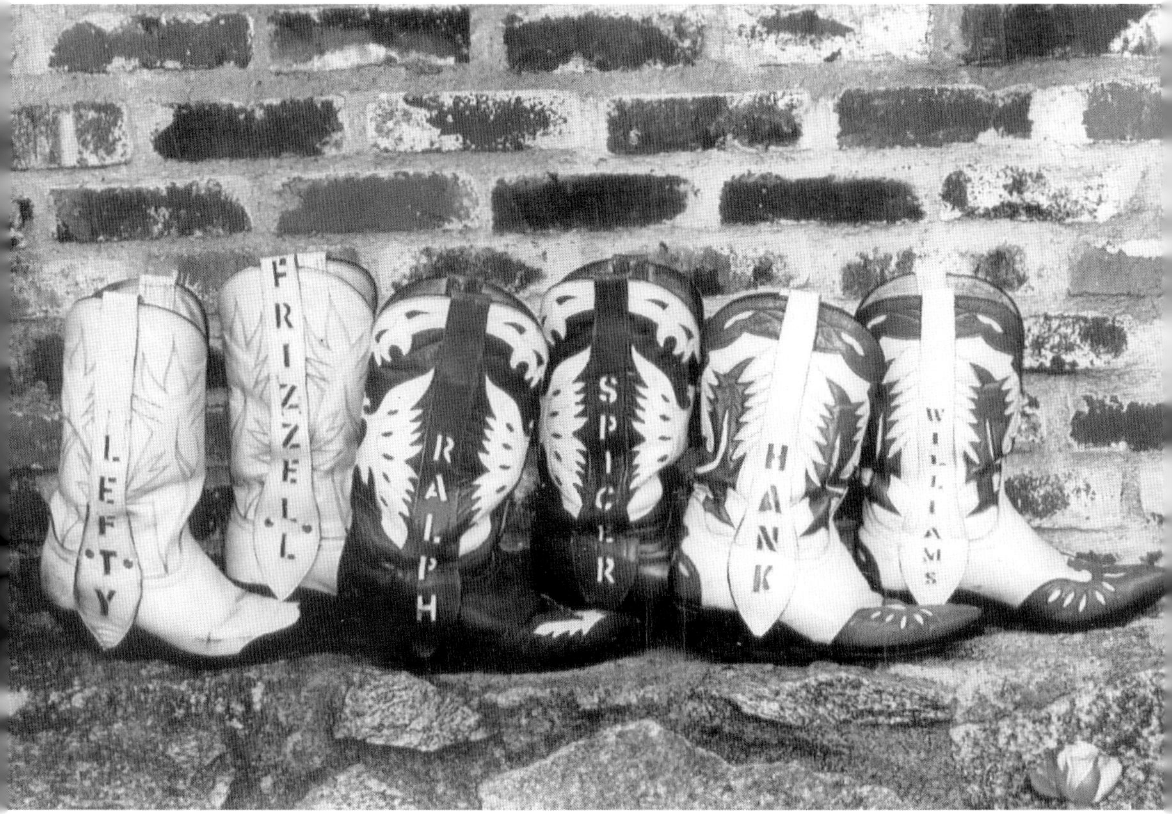

Boots on Spicer's Hearth
Frizzell's, Spicer's, and Williams's boots are resting on the hearth in Spicer's home. The footwear boldly displays the names of the prior owners: Lefty Frizzell, Ralph Spicer, and Hank Williams. (Ralph Spicer.)

Fried Green Tomatoes with Ralph Spicer (OPPOSITE PAGE, BELOW)
Spicer has been in many movies, including *Fried Green Tomatoes* (1991) with Jessica Tandy and Kathy Bates. The marquee announces Spicer's name below the movies playing. Spicer performed with many stars of Westerns. He was in *Silver Spur* with Gene Hackman. The drive to his home on the Cliffside-Six Points Road in Rutherford County bears the name of cowboy star Jimmy Wakely. Spicer has sung and played with such notables as Loretta Lynn, Roy Rogers, Connie Smith, Reba McEntire, and Donna Douglas of *The Beverly Hillbillies*. (Ralph Spicer.)

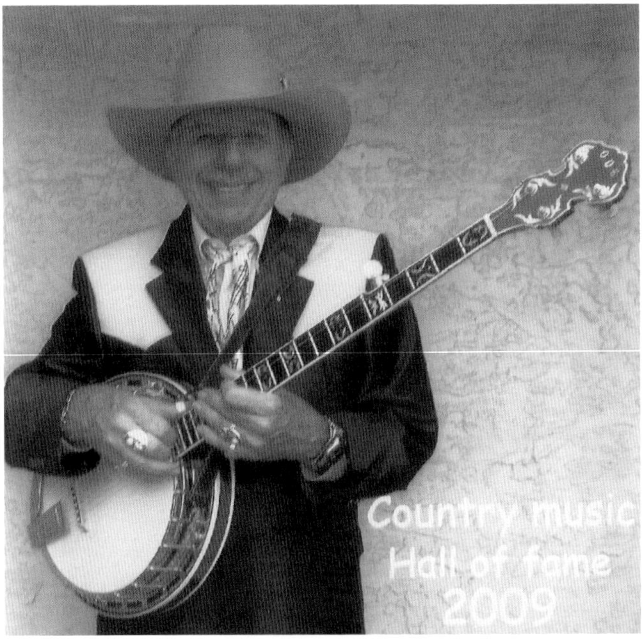

Dan X. Padgett, Country Hall of Fame

If one were to travel north from the home of Cowboy Ralph Spicer on Jimmy Wakely Drive, one would reach Race Path Road in Ellenboro. On that road lives Dan X. Padgett, a revered teacher of 11 instruments, a famed musician, and a vital part of every one of Lester Flatt and Earl Scruggs's television shows. In 2009, the Country Music Hall of Fame inducted the deserving musician Dan X. Padgett into its hallowed membership. (Dan X. Padgett.)

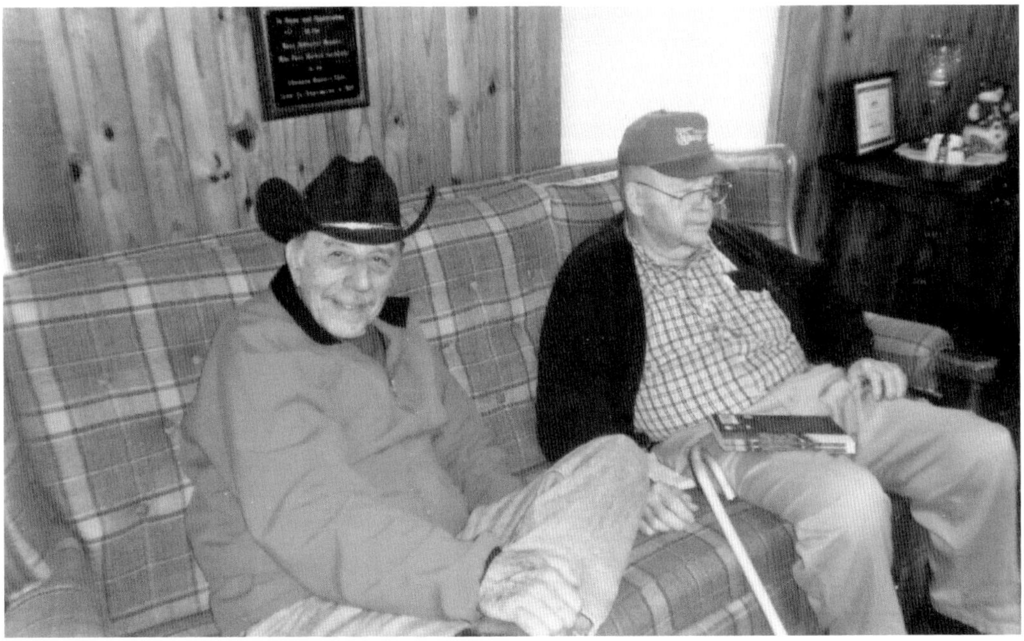

Dan X. Padgett and Joe Stockton

This photograph shows Dan X. Padgett (in cowboy hat) and Joe Stockton in Ellenboro. Padgett has been teaching music for 40 years. He has taught in Shelby, Spartanburg, and on the Race Path Road in Ellenboro. He has played with Bill Monroe and has been a regular on Channel 7 (Spartanburg, South Carolina) and Channel 13 (Asheville, North Carolina). He has performed many times at the Hollis-Ellenboro Fiddler's Convention with Bill Monroe. Dan X. Padgett's performances are still a treat for residents of Rutherford County and elsewhere. Joe Stockton (right) is a respected local historian. (Pat Rhyne.)

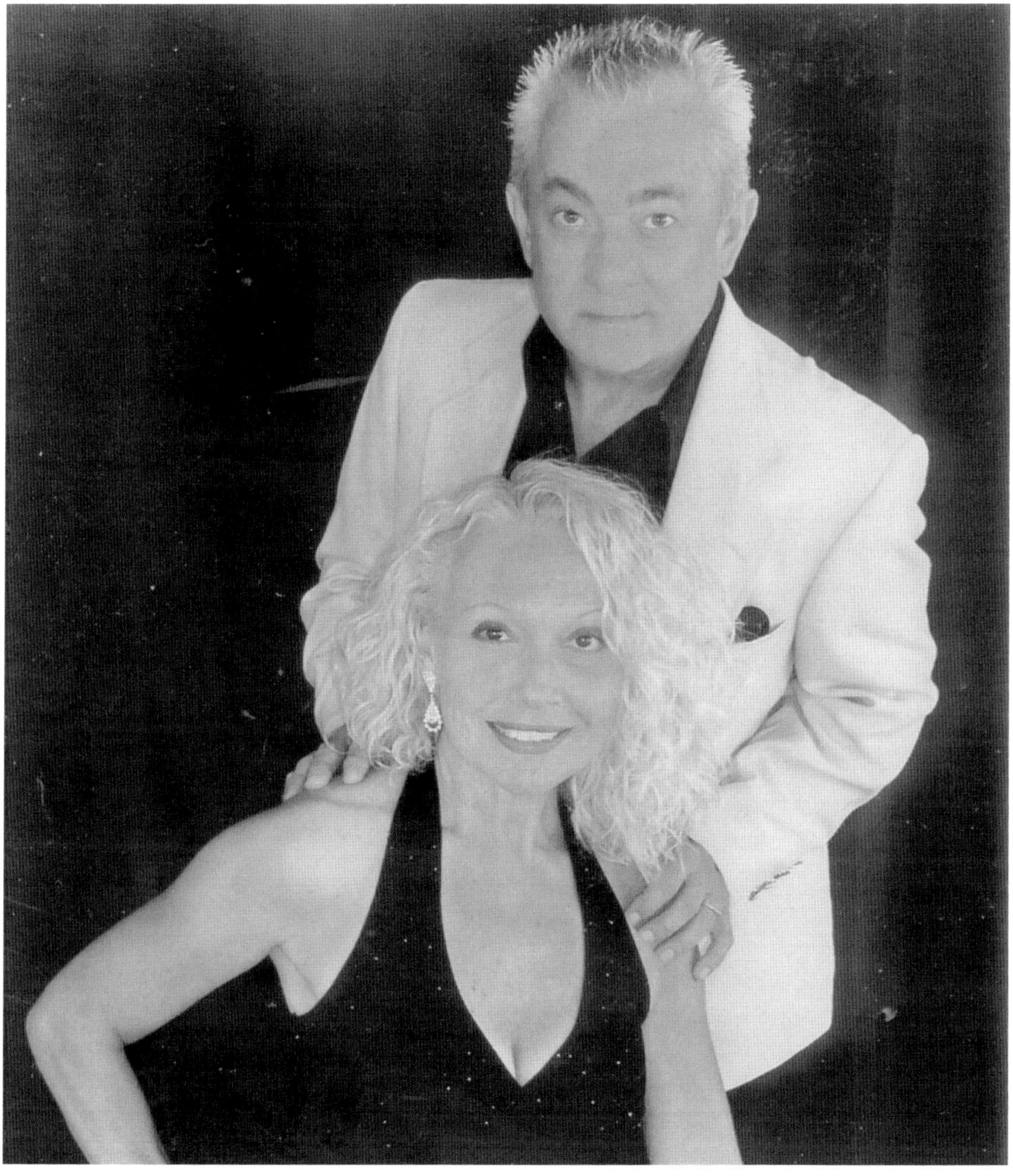

Yvonne and Jimmy Cain
Former Ellenboro resident Jimmy Cain (1943–) has achieved the rank of master magician. Here, he poses with wife/performer Yvonne Savage Cain. Jimmy entered first grade at Ellenboro School in 1949. He had an older brother and a mother who taught fifth-grade there. His father was a pastor, a farmer, and a chaplain in the US Army. At the age of six, Jimmy received a magic kit for Christmas. He was enthralled. After visiting the Ringling Bros. Circus, he decided show business was for him. He studied drama at the University of North Carolina, but he soon found his livelihood in magic. Jimmy (who appeared as Vince Carmen) performed wherever there was an audience: Charlotte, Canada, Mexico, and a three-year tour in North and South America. He played regularly in Madrid, Reno, and Las Vegas. Yvonne (unicycle rider and balancer) and Vince fell in love in Reno at Circus Circus. They were offered a job in Madrid (1980s) and married on the way to the airport. (Yvonne Savage Cain.)

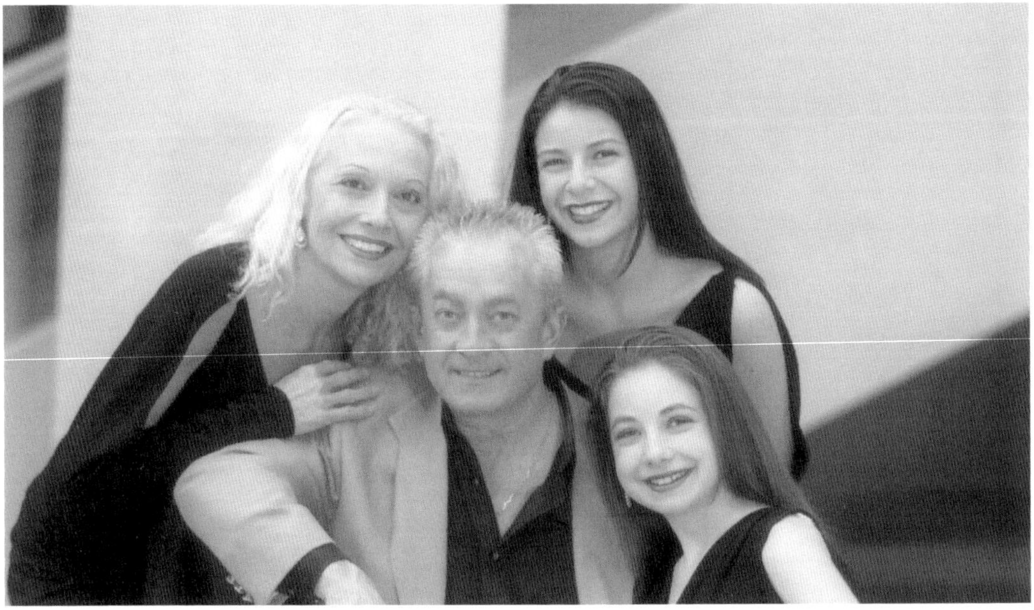

The Cain (Carmen) Family
Jimmy and Yvonne's act would later include two daughters. Here, Vince and "his girls" smile for their fans. The girls are (left to right) Yvonne, Candice, and Erika. Vince and his girls became known as the "first family of magic." In 2004, Vince and family purchased Houdini's Showplace in Sarasota, Florida. Tickets included a buffet, a beverage, and a show for one price. (Yvonne Carmen.)

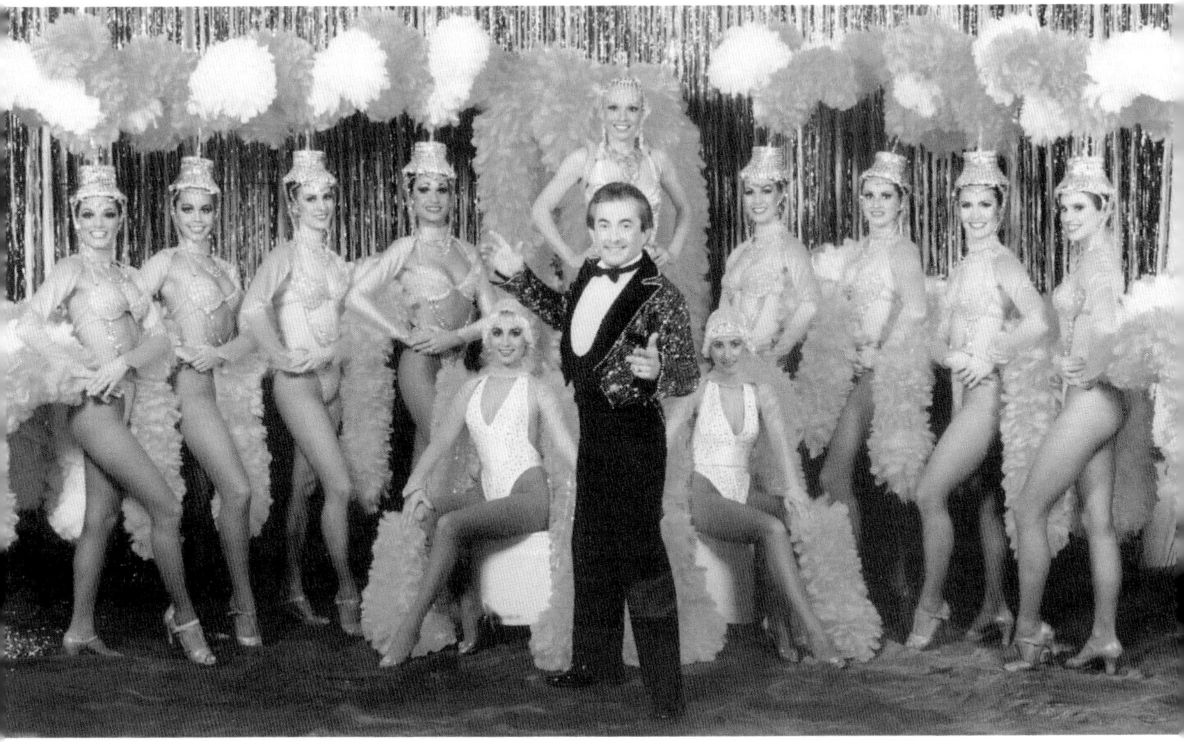

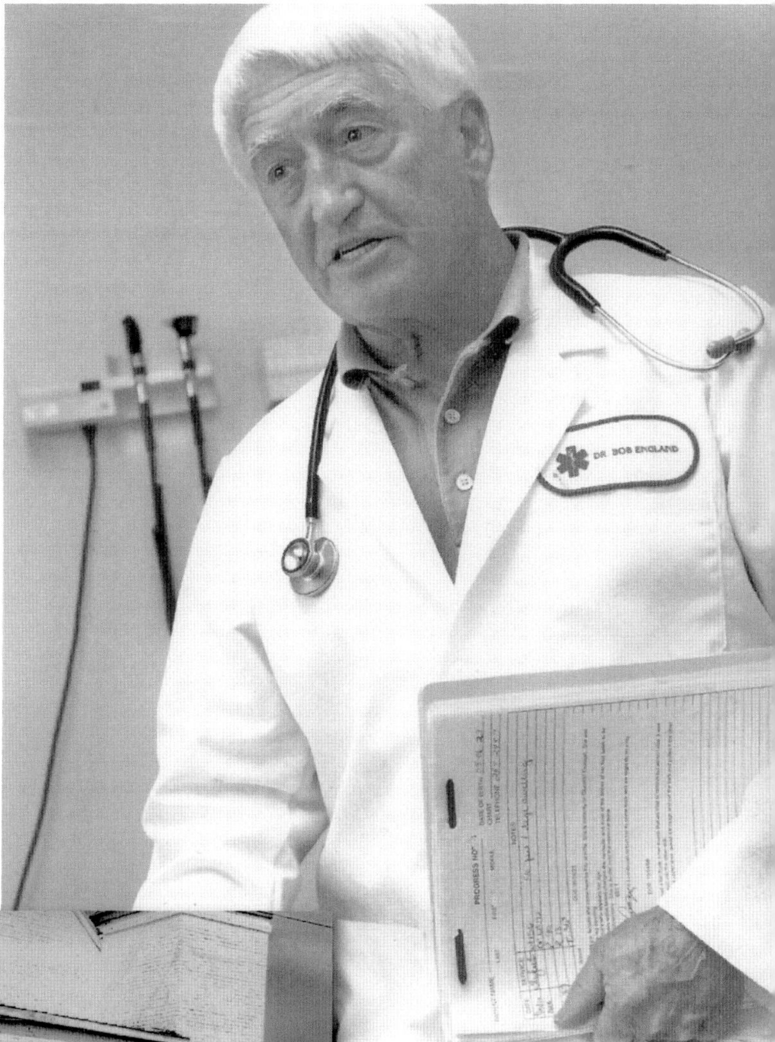

Dr. Bobby F. England, Veteran and State Representative

In 2012, Bobby F. England was an Ellenboro resident, a former area physician, a US Air Force veteran, and a four-time representative of the 112th House District of North Carolina. During one of his four terms in the North Carolina House of Representatives, Dr. England helped to save the life of fellow Representative Becky Carney. On April 2, 2009, Carney suffered cardiac arrest at the North Carolina Legislative Building. England administered CPR immediately. Dr. England continued to apply the lifesaving measure until emergency crews could arrive. (Dr. Bobby F. England.)

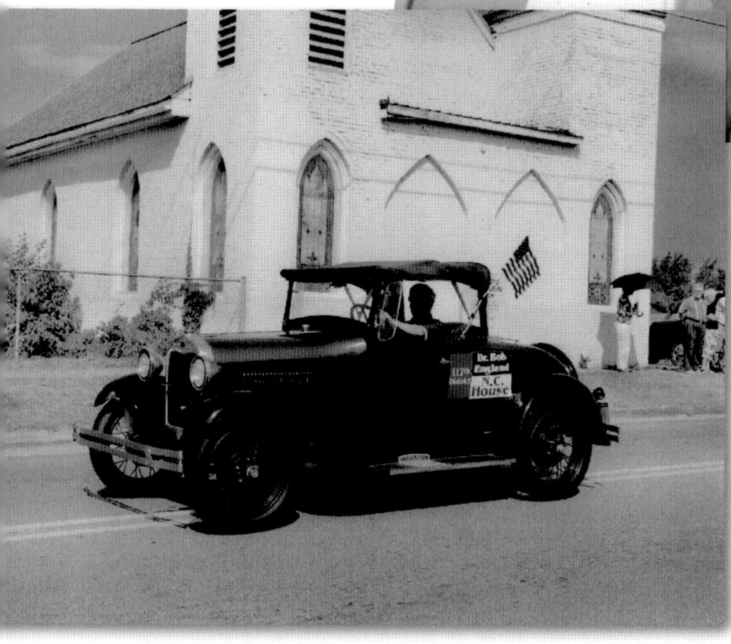

Dr. England Celebrates Big Day

Dr. Bobby England is always present at events in the community. Big Day, which was started by Amos Owens (see pages 22–24), is one of his favorite events. Here, he rides in the Big Day Parade in Ellenboro. (Dr. Bobby F. England.)

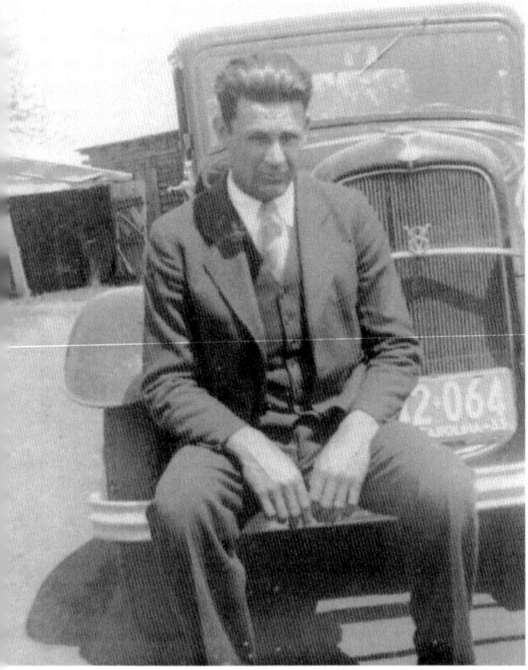

Ewart Burns before the 1934 Chicago Fair

In 1933–1934, the Chicago World's Fair opened. Grover C. Hamrick (May 9, 1888–July 17, 1957) and Robert Ewart Burns of Ellenboro decided to drive to visit the fair despite the Great Depression and despite Grover's current project, which was building a recreation lake for fishing and swimming for local residents who found the distance to Lake Lure an impediment. In the photograph, Burns rests on the bumper of his vehicle purchased for the trip. The plate gives the year of license as 1933. Hamrick planned to purchase some novelty items on the trip and bring them back for use at the lake. Ewart was still telling about the trip when his 13-year-old grandson began asking questions about driving in the 1980s. Hamrick's Sunshine Lake became a popular recreation spot for family gatherings, swimming, and fishing. (Robert Ewart Burns.)

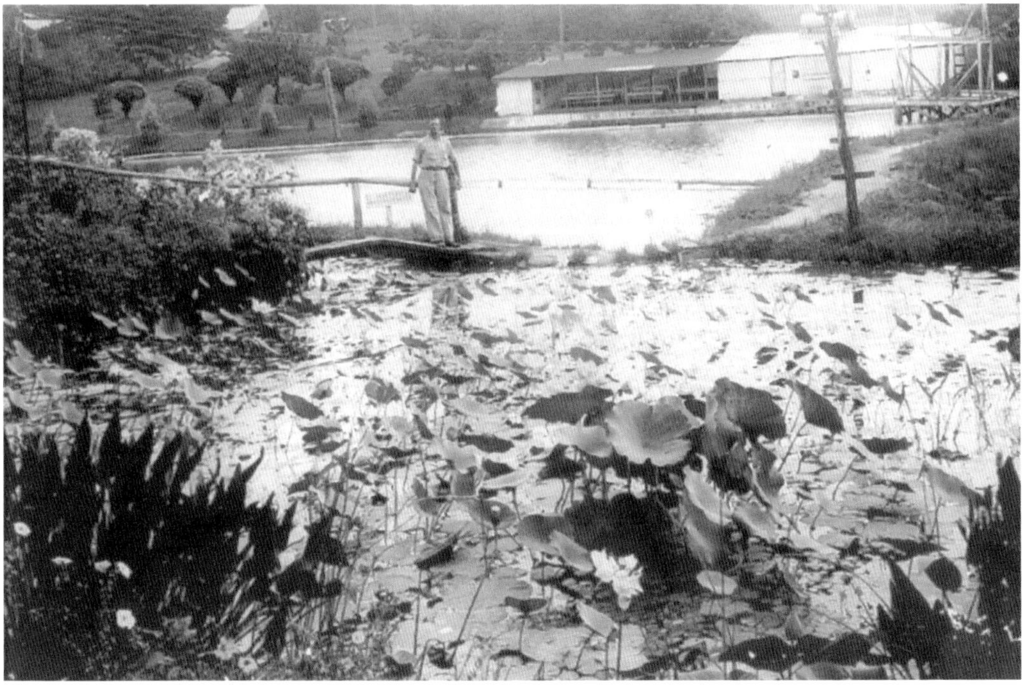

Grover Hamrick on Sunshine Lake Bridge

From a bridge he had constructed at the fishing area of his Sunshine Lake, Hamrick surveys the fruits of his labor. He was particularly proud of the lily pads, shown here, that he had been able to cultivate. Such a public recreation area was unusual for the area. The public was grateful for the diversion that Grover provided, and they used it heavily. (Paul Price, Colfax Museum, and Mike Rhyne.)

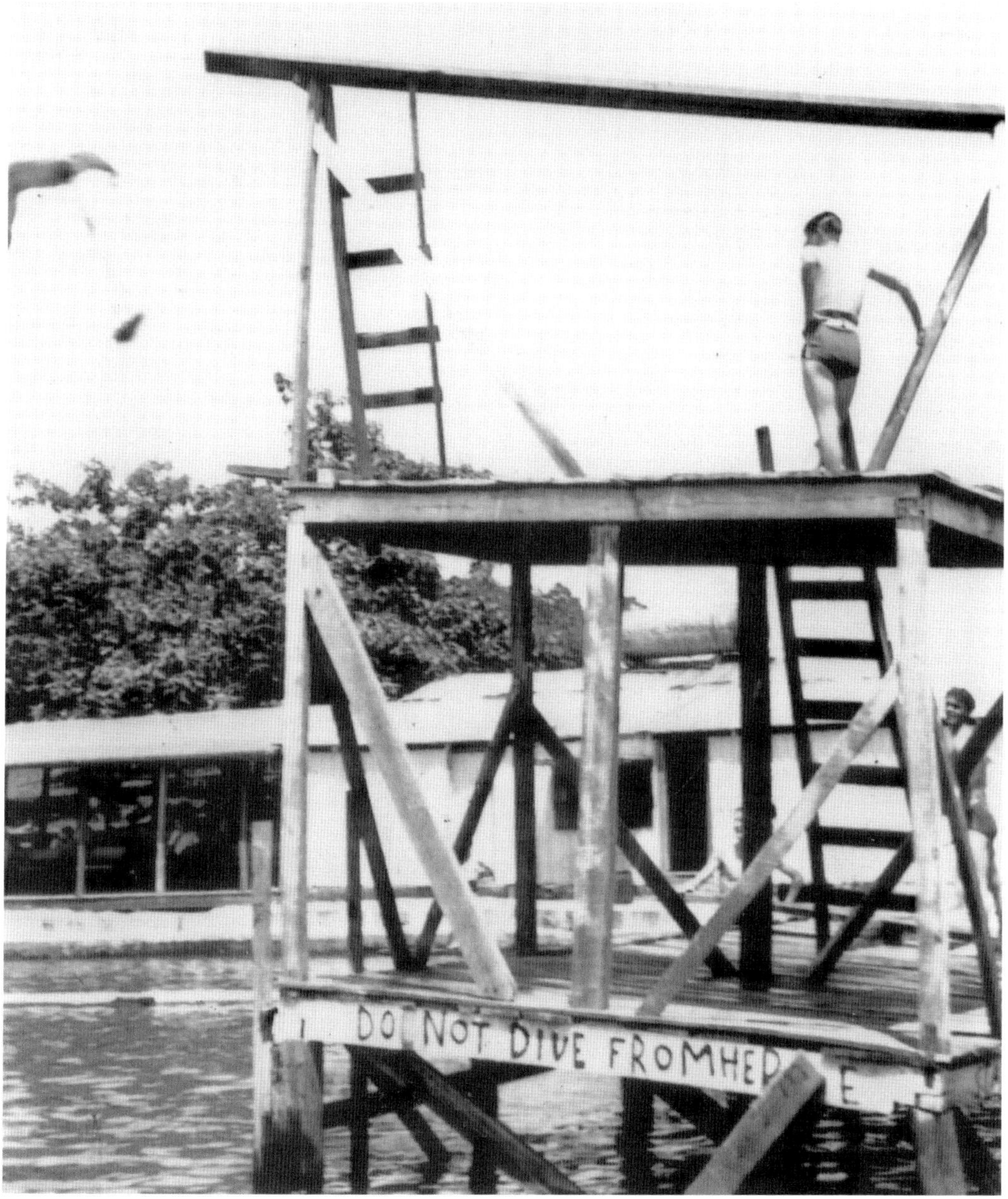

Swimming at Sunshine Lake in the 1930s

Grover Hamrick spared no expense in installing diving boards for visitors to his lake. At a time when public swimming pools were not readily available in the area, the public frequented the swimming area on hot summer days. The author lived across Highway 74 Business from Sunshine Lake Road when the lake was in its heyday. She remembers the lines of cars turning into Sunshine Lake Road from Highway 74 on hot summer days.

Grover closed Sunshine Lake as a swimming lake in 1952 because of the polio epidemic, but he allowed guests to use the lake for fishing for several more years. Visible in the background is a pavilion with jukebox and hardwood floors; Grover continued to make this facility available to the public for family reunions and dances for years to come. (Paul Price, Colfax Museum, and Mike Rhyne.)

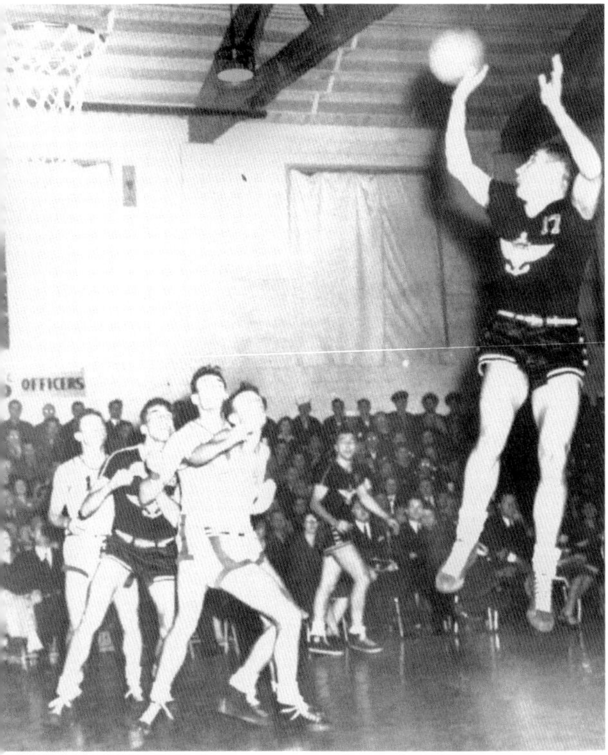

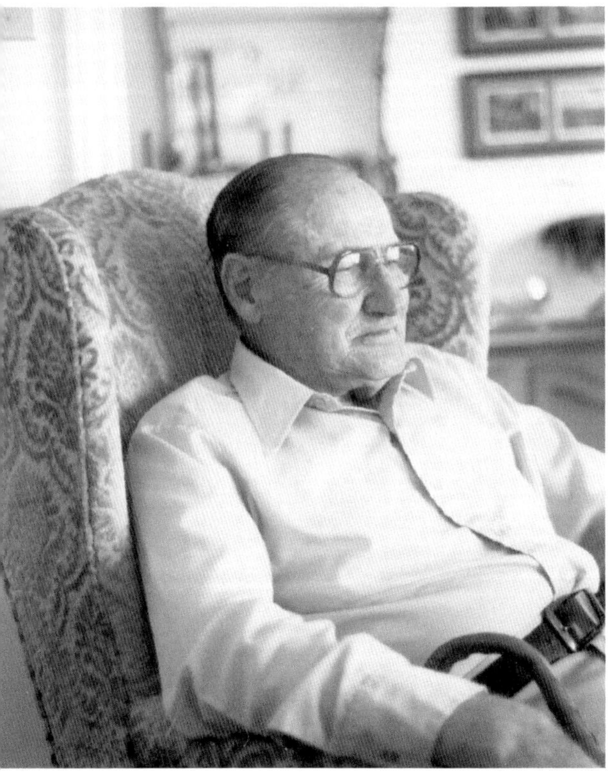

Belus Van Smawley, Basketball Star

Basketball great Belus Van Smawley (March 30, 1918–April 24, 2003) was born in Golden Valley, North Carolina, in 1918. When Belus was 13, his family moved to a small farm two miles south of Ellenboro. The Smawley farm was about half a mile from an abandoned Southern Line Railroad depot. In 1934, Belus developed his unique basketball shot. He would stop suddenly in a dribble, with his back half to the peach-basket goal, leap high into the air, and twist to face the basket as he shot.

At Appalachian State Teachers College (now Appalachian State University), Smawley was a star basketball player. He received credit for inventing the turn-around jump shot; in fact John Christgau suggests he may have been the first even to execute a jump shot. Smawley was a Second-team National Association of Intercollegiate Athletics All-American in 1943 and the Most Valuable Player in 1943 at the NAIA Tournament. Smawley became a member of the NAIA Basketball Hall of Fame. With the military drafts and enlistments, Smawley ended the season as the head coach of the basketball team at Appalachian State Teachers College (ASTC).

Above, Smawley is executing his jump shot at the Norfolk Naval Air Station (1945). Between 1946 and 1952 he played with St. Louis, Syracuse, and Baltimore. During his professional career, Smawley scored 3,316 points and averaged 12.7 points per game, a high total for this era. In 1949, he averaged 15.5 points per game; this was the sixth-best mark in the National Basketball Association. Smawley was an outstanding foul shot shooter; he shot 79.7 percent from the foul line during his career. In 1951, he scored 85 percent, which was third in the league.

After Smawley ended his professional playing career, he served as a school principal and as a basketball coach. In 1992, he received induction into the North Carolina Sports Hall of Fame. Smawley is pictured below in Mooresville in 1999. Having passed away in 2003, Smawley and his contributions to the sport are still remembered. (Both, John Christgau.)

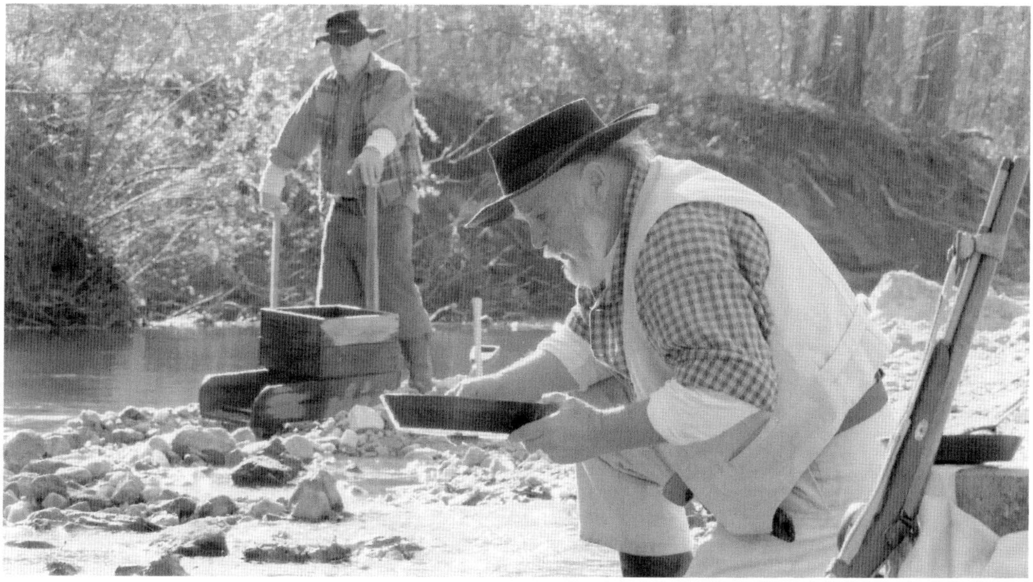

Nanney Family's Gold and Gem Mine

The land where the Thermal City Gold and Gem Mine is now located has passed through five generations of the Nanney family. This gold mine at the Rutherford and McDowell County line is one of the earliest (1830) gold mines in the Southeast. In 1880, Sgt. Amos Nanney (April 8, 1827–May 23, 1906), who fought for the South during the Civil War, bought the mineral deposits and the land. Amos, the son of Shadrach Nanney of Virginia, passed the land and mineral deposits to his son Amos Perminter (December 27, 1860–January 17, 1944). From Perminter Nanney, the land went to J. Reginald Nanney (February 28, 1906–October 22, 1960). All these Nanneys were laid to rest in the Round Hill Cemetery. Reginald passed the land to Paul Nanney. There was little mining on the Nanney land until Lloyd Nanney opened the Thermal City Gold and Gem Mine to the public in 1992. The friendly, helpful staff provides assistance as guests search for gold and gems in the gravel that backhoes take from the pit; equipment is available for rent. There is also a gem fluming operation. Rustic cabins or campgrounds enable visitors to stay overnight. Above, owner Lloyd Nanney (foreground) and friend Bob Coble (background) search for gold on the river at Thermal City Gold and Gem Mine. (Page and Lloyd Nanney.)

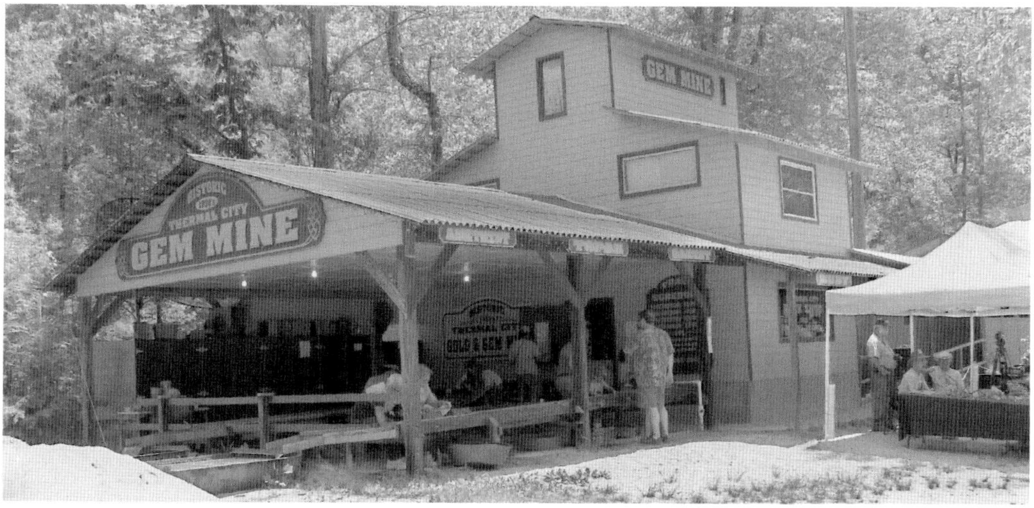

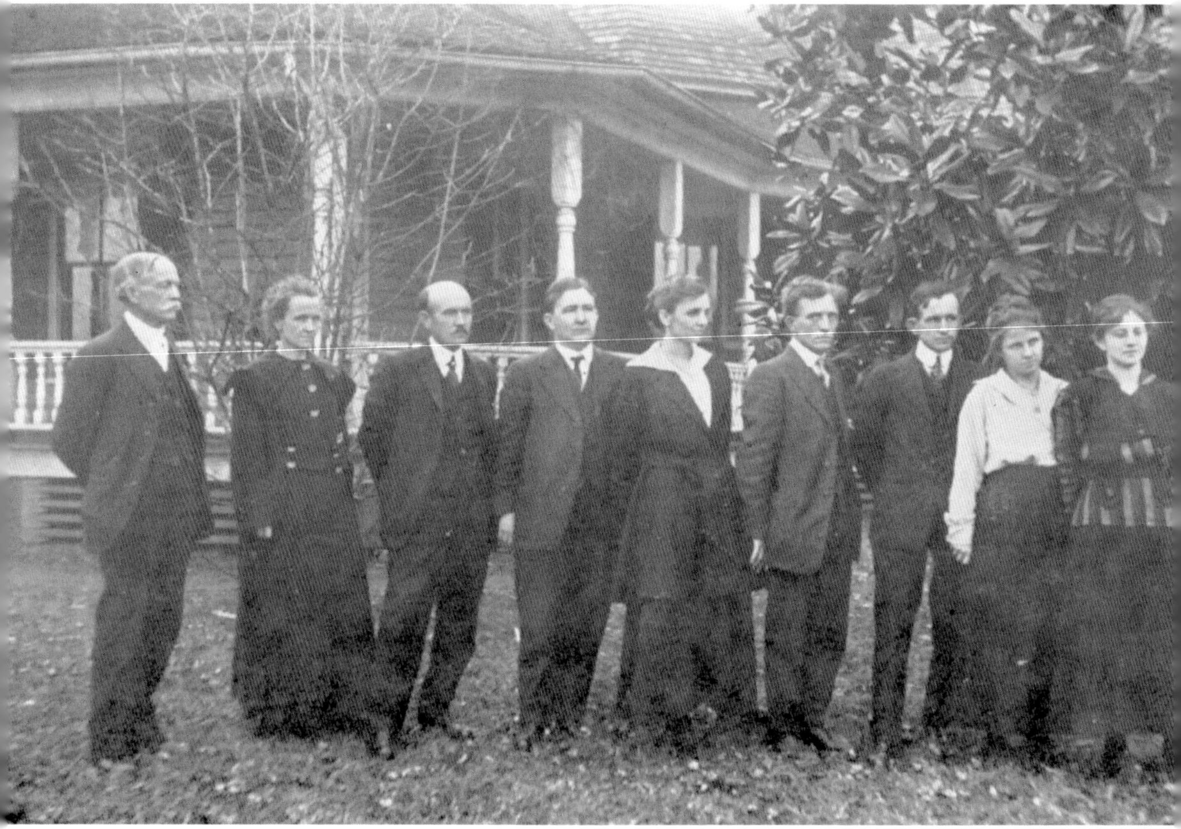

Raleigh Rutherford Haynes and Family

Here, textile executive Raleigh Rutherford Haynes (June 30, 1851–February 9, 1917) and his eight children stand for a photograph on Christmas Day 1916. They are, from left to right, R.R. Haynes, Florence Haynes Jenkins, Robert E. Haynes, Charles H. Haynes, Sara Haynes Love, Walter H. Haynes, Grover C. Haynes, Eula Haynes Shull, and Virginia Haynes Caldwell.

Raleigh Rutherford Haynes was instrumental in the building of mills and mill towns across the county. (See also page 52 in this volume.) Haynes had overseen Cliffside Mills and the town of Cliffside. Haynes oversaw the construction of the Cliffside Mill Village, made sure that there were available medical professionals to ensure the health of the community, contributed to the building of local churches, and planned the education of area youth.

On Christmas Day 1916, R.R. Haynes and his family were planning to celebrate the season at the winter home in St. Petersburg, Florida. Haynes insisted on having all eight of his children pose together with him for a photograph. It would be their last family photograph because Raleigh Rutherford Haynes would pass on February 6, 1917. (Mrs. Grover C. Haynes Sr. and Grover C. Haynes Jr.)

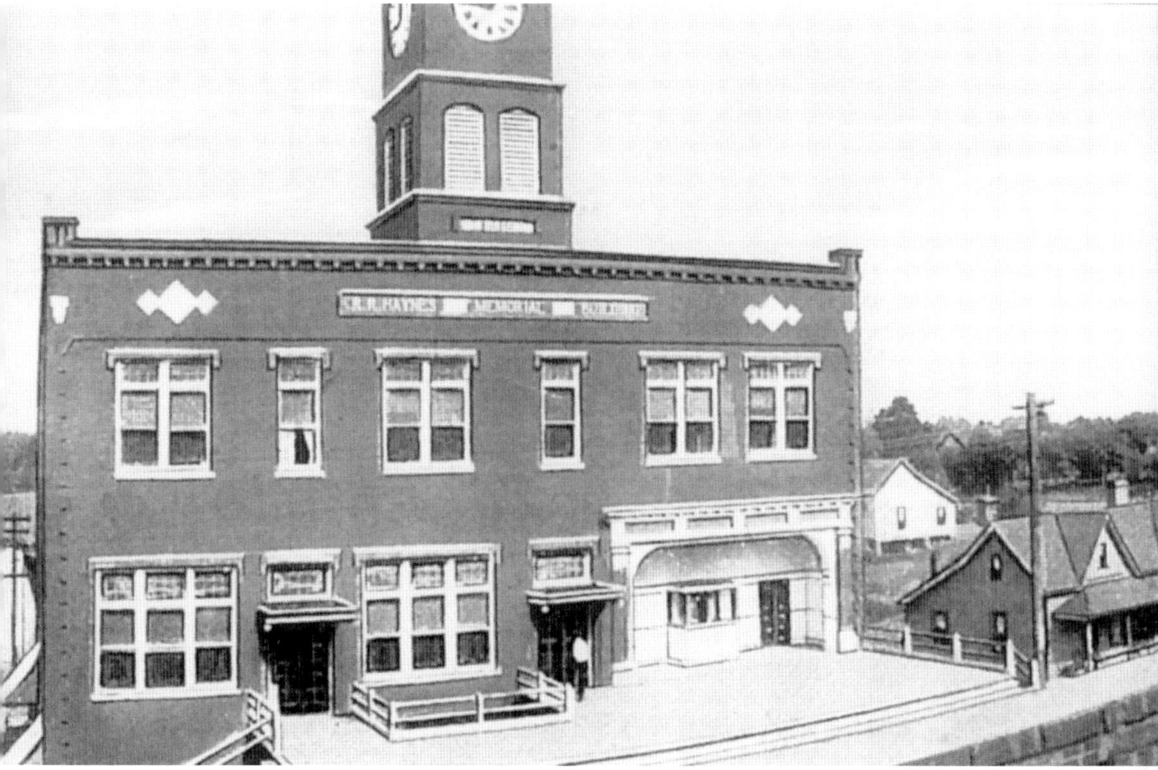

R.R. Haynes Memorial Building (Cliffside)
Haynes had plans to build a $100,000 building for the recreational and relaxation needs of the Cliffside Mill employees. Haynes wanted his employees to have easy access to a movie theater, a library, barber and beauty shops, a gymnasium, a café, a banquet hall, showers, and rooms for overnight stays. He died before he could realize his dreams; however, his son Charles prevailed and completed the building.

Under the direction of Charles H. Haynes, the director of Cliffside Mills after his father's death, ground was broken for a memorial building to honor Raleigh Rutherford Haynes. The dedication of the R.R. Haynes Memorial Building in Cliffside occurred on June 24, 1922. This is the theater where Earl Owensby (page 88) worked in his youth. The Haynes Memorial Building created memories for visitors. When patrons walked inside, they faced the seats; the screen was behind them. (Anne and Paula Cargill.)

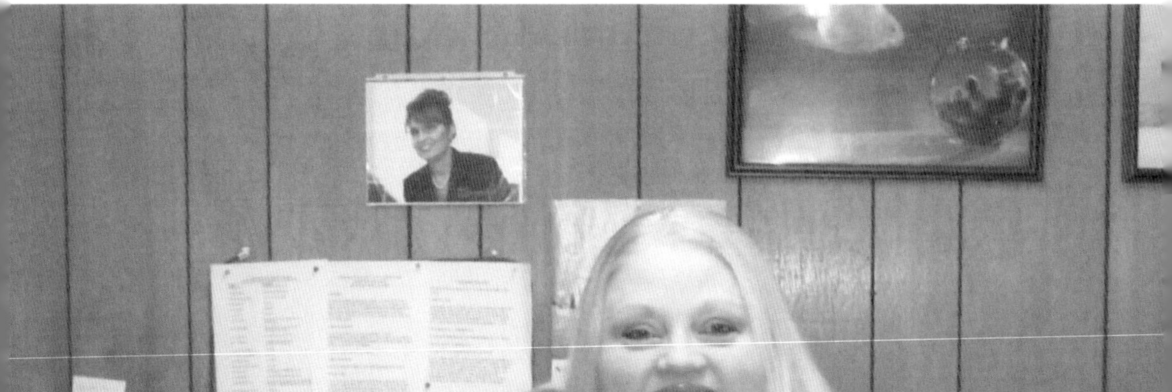

Lou Gilliam
Gilliam has helped to organize the announcements, news, and weather to keep the residents of the county up-to-date for several decades. Gilliam started her radio career at WBBO in Forest City over 30 years ago. It was then she met Jim Bishop before he went to work for Gov. Jim Martin. She is now the office manager, program director, and announcer at WCAB in Rutherfordton. Bishop owns the station and calls her a "record breaker." Even though offered jobs at other stations and larger market stations, she remained in Rutherford County. She has been on the air in the county longer than any other female. (Lou Gilliam.)

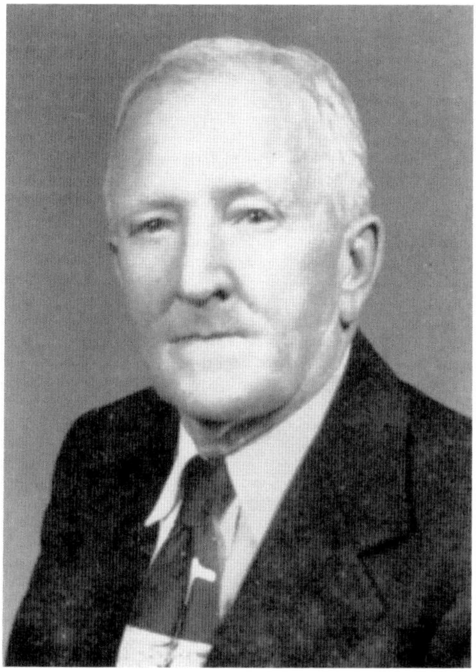

Walter Hodge Haynes

Walter Hodge Haynes (November 28, 1882–June 20, 1957), like his father, Raleigh Rutherford Haynes, was not afraid to try new endeavors. Building a theater with sound was no exception. On January 1, 1929, Walter opened the first theater in the county to be equipped with sound apparatus. (Grove C. Haynes Jr.)

The Romina Theatre

The Romina Theatre was on Main Street in Forest City. Walter spent $125,000 to construct the theater. It had a curtain, a 28-by-14-foot stage, carpeting, leather seats, a domed ceiling, dressing rooms, sound equipment, and vaudeville show equipment. This view of the theater is from 1937. (Reno Bailey and Phillip White.)

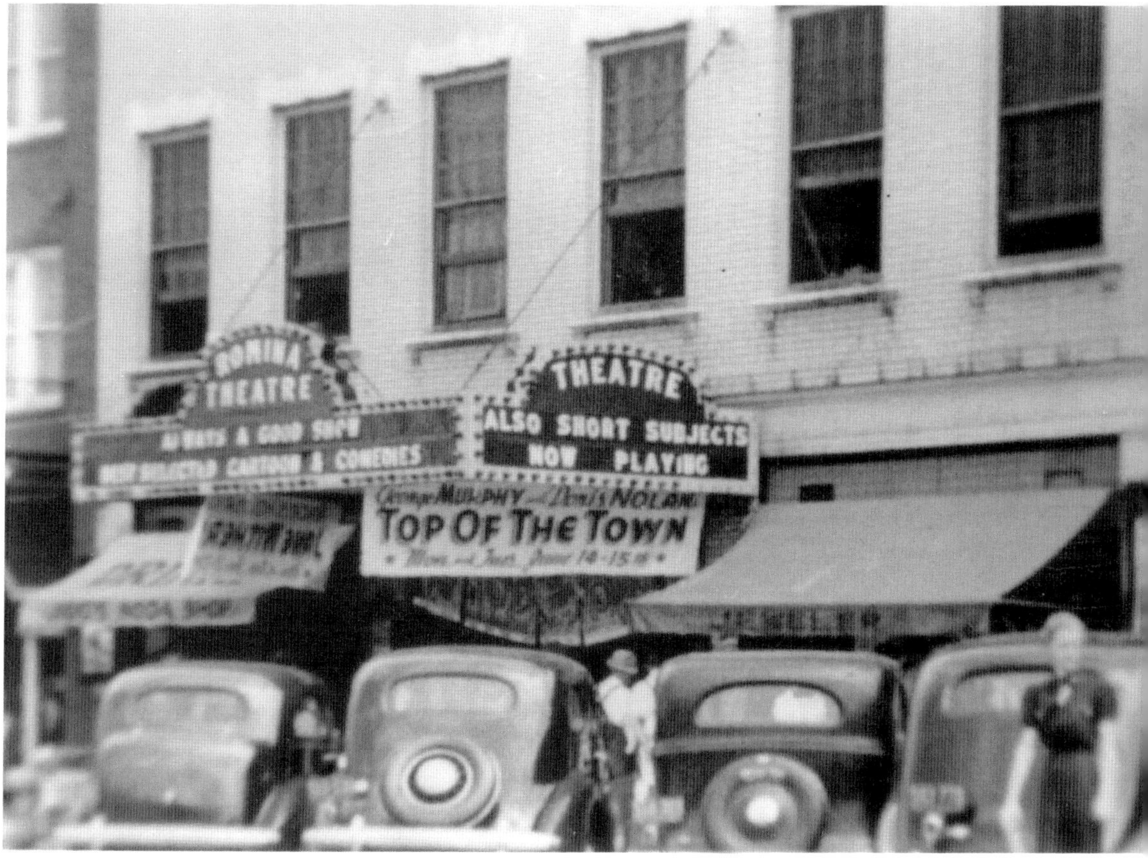

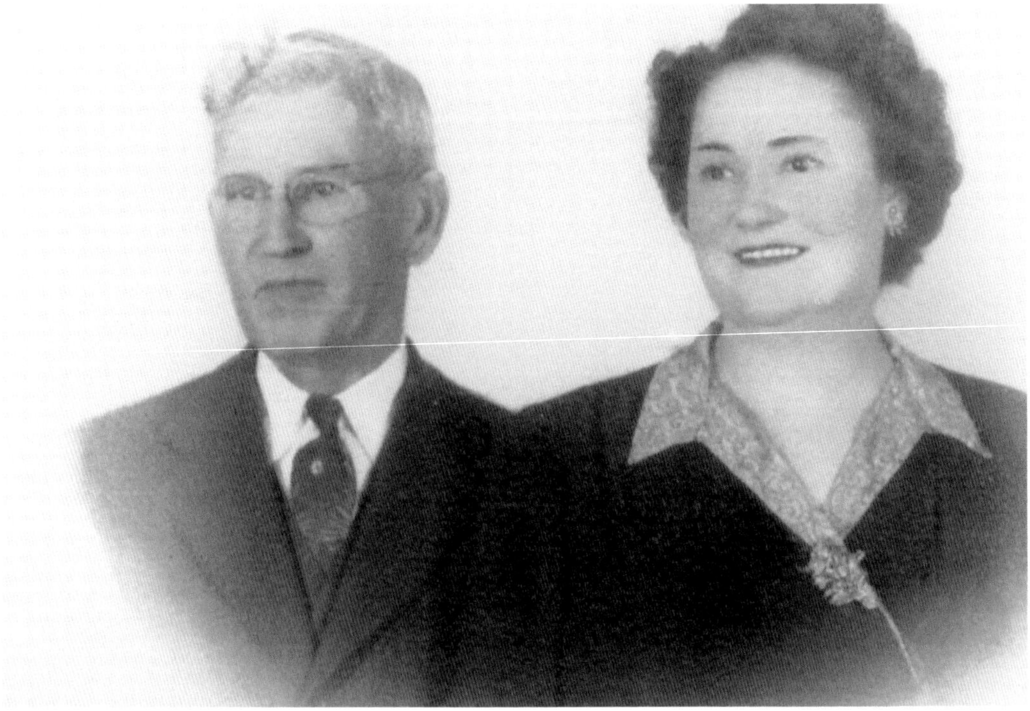

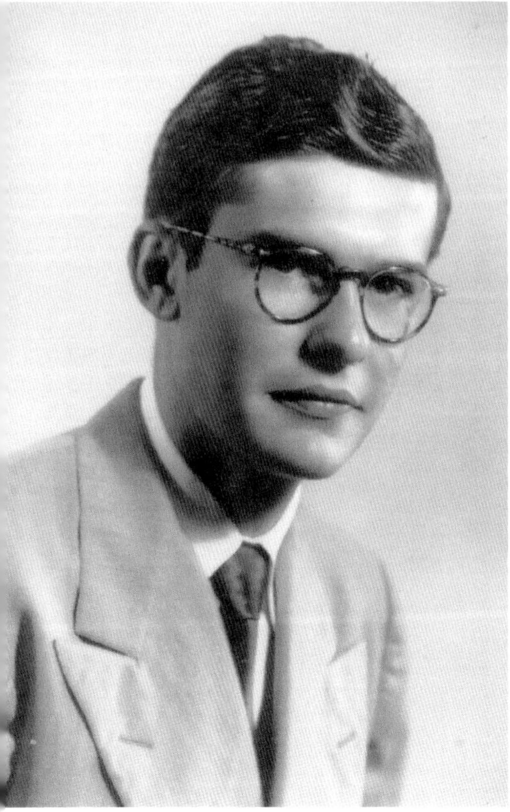

Alice Grace and James Willis Griffin Sr.
Around 1933, entrepreneurs James Willis Griffin Sr. (March 28, 1884–January 13, 1959) and his wife, Alice Grace Griffin (December 10, 1896–October 15, 1956), purchased the Romina Theatre and the Horn Theater (once the Pastime Theater) from Walter Hodge Haynes. The Pastime was across Main Street from the Romina Theatre. Griffin renamed the Pastime Theater the Grace Theater, in honor of his wife, Grace. Grace helped operate both theaters for almost 20 years. Melinda remembers her grandmother scurrying back and forth across the street from one theater to the other, often with a moneybag. Grace carried a pistol with her. (Melinda Griffin Peterson.)

James W. Griffin Jr.
Toward the end of World War II, James and Grace's son James W. Griffin Jr. (December 16, 1920–January 27, 2001) was in the military. Upon returning home, he built a new movie house about five blocks from the Romina. He called it the Griffin Theater in honor of his family and opened it on June 8, 1949. The theater even had a "crying room" for mothers who had young children. In 1972, James closed the Griffin Theater. The Romina and the Grace had been closed for some time. A new cinema at the mall attempted to replace the downtown facilities that the Griffins had begun some 40 years before. (Melinda Griffin Peterson.)

CHAPTER SIX

Medical and Spiritual Caregivers

An integral part of Rutherford County's story has been the kindness, the compassion, the generosity, and the guidance displayed by its medical and its spiritual leaders. These servants of the people have not always been individuals with formal medical or religious education, but they have always cared about their clientele and have done their best. In some of the remote areas of Cherry Mountain, for example, weekly religious services were rare. Weddings and burials sometimes had to wait for the arrival of traveling men of the cloth.

In the 1800s and before, midwives and "granny women" used their remedies and their concern to heal those about them. Caring lay people sought to comfort and help.

In the mid-1860s, for example, Argana Black helped with "laying out" the dead, with attending the ill and injured, and with birthing many babies in the Golden Valley area. The tea leaves that she instructed those with excessive bleeding from a tooth extraction to press on the oozing socket was not just a baseless superstition; tea leaves actually contain tannic acid that does, indeed, help staunch the bleeding.

Dr. Benjamin Earle Washburn found that the oak balls (galls) "granny women" used to treat burns contained tannic acid; this remedy was scientifically sound. Dr. Washburn and Dr. W.C. Bostic will represent the medical profession in this volume.

In the early 1800s, those who ministered spiritually to residents were not always available and trained in formal institutions. Rather these early preachers and clerics were merely caring people who tried to help in times of tragedy, death, and illness. This volume, however, includes Rev. Harold Blake Brown as a representative of the local ministers. He was trained, educated, and caring. Brown, Bostic, and Washburn will be representatives in this section of *Legendary Locals of Rutherford County*.

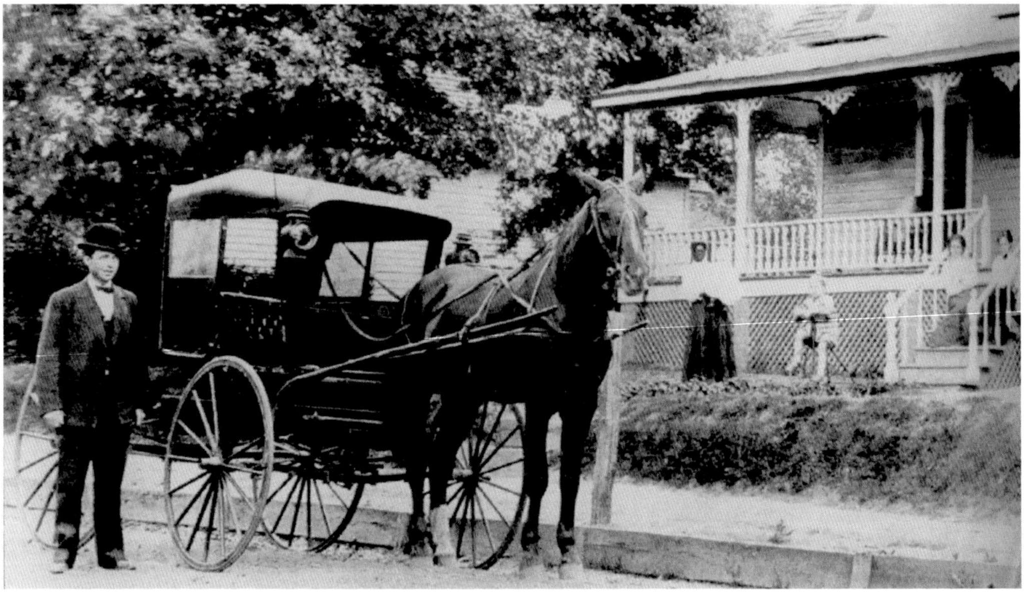

Dr. William Chivous Bostic Sr.

Well-known doctor William Chivous Bostic Sr. (December 20, 1877–September 23, 1957) was born in Black Oak, an area that became Bostick, and still later Bostic, North Carolina. When Bostic was 14 years old, an epidemic of measles struck the area. The young man helped Dr. Guilford E. Young care for those who were ill; Bostic was even allowed to use Young's horse. Bostic helped with the sick's necessary chores, such as carrying wood and drawing water. Residents began to call Bostic "Doc."

At the age of 21, Bostic graduated from the University of Chattanooga Medical College. He practiced medicine briefly in Polk County and in the state of Tennessee before returning to Rutherford County and joining Dr. Young's office. Bostic received further training at the Mayo Clinic and earned Life Membership in the Mayo Surgeon's Club.

Bostic delivered thousands of babies and served at various times as surgeon for Florence Mills and Alexander Manufacturing Company and as a county physician. He was instrumental in founding the Alexander Home for Motherless Children. He advocated the construction of the public square in Forest City before his death. Above, Will McArthur (page 70) photographed Dr. Bostic with his carriage on Cherry Mountain Street in Forest City. Below is the residence of Dr. Bostic on East Main Street in Forest City. (Above, Robert Watkins; below, author's collection.)

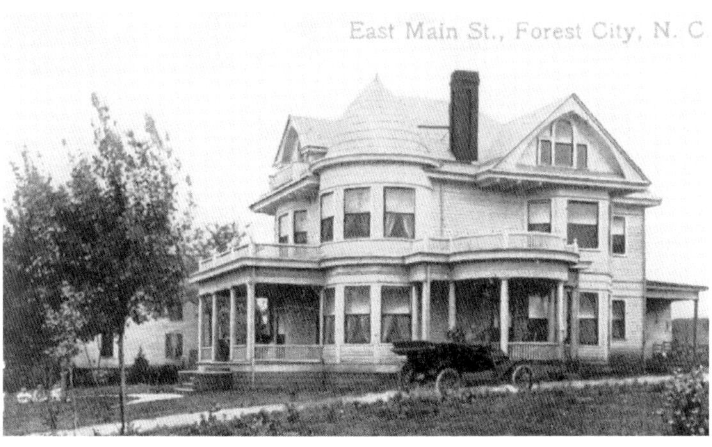

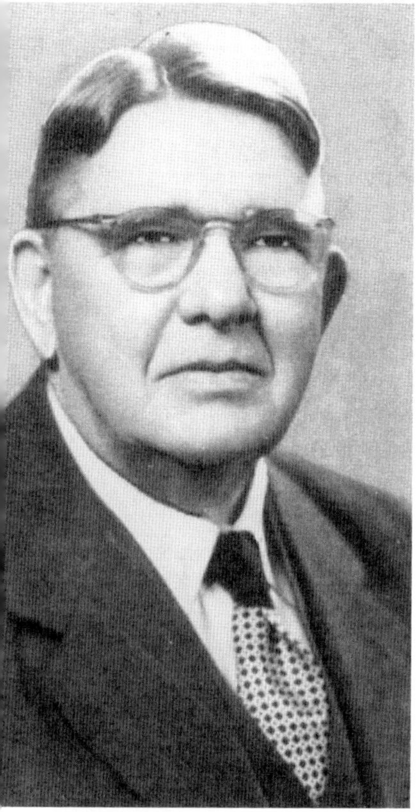

Dr. Benjamin Earle Washburn

A native of Rutherford County, Dr. Washburn (December 29, 1885–December 28, 1979) spent his childhood on the Cleghorn Plantation, which totaled 2,000 acres on Cox Road near Rutherfordton. Washburn graduated from the University of North Carolina and the University of Virginia Medical School. With his wife, Zellah, Benjamin began his medical practice in the South Mountains of Rutherford County in 1913, which he wrote about in *A Country Doctor in the South Mountains* (1955). Dr. Washburn joined the Rockefeller Sanitary Commission in its campaigns against hookworm disease. He organized the Bureau of County Health Work of the North Carolina State Board of Health and became Nash County health officer, one of the first such officers in the United States. He became an officer of the International Health Division of the Rockefeller Foundation from 1915 to 1939. He served in Trinidad, Jamaica, the West Indies, Central America, and two years in England. He worked as health editor of the *Progressive Farmer* (1940–1953) and as district health officer during World War II. He served as a member of the Governor's Committee on Hospitals and Medical Care, as a director of the North Carolina Good Health Association, and as the first physician to serve on the Board of Rutherford County Hospital. In addition to his findings on sickle cell anemia, Washburn wrote *Rutherford County and Its Hospital* (1969) and *To Every Thing a Season* before his 1979 death. His works remain historical references. (The *Progressive Farmer.*)

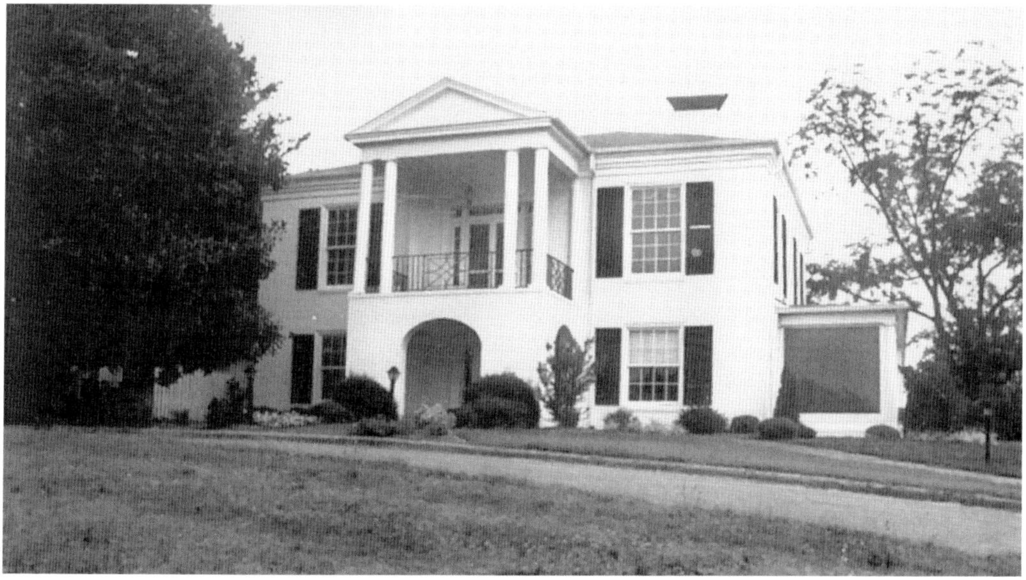

Washburn's Home, Cleghorn Plantation

Washburn's parents, John Rutherford and Camilla Miller Washburn, purchased the hip-roofed house made from stucco and brick from Cleghorn Creek in 1889. Ben would later sell the property to Dr. G.O. Moss (page 50). (James M. Walker.)

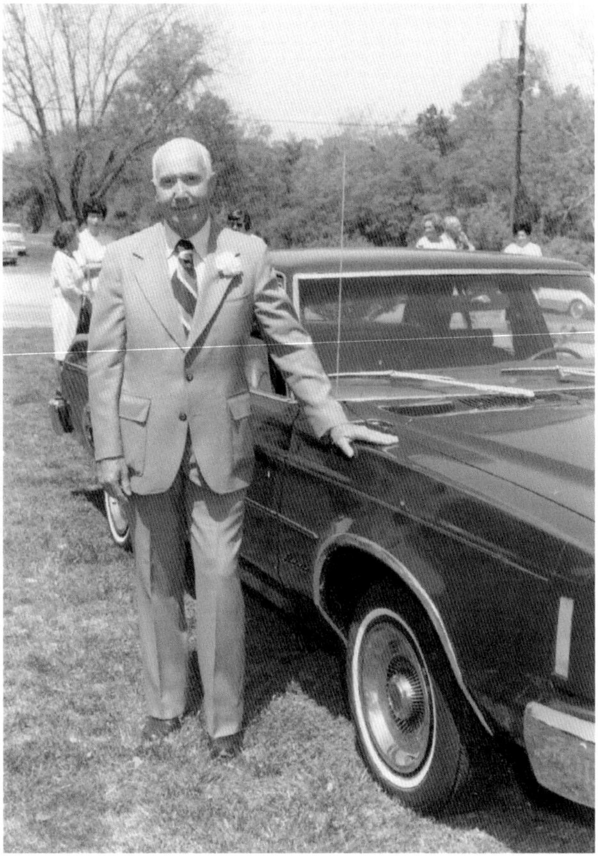

Rev. Harold Blake Brown, People's Pastor

Reverend Brown (November 30, 1912–March 16, 2006) was much loved. He served wherever there was a need and whenever he felt a calling. This meant that he would pastor more than one denomination and more than one church during his years of service. Brown graduated from Holly Springs High School, North Greenville Junior College, and Furman University. His 1944 ordination was at First Baptist Church in Duncan, South Carolina. Brown and his family moved to Bethel Baptist Church in Ellenboro in 1955. To show its love for its pastor, in 1957, the congregation presented him with a gift: a 1957 Plymouth. After retirement in 1978, the Baptist preacher received a call to serve as an interim pastor at Duncan's Creek Presbyterian Church, which he accepted. After his service there, he received a call to serve as an interim pastor again; this time his call was to the Ellenboro Presbyterian Church. Again, he accepted. (Benny Brown.)

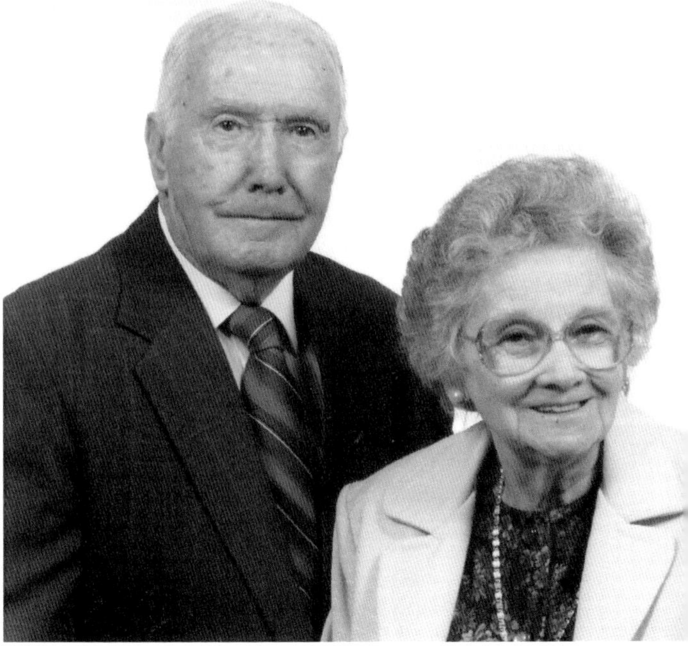

Ruby Miller Brown and Harold Brown

Ruby and Harold were married on January 26, 1935, and celebrated the following 67 years. The Browns had four children, three of whom died shortly after birth. Their one surviving child, Benny Brown, graduated from Ellenboro High School in 1960. (Benny would later serve as a North Carolina State Highway patrolman.) The Browns also adopted four children, Dot, Brenda, Stella, and Doug, before their 1955 move to Ellenboro's Bethel Baptist Church. After full retirement, Reverend Brown lived and worked on his little farm on New House Road until his death. (Benny Brown.)

CHAPTER SEVEN

Servicemen, Law Enforcement, and Government Officials

Many residents of Rutherford County have served others in the nation, the state, and the county through their work in the military, in law enforcement, and in the ranks of the government. The service of these residents has, in many cases, been underpaid and dangerous, and yet these workers have remained dedicated to their professions. Some have given their all. This chapter highlights the sacrificial service of those in the military, law enforcement, and government.

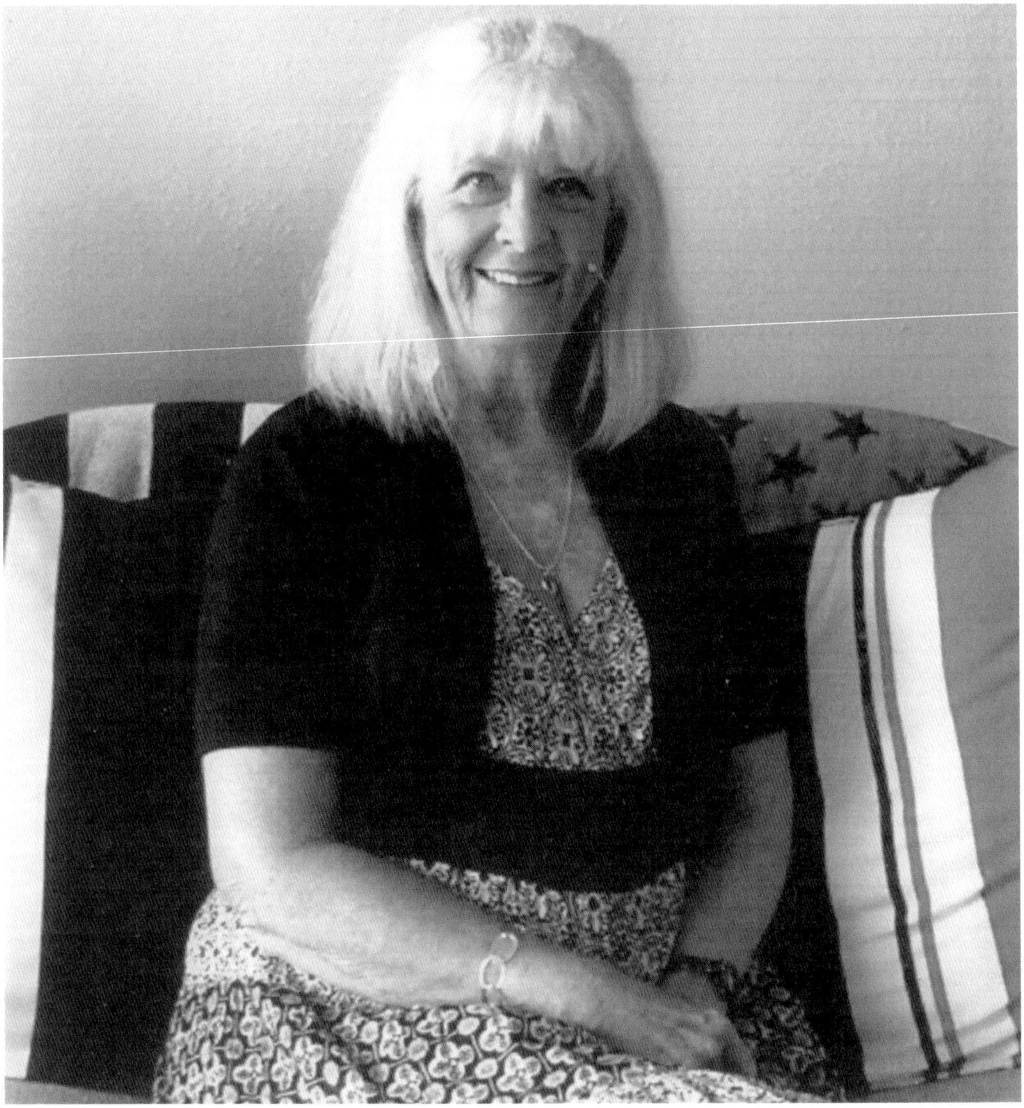

Marie Howard Champion, Veteran Services Director

Champion (June 1, 1950–) was born to Navy veteran Newton E. Howard and Ardith Bedford Howard in 1950. She went to work for Veteran Services officer Herbert Logan Downey (July 27, 1919–December 10, 1991) at the Rutherford County Veteran Services Office on November 5, 1975. Champion worked as his full-time employee until his December 1991 death; two months later Marie Howard Champion received appointment as the Veteran Service officer of Rutherford County.

Marie Howard Champion has served the Rutherford County veterans in the Veteran Services Office for more than 37 years. She has much respect and appreciation for the veterans; she remarks that they have been her support, her friends, and her family during all her years of service.

The veterans in return remark on the respect, support, guidance, and friendship she has offered to them and to their families. They have shared with her all their stories: the sad ones and the happy ones. They have cried and laughed together through the years.

Marie remarks, "The veterans have always been there for me when I have needed support. My heart will always be with them. Thanks to all of them." (Marie Howard Champion.)

SFC George S. Mills

Rutherford County and its people have done their part in many wars. The number of veterans is many. This representative veteran is the highly decorated George S. Mills.

After his 1958 entry, George S. Mills of Union Mills served more than 20 years in the US Army. Upon his retirement, SFC George S. Mills could boast of having two tours in Vietnam, two tours in France, and three tours in Germany. Mills's basic training was at Fort Dix, New Jersey. He completed AIT at Fort Gordon, Georgia, and from there he went to Fort Riley, Kansas, and Paris, France. Mills's other stations included Fort Mead, Maryland; Paris, France; Hunter Air Force Base in Savannah, Georgia; Germany; Vietnam; Fort Campbell, Kentucky; Fort Gordon, Georgia; another tour in Vietnam; another tour in Germany; Fort Dix, New Jersey; and a third tour in Germany.

On December 11, 1970, Sgt. George S. Mills earned the Bronze Star Medal for Meritorious Achievement in Ground Operations against Hostile Forces in the Republic of Vietnam. His other decorations, medals, badges, citations, and ribbons include Expert with the M-16; the Good Conduct Medal (6 times), the National Defense Service Medal, the Vietnam Service Medal with Four Service Stars, the Republic of Vietnam Campaign Medal, the Vietnam Cross of Gallantry with Palm, and four Overseas Service Bars. (Ruby Mills and George S. Mills.)

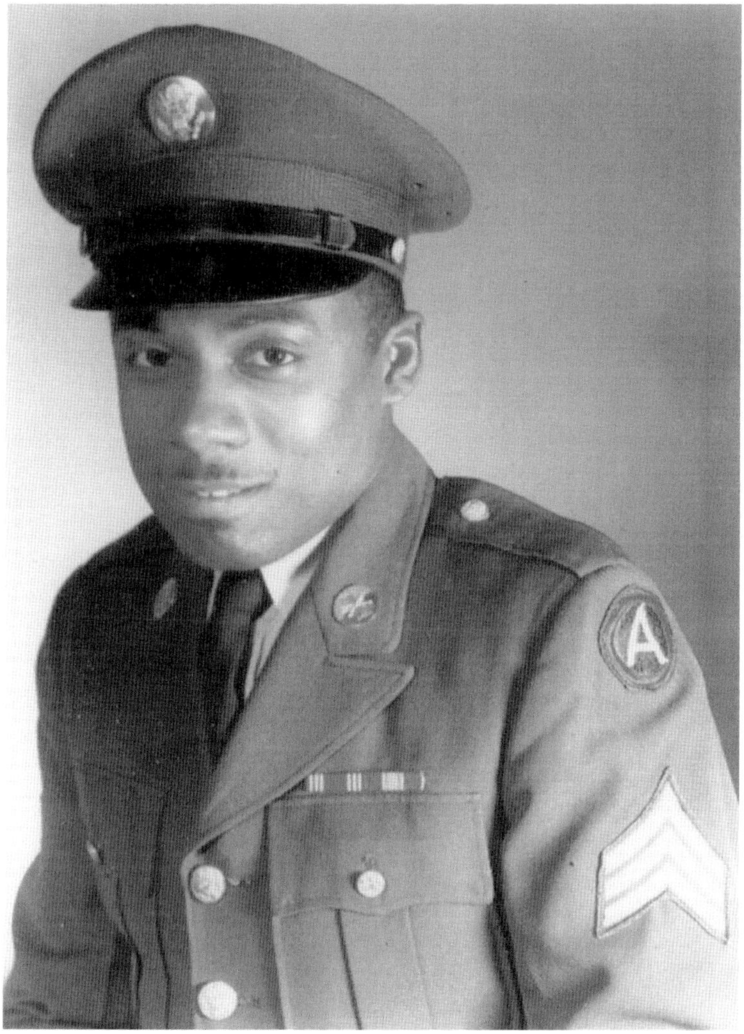

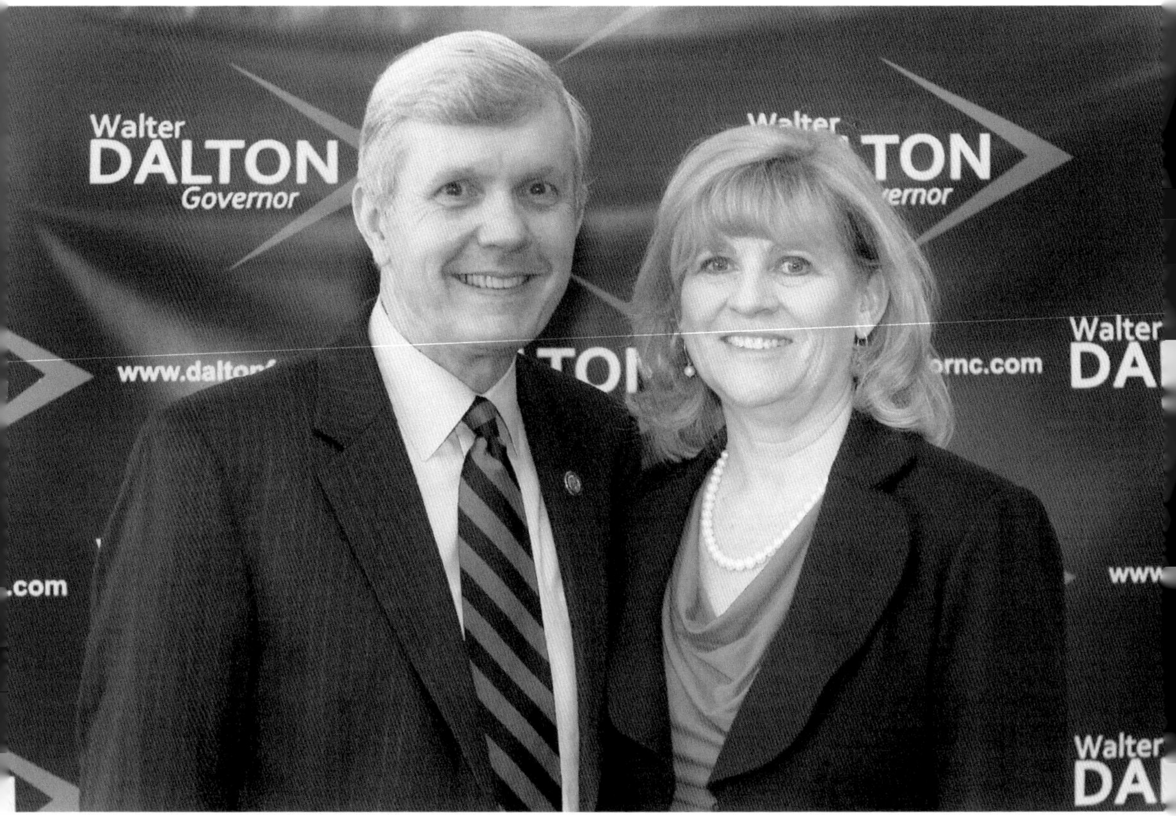

Lt. Gov. Walter and Lucille Dalton
Lieutenant Governor Dalton is the only North Carolina lieutenant governor to come from Rutherford County. Both Dalton, great-grandson of Raleigh Rutherford Haynes (page 52), and Dalton's wife, Lucille Hodge Haynes, grew up in Rutherford County. Both attended the public schools in the county, and both their fathers were World War II veterans. When not in Raleigh, the couple still loves to spend time in the county. Dalton clerked for the Hon. Woodrow W. Jones, US District Court judge, after Dalton's 1975 graduation from the University of North Carolina Law School at Chapel Hill. Dalton practiced law for 30 years and represented Rutherford County for over 20 years as the county attorney. Dalton was a Cub Scout leader, a cofounder of the Child Abuse Prevention Society, member of the American Red Cross, and chair of the Isothermal Community College Board. He received 1996 election to the state senate and the 2008 election as North Carolina's 33rd lieutenant governor.

Lucille Dalton served on the Rutherford County School Board for nine years and was the 1998 North Carolina School Board Member of the Year. She was a recipient of the Raleigh Dingman Award. In the photograph, Lt. Gov. Walter and Lucille Dalton stand before a 2012 campaign banner announcing his candidacy as the 74th governor of North Carolina. Although Dalton's bid for governor was unsuccessful, he plans to continue serving the people of the county and the state. (Lucille H. Dalton.)

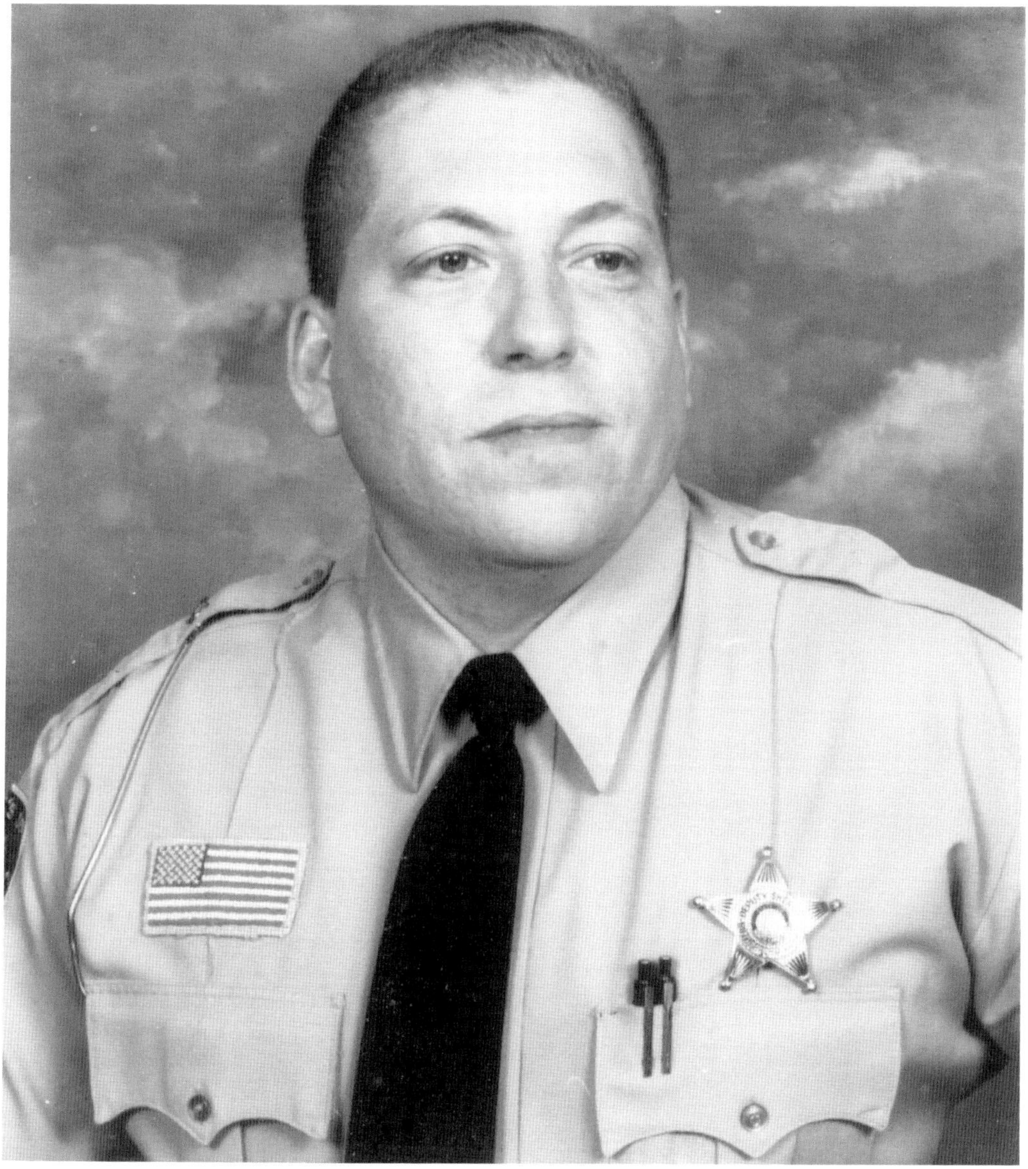

Deputy Sheriff Ronald Dean Bailey

Deputy Sheriff Ronald Dean Bailey (November 19, 1965–), a current member of Rutherford County Sheriff's Department, is a symbol of continued hope for the county.

The son of Frances Gettys Bailey and veteran Palmer Bailey, Ronald attended Ellenboro School and graduated in 1982 from East Rutherford High School. He was enrolled in Isothermal Community College from 1982 to 1983. From 1984 to 1988, Bailey was in the Marine Corps; his stations included Parris Island; Camp Lejeune; Okinawa, Japan; and Korea. After his discharge from the Marines, Bailey worked with the Department of Corrections in Rutherfordton from 1988 to 1994. From 1994 until the present (2012), Bailey has served as a deputy and as a detective in the Rutherford County Sheriff's Department.

To illustrate Bailey's concern for others, he immediately suggested other law enforcement officers in the county for inclusion in this book. His unselfishness is duly noted. (Frances Bailey.)

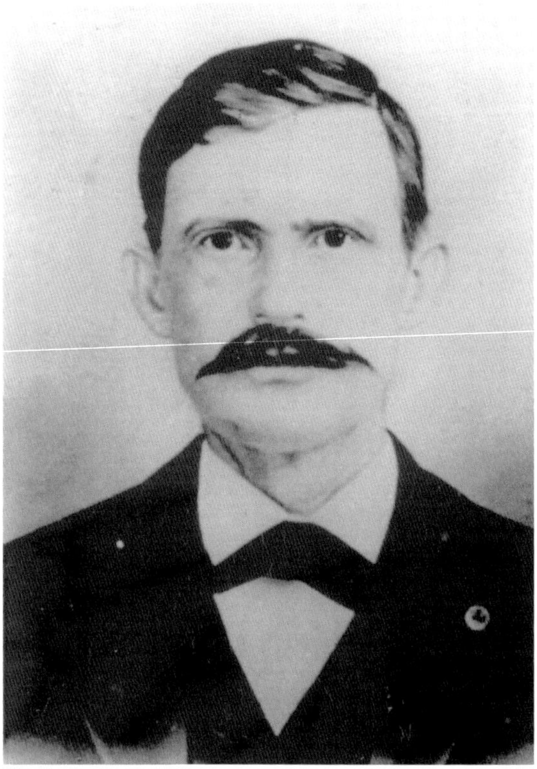

John Landrum Greene, First County Officer Down

There have been four law enforcement officers killed in the line of duty in Rutherford County. The first of these was John Landrum Greene (September 2, 1944–March 13, 1898). Greene and his father, William H. Greene (May 31, 1823–February 22, 1862), enlisted together in the Confederate army on August 22, 1861. John brought his father's body back to Rutherford County for burial after William died of "the fever." After John returned to duty and suffered leg wounds at Gettysburg in July 1863, his mother brought him home from Farmville, Virginia. He was able to return to his unit in February 1865. He performed light duties until the April 1865 surrender at Appomatox. After returning to Rutherford County after the war, John accepted the position of constable. On March 13, 1898, Constable Greene was to serve a warrant in Henrietta. Someone in the group wounded him. Greene killed the wanted man but he also died within the hour. His burial plot is in the Bethel Baptist Church Cemetery. (Mike Rhyne, Polly Condrey, and Susan Todd.)

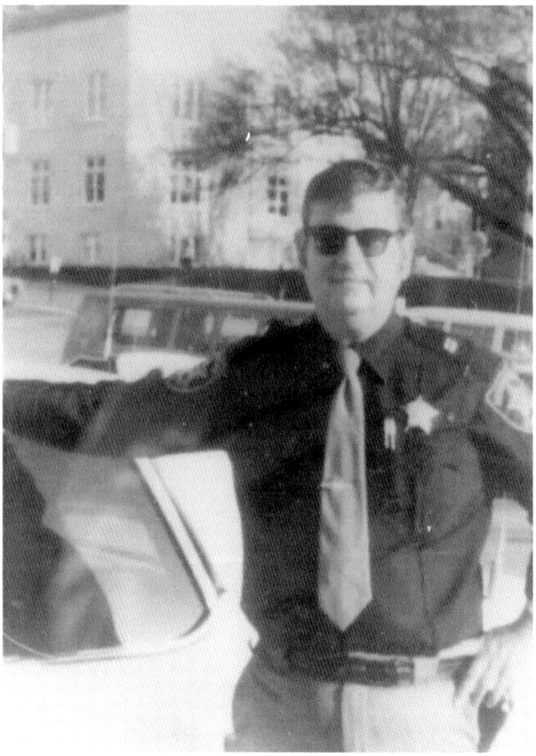

Roy Huskey

Three law enforcement officers died in Rutherford County on the same day: May 31, 1979. The first of the three was Deputy Sheriff Roy Huskey. Huskey—Rutherford County Deputy Sheriff and half-brother of Rutherford County Sheriff Damon Huskey—was shot and killed after responding to a domestic dispute call for a teenage daughter and her father. Deputy Huskey was the first officer dispatched to the home of James Hutchins and his family. Hutchins shot Huskey in the head as the deputy exited his patrol car. Earl Owensby (page 88) filmed the story of the incident in *Rutherford County Line* (1987), later called *Damon's Law*. Deputy Huskey left behind a wife and two children. His burial site is in Sunset Memorial Park in Forest City. A marker for him and the other two law enforcement officers killed on that day is on Main Street in Forest City. (Rutherford County Sheriff's Department.)

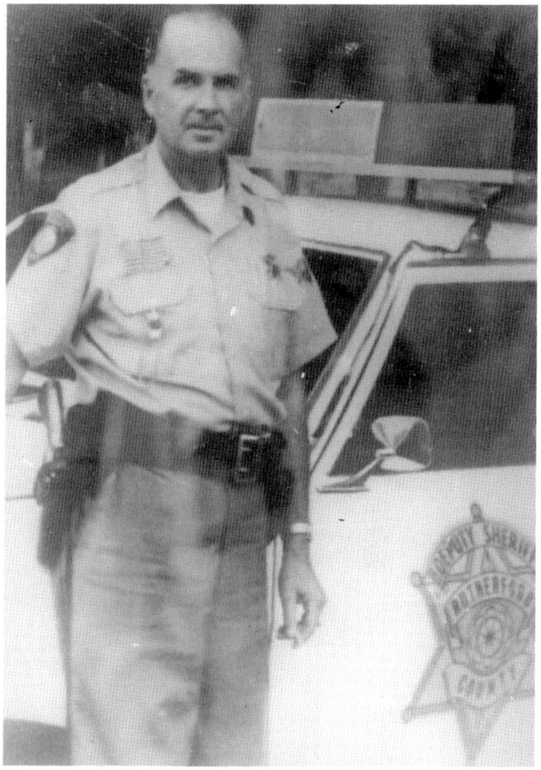

Millard Owen Messersmith
The second to die on May 31, 1979, was Deputy Sheriff Messersmith. After Deputy Sheriff Huskey failed to radio back from the site to which he had responded to the domestic disturbance call, Deputy Sheriff Messersmith responded. Pulling into the driveway, Deputy Messersmith saw Deputy Huskey lying beside the patrol car; Messersmith began backing his car out of the driveway. Hutchins then opened fire on Deputy Sheriff Messersmith. A shot struck Messersmith in the head as he backed away from the scene. Messersmith's burial spot is in the cemetery of the Church of the Transfiguration in Henderson County. (Rutherford County Sheriff's Department.)

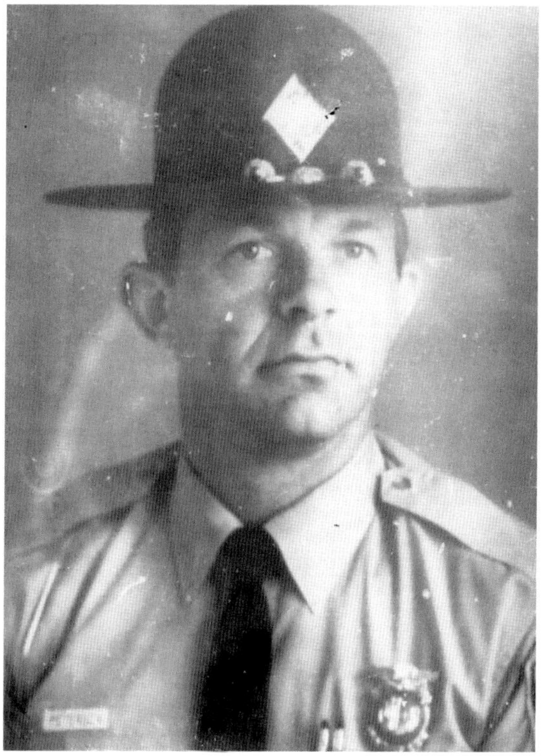

R.L. "Pete" Peterson
North Carolina State Highway patrol officer Robert Lee "Pete" Peterson (January 29, 1942–May 31, 1979) was the next to hear the call on May 31, 1979. One of Hutchins's neighbors had called the Sheriff's Office to report that two deputies had been shot. Because the transmission was not clear, Trooper Peterson decided something was wrong and headed toward Rutherfordton. As Peterson drove into town, Hutchins sped by. Peterson turned his car around and tried to stop the speeding vehicle. The driver of the speeding car jumped out and ran into the woods; Peterson followed. Peterson was found with a gunshot wound to the head. His service revolver had been fired once. The suspect was apprehended, convicted of capital murder, and executed in 1984. Peterson had served with the agency for nine years. He was the longest-assigned physical training instructor in the North Carolina Highway Patrol Training Center. Peterson was laid to rest in Mountain View Memorial Park in Black Mountain. (Rutherford County Sheriff's Department.)

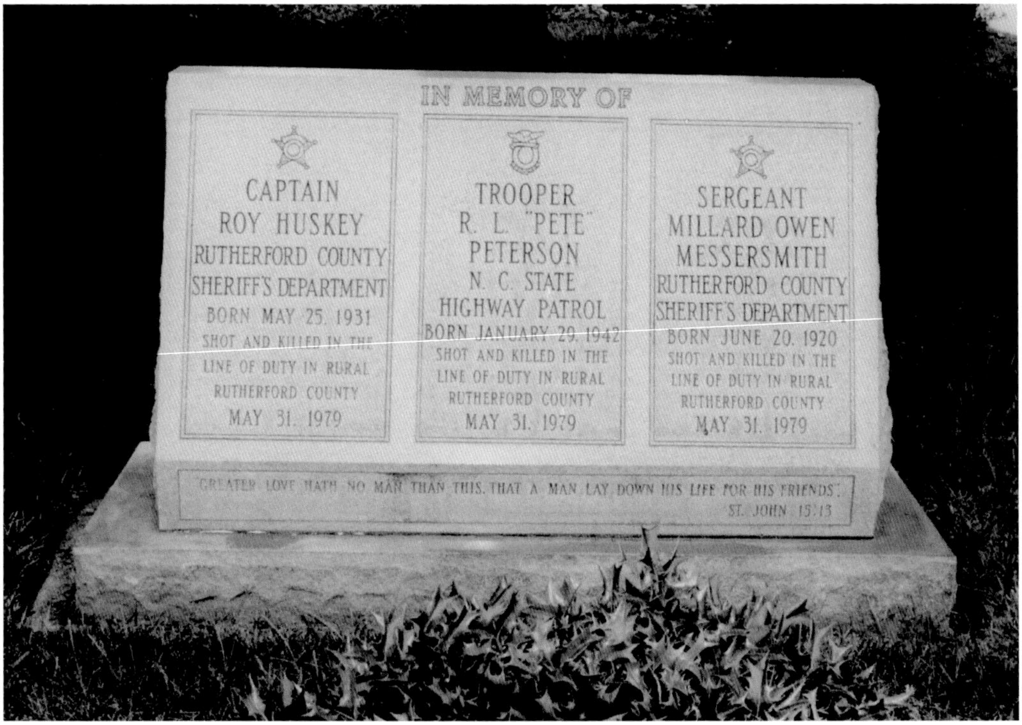

Marker to Law Enforcement Officers Killed (1979)
The public square on Main Street in Forest City has a marker to honor Capt. Roy Huskey (May 25, 1931–May 31, 1979) of the Rutherford County Sheriff's Department, Trooper R.L. Peterson (January 29, 1947–May 31, 1979) of the North Carolina State Highway Patrol, and Sgt. Millard Owen Messersmith (June 20, 1920–May 31, 1979) who died in the line of duty. (James M. Walker.)

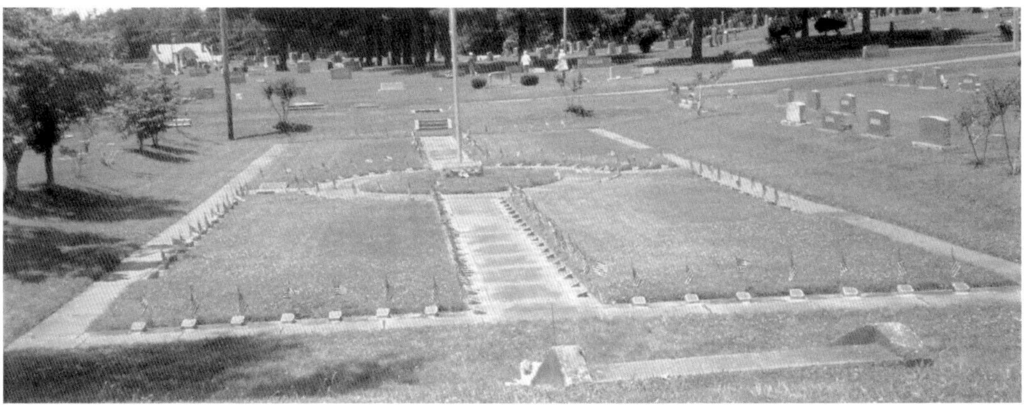

The Rutherford County Memorial Garden
Rutherford County remembers not only the law enforcement officers who have died in the line of duty but also those in service of their country. The Rutherford County Memorial garden is on Wingo Street in Forest City. The garden honors those who made the supreme sacrifice during the 20th century with a plaque bearing each name and other relevant data. (Roy Lewis McKain.)

BIBLIOGRAPHY

Bailey, Alfred Reno. *Cliffside: Portrait of a Carolina Mill Town.* Charleston, South Carolina: Arcadia Publishing, 2005.

Burgess, Larry. "Son of Forrest Harrill 'Smoky' Burgess." Interview. August 11, 2012.

Bynum, William B., ed. *The Heritage of Rutherford County, North Carolina.* Vol. I. Winston-Salem, NC: The Genealogical Society of Old Tryon County, 1984.

Cole, J. Timothy. *Chimney Rock Park and Hickory Nut Gorge.* Charleston, SC: Arcadia Publishing, 2004.

Connor, R.D.W. *History of North Carolina: The Colonial and Revolutionary Period, 1584–1783.* Vol. I. Chicago and New York: The Lewis Publishing Company, 1919.

Davis, Anita Price. *North Carolina During the Great Depression.* Jefferson, NC: McFarland, 2003.

———, and Barry E. Hambright. *Chimney Rock and Rutherford County.* Charleston, SC: Arcadia Publishing, 2002.

———, and James M. Walker. *Forest City.* Charleston, SC: Arcadia Publishing, 2005.

———, and ———. *Rutherford County in World War II.* Vols. I and II. Charleston, SC: Arcadia Publishing, 2004.

———, Mike Rhyne, and Scott Withrow. *Colfax Township.* Charleston, SC: Arcadia Publishing, 2011.

Dill, Alonzo Thomas. *Governor Tryon and His Palace.* Chapel Hill, NC: The University of North Carolina Press, 1955.

Griffin, Clarence W. *History of Old Tryon and Rutherford Counties, 1730–1936.* Asheville, NC: 1937.

Grindstaff, Boyce. Interview. August 11, 2012.

Haywood, Marshall DeLancey. *Governor William Tryon and His Administration of the Province of North Carolina, 1765–1771.* Raleigh, NC: E.M. Uzzell, 1903.

Roberts, Bruce. *The Carolina Gold Rush.* Charlotte, NC: McNally and Loftin, 1971.

Todd, Susan W. *Heroes of the Sixties: Lest We Forget.* Forest City, NC: The Genealogical Society of Old Tryon County, 2004.

toto.lib.unca.edu/WNC_biography/rutherford_griffith.htm

www.baseball-reference.com/bullpen/Smoky_Burgess

www.findagrave.com/cgi-bin/fg.cgi?GRid=7182147&page=gr

www.folkstreams.net/principal,491

www.johnchristgau.com/originsofthejumpshot/originsofthejumpshot.html

www.ncmarkers.com/print_marker.aspx?id=L-21

www.ncpedia.org/biography/governors/Tryon

www.nytimes.com/books/00/06/11/reviews/000611.11gold.html

www.southerngoldsociety.org/thebechtlers.html

INDEX

LEGENDARY LOCALS

AN IMPRINT OF ARCADIA PUBLISHING

Find more books like this at
www.legendarylocals.com

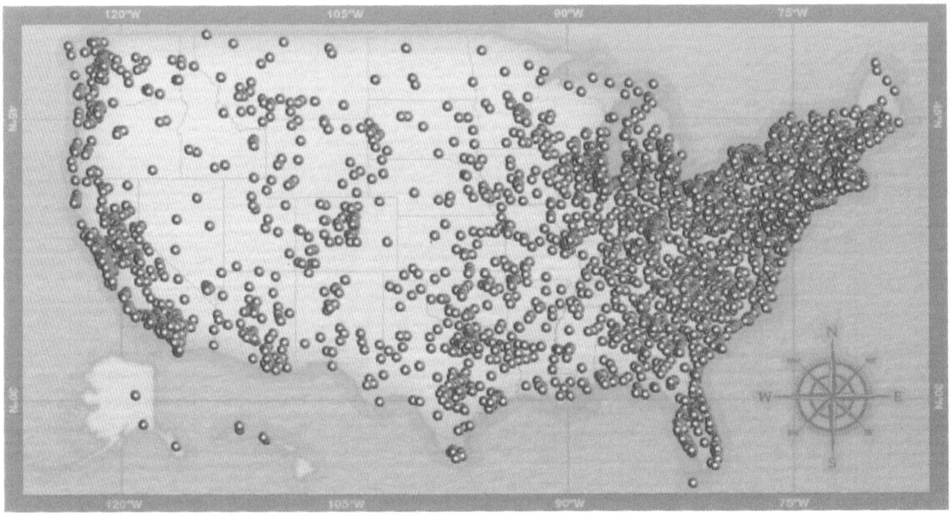

Discover more local and regional history books at
www.arcadiapublishing.com